BICENTENNIAL
1807
WILEY
2007
BICENTENNIAL

THE WILEY BICENTENNIAL—KNOWLEDGE FOR GENERATIONS

*E*ach generation has its unique needs and aspirations. When Charles Wiley first opened his small printing shop in lower Manhattan in 1807, it was a generation of boundless potential searching for an identity. And we were there, helping to define a new American literary tradition. Over half a century later, in the midst of the Second Industrial Revolution, it was a generation focused on building the future. Once again, we were there, supplying the critical scientific, technical, and engineering knowledge that helped frame the world. Throughout the 20th Century, and into the new millennium, nations began to reach out beyond their own borders and a new international community was born. Wiley was there, expanding its operations around the world to enable a global exchange of ideas, opinions, and know-how.

For 200 years, Wiley has been an integral part of each generation's journey, enabling the flow of information and understanding necessary to meet their needs and fulfill their aspirations. Today, bold new technologies are changing the way we live and learn. Wiley will be there, providing you the must-have knowledge you need to imagine new worlds, new possibilities, and new opportunities.

Generations come and go, but you can always count on Wiley to provide you the knowledge you need, when and where you need it!

WILLIAM J. PESCE
PRESIDENT AND CHIEF EXECUTIVE OFFICER

PETER BOOTH WILEY
CHAIRMAN OF THE BOARD

Human Resource Management

Max Messmer and Anne Bogardus

with Connie Isbell

BICENTENNIAL
1807
WILEY
2007
BICENTENNIAL

PUBLISHER Anne Smith	**PRODUCTION EDITOR** Kerry Weinstein
PROJECT EDITOR Brian B. Baker	**CREATIVE DIRECTOR** Harry Nolan
MARKETING MANAGER Jennifer Slomack	**COVER DESIGNER** Hope Miller
SENIOR EDITORIAL ASSISTANT Tiara Kelly	**COPYEDITOR** Camelot Editorial Services
PRODUCTION MANAGER Kelly Tavares	**COVER PHOTO** ©Rene Mansi/iStockphoto

Wiley 200th Anniversary Logo designed by Richard J. Pacifico

This book was set in Berkeley by Aptara, Inc., printed and bound by R. R. Donnelley. The cover was printed by R. R. Donnelley.

To order books or for customer service please call 1-800-CALL WILEY (225-5945).

Library of Congress Cataloging-in-Publication Data

Messmer, Max, 1946-
Human resource management / Harold Messmer and Anne Bogardus ; with Connie Isbell.
   p. cm.
  Includes index.
  ISBN 978-0-470-11120-8 (pbk.)
1. Personnel management.   I. Bogardus, Anne M.   II. Isbell, Connie.   III. Title.
  HF5549.M3497 2008
  658.3—dc22   2007033368

ISBN 978-0-470-11120-8

Printed in the United States of America

10 9 8 7 6 5 4 3

Harold "Max" Messmer Jr. is Chairman and CEO of Robert Half International, the world's largest specialized staffing firm, and one of the foremost experts on human resources and employment issues.

Anne Bogardus, SPHR, has over twenty years experience working with small businesses in developing effective human resource programs to meet organizational needs. She currently works as an HR consultant and is the author of the best-seller *PHR/SPHR Certification Study Guide.*

Connie Isbell is an editor and writer with more than 15 years of experience in magazine and book publishing. Since earning her degree in Journalism from New York University she has been involved with projects that range from business communications and emergency management to pet care and birdwatching. This is her third Wiley Pathways project.

College classrooms bring together learners from many backgrounds, with a variety of aspirations. Although the students are in the same course, they are not necessarily on the same path. This diversity, coupled with the reality that these learners often have jobs, families, and other commitments, requires a flexibility that our nation's higher education system is addressing. Distance learning, shorter course terms, new disciplines, evening courses, and certification programs are some of the approaches that colleges employ to reach as many students as possible and help them clarify and achieve their goals.

Wiley Pathways books, a new line of texts from John Wiley & Sons, Inc., are designed to help you address this diversity and the need for flexibility. These books focus on the fundamentals, identify core competencies and skills, and promote independent learning. Their focus on the fundamentals helps students grasp the subject, bringing them all to the same basic understanding. These books use clear, everyday language and are presented in an uncluttered format, making the reading experience more pleasurable. The core competencies and skills help students succeed in the classroom and beyond, whether in another course or in a professional setting. A variety of built-in learning resources promote independent learning and help instructors and students gauge students' understanding of the content. These resources enable students to think critically about their new knowledge and to apply their skills in any situation.

Our goal with *Wiley Pathways* books—with their brief, inviting format, clear language, and core competencies and skills focus—is to celebrate the many students in your courses, respect their needs, and help you guide them on their way.

CASE Learning System

To meet the needs of working college students, *Human Resource Management* uses a four-part process called the CASE Learning System:

▲ C: Content
▲ A: Analysis
▲ S: Synthesis
▲ E: Evaluation

Based on Bloom's taxonomy of learning, CASE presents key topics in network security fundamentals in easy-to-follow chapters. The text then prompts analysis, synthesis, and evaluation with a variety of learning aids and assessment tools. Students move efficiently from reviewing what they have learned, to acquiring new information and skills, to applying their new knowledge and skills to real-life scenarios.

Using the CASE Learning System, students not only achieve academic mastery of network security *topics,* but they master real-world *skills* related to that content. The CASE Learning System also helps students become independent learners, giving them a distinct advantage in the field, whether they are just starting out or seeking to advance in their careers.

Organization, Depth, and Breadth of the Text

▲ **Modular Format.** Research on college students shows that they access information from textbooks in a non-linear way. Instructors also often wish to reorder textbook content to suit the needs of a particular class. Therefore, although *Human Resource Management* proceeds logically from the basics to increasingly more challenging material, chapters are further organized into sections that are self-contained for maximum teaching and learning flexibility.

▲ **Numeric System of Headings.** *Human Resource Management* uses a numeric system for headings (e.g., 2.3.4 identifies the fourth subsection of Section 3 of Chapter 2). With this system, students and teachers can quickly and easily pinpoint topics in the table of contents and the text, keeping class time and study sessions focused.

▲ **Core Content.** The topics in *Human Resource Management* are organized into 13 chapters.

Chapter 1, Managing Human Resources Today, looks at the evolving role of human resources managers in today's changing business environment, including the value that is placed on employees in an organization's success. Also examined is the increasing emphasis on strategic thinking and technology in the field of human resources.

Chapter 2, Equal Opportunity and the Legal Environment, outlines the legal implications of U.S. employment laws and the role of the Equal Opportunity Employment Commission. Students learn proactive measures for preventing workplace discrimination; information is presented on preventing sexual harassment and providing a reporting system for sexual harassment complaints.

Chapter 3, Building a Strategic Staffing Plan, explains how to evaluate workflow and staffing needs based on a strategic approach that takes into account both the immediate and long-term needs of an organization. How to conduct a job analysis and create a job description is presented. Discussions of job titles and employment classifications are also included in this chapter.

Chapter 4, Recruiting and Evaluating Prospective Employees, covers the various ways in which a company can recruit potential new employees, including guidelines for writing job advertisements, using recruiters, and utilizing the Internet. Tools available for evaluating candidates—applications, resumes, and testing—are also presented. Tips are provided for spotting areas of concern in candidates.

Chapter 5, Interviewing and Making Selection Decisions, helps students navigate through the interview process, with tips on preparation and questioning. It examines the value of setting up a system for applicant evaluation as well as how to use a weighted rating system. How to determine the usefulness of reference checks and background checks is presented, along with guidelines for job offers and negotiations.

Chapter 6, Training Employees, outlines the various employee training approaches as well as common topics of training. Ways of assessing the training needs of an organization are covered, including the use of a needs assessment worksheet. Techniques for measuring the effectiveness of a training program are explained.

Chapter 7, Assessing and Appraising Performance, examines the benefits of using a performance appraisal system and offers guidelines for creating a successful system. It covers the types of appraisal systems and the applicable uses of each. Tips are included for managing negative reactions of employees during difficult evaluation meetings. The importance of follow-up is presented as is ways of assessing the effectiveness of a program.

Chapter 8, Compensation Strategies and Practices, reviews the types of compensation philosophies employed by organizations. The implications of the Fair Labor Standards Act are discussed, as well as the use of exemption status in compensation practices. Pay scale options, total rewards systems, and the role of incentives are included in this chapter.

Chapter 9, Designing and Administering Benefits, explains the need for benefit programs that will attract and retain the type of employees needed by an organization to achieve its goals. The types of benefit programs are outlined, including both those that are legally mandated and those that are voluntary. It reviews the ways in which employees provide health and welfare benefits as well as help employees prepare for retirement.

Chapter 10, Developing Employee Relations, discusses the importance of employee relations to an organization's strategic plan. It explores the characteristics of employee-friendly workplaces, including types of alternative work arrangements that are attractive to employees. Ways of evaluating the effectiveness of employee relations programs are presented. The chapter offers ways in which employee recognition programs would benefit an organization.

Chapter 11, Managing Discipline and Employee Rights, covers how to address employee discipline issues in a fair and effective manner; in particular, how to avoid legal issues in the process. Guidelines for implementing a grievance procedure as well as for forming a termination approach are offered. The realities of layoffs are explored, with tips on creative alternatives to layoffs.

Chapter 12, Managing Workplace Health and Safety, explains what is required to make the workplace a healthful, safe, and secure environment. It describes the legal requirements of the Occupational Safety and Health Act, discusses the various occupational health hazards, and covers some of the issues employers face in providing a hazard-free workplace.

Chapter 13, Working With Organized Labor, explores how the history of unionization affects labor relations today. The chapter covers the major union-related laws and regulations and outlines the steps of the union-organization process. The role of a collective bargaining agreement is explained. Examples of unfair labor practices are presented as well as examples of strikes and other union actions, both lawful and unlawful.

Pre-reading Learning Aids

Each chapter of *Human Resource Management* features the following learning and study aids to activate students' prior knowledge of the topics and to orient them to the material.

▲ **Pre-test.** This pre-reading assessment tool in multiple-choice format not only introduces chapter material, but it also helps students anticipate the chapter's learning outcomes. By focusing students' attention on what they do not know, the self-test provides students with a benchmark against which they can measure their own progress. The pre-test is available online at www.wiley.com/college/messmer.

▲ **What You'll Learn in This Chapter.** This bulleted list focuses on subject matter that will be taught. It tells students what they will be learning in this chapter and why it is significant for their careers. It will also help students understand why the chapter is important and how it relates to other chapters in the text.

▲ **After Studying This Chapter, You'll Be Able To.** This list emphasizes capabilities and skills students will learn as a result of reading the chapter. It sets students up to synthesize and evaluate the chapter material, and to relate it to the real world.

Within-text Learning Aids

The following learning aids are designed to encourage analysis and synthesis of the material, support the learning process, and ensure success during the evaluation phase:

▲ **Introduction.** This section orients the student by introducing the chapter and explaining its practical value and relevance to the book as a whole. Short summaries of chapter sections preview the topics to follow.

▲ **"For Example" Boxes.** Found within each section, these boxes tie section content to real-world examples, scenarios, and applications.

▲ **Figures and tables.** Line art and photos have been carefully chosen to be truly instructional rather than filler. Tables distill and present information in a way that is easy to identify, access, and understand, enhancing the focus of the text on essential ideas.

▲ **Self-Check.** Related to the "What You'll Learn" bullets and found at the end of each section, this battery of short answer questions emphasizes student understanding of concepts and mastery of section content. Though the questions may either be discussed in class or studied by students outside of class, students should not go on before they can answer all questions correctly.

▲ **Key Terms and Glossary.** To help students develop a professional vocabulary, key terms are bolded when they first appear in the chapter. A complete list of key terms with brief definitions appears at the end of each chapter and again in a glossary at the end of the book. Knowledge of key terms is assessed by all assessment tools (see below).

▲ **Summary.** Each chapter concludes with a summary paragraph that reviews the major concepts in the chapter and links back to the "What You'll Learn" list.

Evaluation and Assessment Tools

The evaluation phase of the CASE Learning System consists of a variety of within-chapter and end-of-chapter assessment tools that test how well students have learned the material. These tools also encourage students to extend their learning into different scenarios and higher levels of understanding and thinking. The following assessment tools appear in every chapter of *Human Resource Management:*

▲ **Summary Questions** help students summarize the chapter's main points by asking a series of multiple choice and true/false questions that emphasize student understanding of concepts and mastery of chapter content. Students should be able to answer all of the Summary Questions correctly before moving on.

▲ **Applying This Chapter Questions** drive home key ideas by asking students to synthesize and apply chapter concepts to new, real-life situations and scenarios.

▲ **You Try It Questions** are designed to extend students' thinking, and so are ideal for discussion or writing assignments. Using an open-ended format and sometimes based on web sources, they encourage students to draw conclusions using chapter material applied to real-world situations, which fosters both mastery and independent learning.

▲ **Post-test** should be taken after students have completed the chapter. It includes all of the questions in the pre-test, so that students can see how their learning has progressed and improved.

Instructor Package

Human Resource Management is available with the following teaching and learning supplements. All supplements are available online at the text's Book Companion website, located at www.wiley.com/college/messmer.

▲ **Instructor's Resource Guide.** Provides the following aids and supplements for teaching a human resource management course:

- *Teaching suggestions.* For each chapter, these include a chapter summary, learning objectives, definitions of key terms, lecture notes, answers to select text question sets, and at least 3 suggestions for classroom activities, such as ideas for speakers to invite, videos to show, and other projects.

▲ **PowerPoint Slides.** Key information is summarized in 10 to 15 Power-Point® slides per chapter. Instructors may use these in class or choose to share them with students for class presentations or to provide additional study support.

▲ **Test Bank.** One test per chapter, as well as a mid-term, and two finals: one cumulative, one non-cumulative. Each includes true/false, multiple choice, and open-ended questions. Answers and page references are provided for the true/false and multiple choice questions, and page references for the open-ended questions. Questions are available in Microsoft Word and computerized test bank formats.

Taken together, the content, pedagogy, and assessment elements of *Human Resource Management* offer the career-oriented student the most important aspects of the human resource field as well as ways to develop the skills and capabilities that current and future employers seek in the individuals they hire and promote. Instructors will appreciate its practical focus, conciseness, and real-world emphasis.

We would like to thank the reviewers for their feedback and suggestions during the text's development. Their advice on how to shape *Human Resource Management* into a solid learning tool that meets both their needs and those of their busy students is deeply appreciated.

We would especially like to thank the following reviewers for their significant contributions:

Christine Mooney, Queensborough Community College
Shawn D. Allison, Central Piedmont Community College
Dr. Michal Settles, City College of San Francisco
Rieann Spence-Gale, Northern Virginia Community College

BRIEF CONTENTS

CONTENTS

1

MANAGING HUMAN RESOURCES TODAY

Strategies for a Changing Business Environment

Starting Point

Go to www.wiley.com/college/messmer to assess your knowledge of the basics of human resources today.

Determine where you need to concentrate your effort.

What You'll Learn in This Chapter

▲ The value of employees in company performance
▲ Responsibilities of human resources managers
▲ Legal implications of corporate ethics
▲ The role of strategic thinkers
▲ Examples of technological change in human resources

After Studying This Chapter, You Will Be Able To

▲ Examine how a company balances its strategic needs with its people needs
▲ Compare the human resources responsibilities of a small company to those of a large company
▲ Assess the effectiveness of a human resources department's ethics enforcement
▲ Differentiate between strategic thinkers and non-strategic thinkers
▲ Prepare to purchase updated human resources management software

INTRODUCTION

As business has become more complex, so has the field of human resources, which now encompasses everything from strategic staffing to recruiting and launching effective training initiatives, as well as implementing ethic codes, policies, and benefits that safeguard workers. At the same time, a major function of human resources is to protect a company's interests and improve the bottom line.

1.1 Human Resources and Company Performance

A company's ability to grow and succeed has always depended heavily on the quality of its people. In today's market, this relationship is even more relevant. Employees are the talent base, or **intellectual capital**, that can make or break a firm's efforts to remain competitive. Businesses recognize the value of a skilled and motivated workforce as well as the challenge involved in finding and keeping top talent.

1.1.1 The Business of People

Most people in business would agree that finding and keeping a quality workforce is harder to achieve today than in the past. To that end, human resources has become a business unto itself. And the principal asset of this particular business is people.

In any job market, those in human resources recognize that competition exists for the most desirable candidates, and, once hired, they are only a phone call away from another job offer. Recruiting and managing a first-rate staff takes more skill and effort than ever before.

1.1.2 Standing Out From the Competition

The way a business manages its employees can make all the difference in its ability to differentiate itself from the competition. It is the job of a human resources manager (or, in some cases, a business owner or executive responsible for the HR function), to focus on the practices and policies that directly affect the welfare and morale of a company's most important asset—its employees.

1.1.3 Balancing Act

Those in human resources help a firm strike the optimal balance between two aspects:

▲ The **strategic needs** of a business—those actions or measures that ensure the successful attainment of an organization's goals or mission.
▲ The basic **people needs** of a workforce—everything from a safe working environment to fair compensation and competitive benefits.

FOR EXAMPLE

Creative Incentives

OneStop, a company that sells and services office equipment in Delaware, is facing stiff competition from a big-name superstore that has moved into the area. Though sales representatives are being asked to put in extra hours to reassure their current customers and secure new business, Charlie DiCielo, the company's president, has taken steps to keep morale up and staff motivated. Those working long hours can now bank that time to use around the holidays. In addition, a new e-newsletter is being sent out that will highlight the efforts of a different employee each month, giving many behind-the-scenes staffers a chance to shine.

Being sensitive to—and doing your best to meet—the "people needs" of a company's employees is in the best interest of an employer. But many in business debate just how much responsibility a company needs to assume—and how much time (and money) a company must devote to the needs and priorities of employees as opposed to the needs and priorities of its business operations and customers.

SELF-CHECK

1. Define *intellectual capital.*
2. Stock options are a company's most important assets. True or false?
3. Give three examples of a company's "people needs."

1.2 Responsibilities of Human Resource Departments

Human resources management is the phrase most often used to describe a set of functions that once fell under the category of "personnel administration" or "personnel management." Regardless of the name, you can sum up this particular aspect of business as the decisions, activities, and processes that must meet the basic needs and support the work performance of employees.

HR management is one of the five basic functions that make up modern organizations. In addition to human resources, an organization will have sales

Figure 1.1

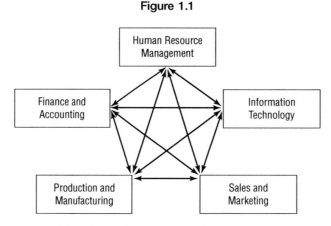

The interrelationship between information systems.

and marketing, information technology, operations and manufacturing, and finance and accounting. Each area plays a vital role in the operation of any company; Figure 1-1 illustrates the interrelationship of these functions.

1.2.1 A Range of Focus

The most common areas that fall under HR management include the following:

- ▲ **Staffing:** Strategically determining, recruiting, and hiring the human resources you need for your business.
- ▲ **Basic workplace policies:** Orienting your staff on policies and procedures, such as schedules, safety, and security.
- ▲ **Compensation and benefits:** Establishing effective—and attractive—wages and perks.
- ▲ **Retention:** Continually assessing the quality of your workplace and HR policies to ensure people want to stay with your company.
- ▲ **Training and developing employees:** Ensuring that your staff grows in knowledge and experience to help your company expand and continue to meet the changing needs of customers.
- ▲ **Performance and behavior issues:** Resolving conflicts, handling disputes, and managing discipline problems.
- ▲ **Regulatory issues:** Complying with the ever-increasing number of federal, state, and local regulations.
- ▲ **Human resources information systems:** Using technology to enhance the efficiency of human resources operations (see Section 1.5).

1.2.2 Customizing Human Resources

No cookie-cutter formulas for effective HR management are available. Every company—regardless of size, location, or purpose—must deal with human resources issues in a way that's best suited to its needs and situation. A company's size is a significant determining factor.

▲ If you run a small business, you probably function as your own HR manager. You personally oversee and conduct all the classic human resources functions of your company:

- You recruit and hire.
- You set up the compensation and benefits package.
- You write the paychecks and keep the appropriate records.
- You're likely the person responsible for training and developing the people you hire.
- You keep the people who work for you informed about what's going on in the company, through a newsletter or other means.

▲ Bigger companies face the same basic challenges and carry out the same general activities. The only difference is that larger companies employ individual specialists—or sometimes entire departments—to handle these same functions.

The human resources function in general has undergone enormous changes in the past twenty years. Some companies still take a highly structured, largely centralized approach to human resources management. The majority of companies today, however, take a far more decentralized approach, with HR practitioners and line managers working cooperatively to set basic policies and carry out programs.

1.2.3 Skills of Human Resource Professionals

To be successful in human resources management you must possess the skills necessary to work—*really* work—with people: find and recruit them; hire them; train and develop them; pay them; retain them; create a safe, healthy, and productive environment for them; communicate with them; and do what it takes to find that delicate balance between what best serves the basic needs of employees and what best serves the needs of the company.

Because of the increasing complexity of HR issues today, larger companies have boosted the size of their departments and typically employ **specialists** in areas such as benefits administration or 401(k) retirement plans. But smaller firms that don't have the resources for such specialization must ensure that the people who handle their HR functions are solid **generalists**—that is, they possess skills in several areas of HR rather than in one particular specialty.

FOR EXAMPLE

Specialist Needed

As the staffing needs for Samuel Merritt College began to change, it became clear to the administration that an HR specialist was needed to handle the college's independent contractors. However, in addition to managing and administering all independent contracts, the person hired would also be required to handle the following: provide administrative support to the human resources department, including recruitment and employment, employee records, employee relations, job evaluation, compensation management, benefits administration, organization development, and training.

SELF-CHECK

1. Define *human resources management*.
2. A large company is more likely to require the services of an HR specialist than a smaller company. True or false?
3. Explain the role of an HR generalist.
4. List five areas of human resources management.

1.3 Ethics in Human Resource Management

Ethics refers to a set of rules or principles that define right and wrong conduct. The much-publicized cases of unethical and illegal organizational practices at companies such as WorldCom and Enron have brought the issue of ethical conduct to the attention of the government, media, and the public. People question how such unethical actions could have taken place and whether proper controls would have prevented them.

1.3.1 Government and Corporate Ethics

Government-mandated regulations touch almost every aspect of the human resource function, including safety and health, equal-employment opportunity, sexual harassment policies, pension reform, and environmental issues. Among recent legislation, the Sarbanes-Oxley Act of 2002 has had a widespread effect on workplace cultures. The primary objective of the act was to create stronger forms of financial accountability and internal controls in organizations. But the overall spirit of Sarbanes-Oxley is one of ethics and responsibility. To that end, it mandates that every publicly traded company create and articulate a strong code of conduct or **code of ethics**. Many private companies, attuned as well to the spirit of the legislation, are voluntarily complying with some of the regulations, including placing a stronger emphasis on the ethical behavior of their employees.

1.3.2 The HR Role

No single department is better equipped than HR to deliver on this new spirit and vision of ethical conduct. Consider the ways in which human resources can inform and enforce a code of ethics:

▲ Company-wide communications.

▲ Training programs and careful ongoing monitoring efforts.

In the HR role for your company, you have the chance to be at the forefront of creating a corporate culture of accountability and personal integrity with a strong spirit of ethical behavior at its heart. Helping your organization understand the importance of putting ethics first is a way in which you can begin to make HR more than a function as you take on the role of strategic counselor.

CRACKING THE CODE

In performing their duties, HR practitioners must operate within a code of ethics that allows them to maintain credibility in their organization. The Society for Human Resources Management (SHRM) has established guidelines for conduct and sets a high standard for dealing with conflicts that arise between the multiple roles often played by those in human resources. You can visit the SHRM website at www.shrm.org/ethics/code-of-ethics.asp to read the entire code of ethics.

FOR EXAMPLE

Corporate Clean

In October 2006, the CEO of Whirlpool Corporation released the following code of ethical conduct: "Whirlpool's code of ethics requires each of us to act responsibly and maintain the highest levels of personal, business, and legal conduct. That means walking away from a business agreement rather than violating the law or compromising our standards. We are ever mindful that there is no right way to do a wrong thing." The announcement also included instructions for employees to obtain additional information or to report any potential issues—either by contacting a supervisor or by contacting a "hotline" maintained by a specialized company to receive inquiries on a confidential basis. Employees can contact the hotline by telephone, by email, or by regular mail.

1.4 Focusing on Strategy

Given the increasing recognition in corporate America that the most important asset a company has is not its products, factories, or systems, but its people, today's HR professionals are assuming an increasingly broad role in their companies, becoming strategic advisors to the senior management team.

Companies no longer take the "human" side of business for granted. For several decades now, people responsible for the human resources function have ceased to be viewed merely as "personnel administrators" or strictly "support." Top company managers now look to HR for help in other ways:

▲ Formulating long-term staffing strategies.
▲ Introducing practices that help ensure that employees are able to meet the increasing demands of their jobs.
▲ Providing assistance with a wide range of legal and regulatory issues.
▲ Following through on the necessary support and training.

In short, senior management is looking to HR for insights on how to tap into the potential of every individual within the organization.

1.4.1 A Strategic Skill Set

These new expectations create new opportunities for those in human resources. They also create a need for additional key skills, in particular, the ability to think strategically.

No doubt you've heard the term **strategic thinkers**. But what does it really mean? Certainly, strategic thinkers spend plenty of time setting objectives and getting work done, but they also do much more:

▲ They try to look ahead, attempting to anticipate which issues and information will be most relevant.
▲ They don't look at their work merely as a series of tasks or simply react to events.

COPING WITH AN AGING WORKFORCE

Probably no generation has more greatly influenced the history of American business than the baby boomers, the 76 million men and women born between 1946 and 1964. Increasing numbers of them are nearing retirement age, creating a potential drain of knowledge within your corporation and the need to ensure proper training for the next generation of leaders. For many of these boomers, their financial, emotional, and mental resources are spread thin as they attempt to simultaneously care for their children and parents. And others who've been focused on their careers for many years are beginning to ponder different directions. All these factors have profound implications for the kind of HR programs you build—from management skills training to flexible work arrangements to broader, strategic initiatives that help shape your firm's overall culture.

▲ They examine trends, issues, opportunities, and long-term needs—and shape what they discover into policies and recommendations.

To borrow from the restaurant industry, strategic thinkers do more than cook; they help shape the menu.

1.4.2 Strategy in HR

So how does the concept of strategic thinkers apply to the HR world? In effect, strategic HR professionals act as consultants to the rest of the business.

▲ They help set a vision of how to ensure HR effectively delivers on its mission. Others may not want to deliberate when they're in a hurry to move forward, but strategic thinkers know it's wise to look before they leap, and this philosophy helps them offer valued counsel.

▲ They carefully examine and explain the long-term cost-benefit ratio of saying "yes" to a proposed direction.

▲ They expand the range of people they talk and listen to, drawing insights not just from HR but from finance, marketing, legal counsel, manufacturing, sales, and others who can help them better understand what makes their company tick. They do so with people at all levels, ranging from experienced senior managers to entry-level employees.

This approach is not easy. But it is a great opportunity—the chance to be regarded as a vital source of counsel and a central part of your firm's management team. Even taking just fifteen minutes a day of solitary "think time" and research time can make a big difference in effectively shaping your work.

1.4.3 Putting Strategy to Work

The following list offers some general guidelines on how to be more successful overall in your HR efforts:

▲ **Know your business.** Find out everything you can about your company's business, particularly in terms of revenues and profits. The more broad-minded you can be in how you approach everything you do in your job, the more credibility you will have as a strategic business professional—and the easier it will be to get senior managers and line managers to endorse the initiatives you recommend.

▲ **Don't ignore the basics.** Regardless of how committed you are to bringing new ideas to your organization, don't overlook the traditional needs such as policies regarding benefits, computers and the internet, dress code, and privacy. Make sure that every employee in the company is familiar with your company's basic practices. If there's an employee manual, it should be up to date. If the company doesn't have an employee manual, make it a priority to create one.

▲ **Focus on quality hiring.** Make a commitment—and try to secure a similar commitment from other managers in other departments—that your company will devote the time and energy needed to ensure that each new employee you recruit and hire is the right person for that particular job.

▲ **Keep your finger on the pulse.** One of the most valuable contributions you can make to the senior managers of your company is to keep them apprised of all workplace issues and concerns that may affect your company's ability to meet the needs of customers. Taking on this role doesn't mean that you're constantly looking over the shoulders of the line managers in your company. It does mean, however, that you aware, for example, when morale is starting to slip, or when the workload is starting to burn out people.

▲ **Stay current.** Be aware of new developments in human resources administration, including technological advances and key trends in pay practices and benefits programs. When you come across new and promising ideas, make sure that you let senior management know. Be particularly diligent about keeping pace with what is going on in the legal and regulatory side of HR, making sure that you're aware of any laws or regulatory changes that apply to your company.

FOR EXAMPLE

A Better HR Recipe

As the head of the advertising sales team of a major wine publication, Deborah's work day consists of racing to meetings, making sales calls, and ensuring that she and her team meet all their deadlines. Like other managers at her level, she is so busy and focused on doing and achieving in the present that it is easy to overlook her staff's strategic needs—training, support, long-term staff planning—that are ultimately essential to improving performance. It's not that she doesn't care. She just doesn't feel she has time because of the demands of the moment. In Deborah's case, her company has put together a human resources team that has a real understanding for the situation that the department managers find themselves in, and both parties feel comfortable sharing those important responsibilities.

SELF-CHECK

1. Define *strategic thinker.*
2. List three examples of how human resources management has changed in recent decades.
3. List three strategic functions for HR professionals.

1.5 Keeping Pace with Technology

As it has in other fields, technology has revolutionary development for people in HR management, changing the way human resource managers work. Email quickly replaced the cork bulletin board as the primary communication between management and employees, and it has gone on to do far more. Computers have streamlined the administrative aspects of every HR function. Technology has redefined the image of the "office," with fax machines, modems, and intranets allowing staff to do their work anytime, anyplace in decentralized work locations.

The following are some specific examples of how technology has helped HR managers carry out human resource plans, make decisions, define jobs, and improve communications.

▲ **Recruiting:** Job postings on the internet—company websites, job-search websites, etc.—help human resource managers disseminate information to individuals. In many cases this technology is even replacing traditional methods such as newspaper advertisements. This technology also allows HR managers to quickly and electronically screen an applicant's resume for job relevance.

▲ **Benefits administration:** HR professionals today have more efficient ways of processing changes in enrollment.

▲ **Management assistance:** Companies have the technology to improve performance review systems as well as monitor and deal with discipline issues.

▲ **Training and development:** The internet enables human resource managers to deliver orientation, training, and career development information, without physically transporting materials or employees.

▲ **Employee efficiency:** Companies can use technology to monitor, when necessary, an employee's computer activity; for example, if any time is being spent on recreational internet use.

▲ **Communication:** Employees today can communicate instantly anytime, with anyone, anywhere. In doing so, this technology has redefined traditional communication patterns and redefined how meetings, negotiations, and even chatting are conducted.

▲ **Decentralization:** Thanks to technology, many employees are no longer tied to a specific work location or work hours. This offers greater flexibility, but with less one-on-one supervision comes changes in management and production techniques.

FOR EXAMPLE

High-Tech Help Wanted

Thanks to job search engines such as Monster.com, HotJobs.com, and CareerBuilder.com, both employers and prospective employees have the means to make contact with one another. A quick search for human resources manager positions within twenty miles of your home may yield dozens of employment possibilities. It's a far cry from the days of scouring the newspaper's help wanted ads.

1.5.1 Facing the Challenges of Technology

With the benefits of technology come new challenges. The software that enables companies to process large amounts of information is complex and can be expensive. It has also introduced training and security issues that didn't affect HR professionals in the days of the typewriter.

In addition, as work processes have become more technically sophisticated, the need for skilled employees has intensified. **Knowledge workers** are employees who jobs are designed around the application and acquisition of information. Such workers possess the skills and knowledge needed to perform the jobs and functions most affected by technological advances, tasks that in turn require significant levels of education. It is estimated that knowledge workers make up about a third of the U.S. workforce. Consider the potential range of knowledge workers required to staff a large corporation:

▲ Analysts.
▲ Database administrators.
▲ Programmers.
▲ Systems analysts.
▲ Technical writers.
▲ Academic professionals.
▲ Librarians.
▲ Researchers.
▲ Lawyers.

According to the U.S. Bureau of Labor Statistics' 2006–2007 Occupational Handbook projections, more than 75 percent of the 25 fastest-growing occupations require a college degree. Companies are looking more and more to their HR departments to simultaneously enhance the skills of existing employees and identify job candidates who possess the necessary level of expertise.

1.5.2 Playing It Safe with HR Technology

One of the great success stories of the last ten years has been the way HR professionals have been able to maximize the benefits of information technology. You can manage everything from payroll to benefits administration to staffing quite efficiently on your desktop. So with all these bells and whistles at your disposal, what should your priorities in maximizing their value be?

▲ **Security:** With so many people in an organization now having access
   to more information, any system you use must be properly safeguarded
   against intrusion. This security is especially important in human
   resources, which houses such sensitive information as employee compensation, performance reviews, health records, and other important data.
▲ **Accessibility:** The ability to consistently, smoothly and affordably
   upgrade and integrate technology into the rest of the organization is
   a key concern. Because HR professionals work with every department

within the company, make sure that any software products you implement are easily understood and used by others.

1.5.3 Staying Ahead with HR Software

Computer software has been very good to HR professionals in recent decades. Many labor-intensive functions involved in tracking employee information—time reporting, payroll calculation, tax computation, and tax reporting—are now processed quite rapidly.

The scope, flexibility, and versatility of HR-related software—formally known as **Human Resource Information Systems (HRIS)**—continues to accelerate. New training and development software, for example, not only tracks such aspects of training as scheduling, enrollments, vendor data, and costs, but it also integrates that data with information relating to career development and assessment.

The evolution of HRIS has not only enhanced the efficiency of human resources operations in general, but it has also enabled HR departments to lower their administrative costs and make better and timelier use of data in strategic planning (see Section 1.4).

1.5.4 Heeding HRIS Hazards

With so many products and applications evolving at such a rapid pace (the number of HR-related software products on the market, according to WorldatWork, now exceeds 3,000 and shows no signs of ebbing), it has become increasingly difficult for HR professionals to make basic buying decisions.

Depending on the size of your company, the level of customization you require, and the number of functions you're interested in, the cost can run anywhere from just under $500 to more than $1 million. And that doesn't include what you may have to spend on additional computer hardware, the time it takes your employees to learn the new system, the potential operational problems during the transition period, as well as any program maintenance that is required.

The challenge you face when you're in the market for an HR software application is not simply a matter of deciding which product has the niftiest features or which vendor is the most supportive. It's much more a matter of figuring out an overall strategy to ensure that the transition from the old way to the new way goes as smoothly as possible.

Of course, all software decisions should be driven by the strategic and operational needs of the business, as opposed to the capabilities of the software. The system must ultimately produce a business payoff, in any or all of the following areas:

▲ Increased productivity.
▲ Cost savings.

▲ Quicker response time.

▲ Improved employee morale.

1.5.5 Making HRIS Decisions

Before you move ahead on any software initiative, be prepared to go through a disciplined needs assessment, followed by a cost/benefit analysis. In other words, instead of thinking about this purchase as an administrative matter of implementation, step back and assess it strategically.

Ask the following key questions when you're going through this process:

▲ What business benefits does your company stand to gain once the software is in place?

▲ How much is the software going to cost?

▲ How long will it take before the investment is recouped?

▲ What can you expect in terms of downtime or reduced productivity while employees are learning the new system?

Don't get so swept up in the remarkable capabilities of today's HRIS products that you lose sight of what the technology is meant to do: help your company operate more efficiently and profitably. Think it through.

1.5.6 HRIS Research

If your company is seriously exploring a major software purchase, you should have at least a general idea of what various products are meant to do and what features distinguish one system and one vendor from another.

The internet offers a wealth of information on technology products. Two useful websites are the Society for Human Resource Management (www.shrm .org) and hrVillage (www.hrVillage.com). These sites contain useful information about HRIS, including data from vendors and tutorial advice.

No secret formulas ensure that your HRIS buying decisions will give you the results you seek. But the following suggestions stack the odds in your favor.

▲ **Rely on teamwork:** Instead of taking sole responsibility for making the final decision, put together a team of employees who represent different areas of the company (IT staff, department managers, etc.) and who are interested in being a part of the process. Use this group to investigate and review issues of compatibility and implementation.

▲ **Research the vendors:** Find out how long potential vendors have been in business, how established they are, how committed they are to research and development, and how diligent they are when it comes to support.

▲ **Get proof:** Insist that a vendor demonstrate how the software you're considering performs those specific functions that you believe are most important to your business (through case studies or pilot programs).

▲ **Ask questions about development:** Find out, in particular, whether the development team included people who were familiar with those business functions that are your chief priority.

▲ **Get references:** Consider getting the names and telephone numbers of at least five current users of any product you're considering to get a real-world perspective. When you talk to those users, ask for additional names that weren't given to you by the vendor.

FOR EXAMPLE

Technological Change

Times have changed in the world of publishing. Ten or fifteen years ago, an office and in-house staff were required to write, edit, illustrate, and design a niche birdwatching magazine. Today, thanks to advances in technology and the changing culture of business, this is no longer the case. An editor in chief can work in one state, a managing editor in another, and an art director in yet another; at the same time, these staffers contract with freelance writers and photographers all over the world to fill the magazine with great photographs and articles. Frequent emails and phone calls keep everyone on the same page, and layouts can be transferred over the internet and reviewed at leisure. When subscribers get their issues months later, they don't notice any difference.

SELF-CHECK

1. Explain how human resource information systems are used.
2. Which of the following can help ensure a successful HRIS purchase?
   a. vendor research
   b. information about product development
   c. references
   d. all of the above
3. Advances in technology allow HR managers to spend more time on strategic planning. True or false?
4. Explain the value of teamwork in HRIS decisions.

SUMMARY

Like other areas of business, human resources has become increasingly complex. In today's market, the way an organization manages its employees can make all the difference in its ability to stand out from the competition. Because a company's employees are its greatest assets, HR must address its employee's needs as it addresses the company's strategic needs, requiring HR managers to take on new responsibilities. An effective human resources department will be customized to best serve the needs of each organization and will include such areas as staffing, compensation, retention, training, and conflict resolution, and strategic thinking. As such, the skills required of HR professionals can vary, with certain areas of specialty becoming more prevalent. In addition, in response to government regulations, many human resource professionals are now responsible for informing and enforcing an organization's code of ethics, which sets principles of conduct for employees. Finally, as part of an organization's effort to keep pace with advances in technology, those in HR are taking advantage of improved information systems to increase their effectiveness in managing many aspects of HR, including recruiting, benefits administration, and communication.

KEY TERMS

Code of ethics	Company policies that place a strong emphasis on the behavior of their employees.
Ethics	A set of rules or principles that define right and wrong conduct.
Generalists	People who possess skills in several areas rather than in one particular specialty.
Human Resource Information Systems (HRIS)	Software designed for human resources management purposes.
Human resources management	The decisions, activities, and processes that meet the basic needs and support the work performance of employees.
Intellectual capital	The knowledge, applied experience, and professional skills that translate into customer relationships and provide an organization with a competitive edge in the marketplace.
Knowledge workers	An employee who possesses the skills and knowledge needed to perform the jobs and functions most affected by technological advances, tasks that in turn require significant levels of education.

People needs	The requirements of a workforce, ranging from a safe working environment to fair compensation and competitive benefits.
Specialist	A person who specializes in one area of human resources or other field.
Strategic needs	Those actions or measures that ensure the successful attainment of an organization's goals or mission.
Strategic thinkers	People who set objectives and get work done, while anticipating future issues; examine trends and long-term needs.

ASSESS YOUR UNDERSTANDING

Go to www.wiley.com/college/messmer to assess your knowledge of the basics of human resources today.
Measure your learning by comparing pre-test and post-test results.

Summary Questions

1. A company's intellectual capital is its skilled and motivated workforce. True or false?

2. Human resources programs care for the people needs of its employees by
   (a) raising product prices.
   (b) cutting healthcare benefits.
   (c) improving morale.
   (d) extending work hours.

3. Assessing the quality of your workplace and policies to ensure that employees stay with a company is
   (a) regulation.
   (b) training.
   (c) retention.
   (d) development.

4. Small companies typically employ specialists to handle particular aspects of HR. True or false?

5. Explain the difference between an HR generalist and an HR specialist.

6. A company's code of ethics refers to its
   (a) mission statement.
   (b) expectations of conduct.
   (c) HR policies.
   (d) stockholder privileges.

7. Name the regulation passed in 2002 that addresses employee behavior.

8. A strategic thinker is able to formulate HR policies that address long-term needs. True or false?

9. In human resources, strategic thinkers utilize coworkers in other departments. True or false?

10. Knowledge workers are
    (a) analysts.
    (b) librarians.
    (c) programmers.
    (d) all of the above.

11. Advances in technology have limited recruiting practices. True or false?
12. Decentralization has increased because of
    (a) strategic thinking.
    (b) rising fuel costs.
    (c) use of teams.
    (d) online communications.
13. Improved HR information systems guarantee a company increased efficiency. True or false?

Applying This Chapter

1. TLC Physical Therapy is experiencing a high rate of turnover—most of the assistant therapists stay with the company for less than six months. Develop a list of potential people needs that should be addressed by TLC's human resources department.
2. The shipping company where you've worked for ten years has bought out a competing company in another state. Now instead of managing five HR employees, you'll be managing ten. Given that the company will have offices in two different states, what new HR challenges might you face?
3. You've been chosen to create a code of ethics for the software development company you work for. Evaluate the particular needs of that industry and choose three areas of ethical emphasis.
4. Assume that you head the HR department of a small hospital. Strategic thinking is increasingly becoming a part of your work. Determine which other hospital employees should also be strategic thinkers.
5. Again, as the human resources manager of the same small hospital evaluate the hospital's need for HR information systems. In this age of patient confidentiality, what areas of HRIS should be of concern to you?

YOU TRY IT

Getting Ahead in HR

Using the Society of Human Resource Management's website (www.shrm.org) research what types of training programs or advanced certifications are available for HR professionals who need to get up to speed with the strategic responsibilties of this changing field. Determine the cost and time involved; indicate which level of HR a program might apply to.

What's in a Job?

Interview someone in human resources—by phone, email, or in person.

- What is that person's job title and responsibilities?

- Evaluate how that person's position fits into the more updated HRM profile covered in this chapter.
- Create a job description for the position, then propose changes or additions to the position to bring it up to date.

Technological Update

A small law firm is in need of an HRIS update: recruiting, training, management software, etc. Using the internet, including hrVillage.com, research purchasing options and create a plan. Determine who will be involved in the decision making, what you'll need, and a timeline.

2

EQUAL OPPORTUNITY AND THE LEGAL ENVIRONMENT

Staying in Line with Employment Regulations

Starting Point

Go to www.wiley.com/college/messmer to assess your knowledge of the basic employment regulations.
Determine where you need to concentrate your effort.

What You'll Learn in This Chapter

▲ The role of the Equal Opportunity Employment Commission
▲ Implications of major U.S. employment laws
▲ The value of acting proactively to prevent workplace discrimination
▲ The steps of the Equal Opportunity Employment Commission's process after a case has been filed
▲ Ways in which sexual harassment can be prevented

After Studying This Chapter, You Will Be Able To

▲ Review the Equal Opportunity Employment Commission's three key requirements for employers
▲ Evaluate the relevance of various employment laws to corporate situations
▲ Assemble research materials and case studies from EEOC resources
▲ Differentiate between disparate treatment and disparate impact
▲ Propose a reporting system for sexual harassment complaints

INTRODUCTION

The legal aspects of human resources are complicated, and they can be more than a bit daunting—especially when you first encounter them. Employment laws affect virtually everything you do in the field of HR: hiring, determining compensation, choosing how to evaluate employee performance. All these activities carry significant legal implications. Failing to fully understand the law can prove costly.

2.1 Equal Employment Opportunity Concepts

Although earlier attempts were made to promote fair employment practices in the history of the United States, it was not until the 1960s that significant change occurred. A landmark piece of employment legislation, the 1964 Civil Rights Act, paved the way to a new era of government regulation of employment practices.

Federal, state, and local laws now make it illegal to discriminate on the basis of a number of factors, including, but not limited to, race, religion, sex, age, disability, veteran status, pregnancy, and marital status. Some states, counties, and cities prohibit discrimination on the basis of sexual preference.

2.1.1 What Is Discrimination?

Discrimination is the unfair treatment of a person or group on the basis of prejudice. Discrimination laws cover areas ranging from **racial bias** to appearance (whether an employee can wear a certain hairstyle, for example). The key is that, no matter how trivial an issue may seem to you, all forms of discrimination are unacceptable, and it's your responsibility to be familiar with federal, state, and local laws which address discrimination.

2.1.2 The Equal Employment Opportunity Commission

The **Equal Employment Opportunity Commission (EEOC)** is the federal agency responsible for enforcing federal antidiscrimination laws in employment.

Regardless of how disciplined you are in your company about following equal opportunity employment principles, you must meet the EEOC's three key requirements:

▲ Post federal and state Equal Employment Opportunity notices.
▲ Depending on the size of your company and the nature of its business, you may be required to file an annual form (the Employer Information Report, EEO-1) that communicates to the EEOC the demographics of your company's workforce broken out into specific job categories.

FOR EXAMPLE

To Show or Not to Show

Although employees have had success claiming company dress codes violate religious discrimination laws (an employee's religious need to wear a beard, for example), many employees mistakenly believe that they have a right to show tattoos and body piercings in the workplace. Though they may be examples of employee self-expression, tattoos and piercings are not generally recognized as an expression of religion and are not protected under federal discrimination laws.

▲ Keep on file copies of all documents (job applications, payroll records, discharges, and so on) that may conceivably become relevant in the event your company is ever involved in a discrimination suit. The recommended minimum period for maintaining these records is three years. Keep on file records of hiring practices, identifying total hires within a particular job classification, and the percentage of minority and female applicants hired.

SELF-CHECK

1. Define *discrimination.*
2. The Equal Opportunity Employment Commission regulates state laws in the United States. True or false?
3. List the three EEOC requirements for all companies.

2.2 Major Equal Employment Laws

More than a dozen pieces of major, HR-related federal legislation have passed since 1963, all relating in some way to equal opportunity. In addition, hundreds of statutes and guidelines exist on the local, state, and county level. If the state or states in which your organization operates have additional laws with different requirements, your organization must comply with the most stringent requirement.

The focus of this legislation and the type of business covered by each piece of legislation vary, and a good deal of overlap occurs. The following offers a quick glimpse of key federal actions.

FLSA: Fair Labor Standards Act (1938)

Purpose: Establishes the minimum wage, requires overtime for certain employees, provides restrictions on the employment of children, and requires certain forms of record-keeping.

Application: Most companies.

FUTA: Federal Unemployment Tax Act (1939)

Purpose: Stipulates that employers must contribute to a government tax program that offers temporary benefits to employees who have lost their jobs. In most cases, includes both a federal and state tax.

Application: Generally, companies that paid wages of $1,500 or more in any calendar quarter.

Equal Pay Act (1963)

Purpose: Prohibits any discrepancies in pay between men and women who are assigned to or perform the same job.

Application: Private employers or labor organizations who have two or more employees, and who are engaged in interstate commerce or in the production of goods for interstate commerce.

Title VII of the Civil Rights Act (1964)

Purpose: Prohibits any employment and other practices that discriminate against people on the basis of race, sex, color, religion, or national origin.

Who the legislation applies to: Almost all government institutions, employment agencies, labor unions, and private employers with fifteen or more employees who work twenty or more weeks per year.

Application: The Civil Rights Act of 1991 gives employees who believe they've been intentionally victimized by discrimination the right to seek compensation and damages before a jury.

ADEA: The Age Discrimination in Employment Act (1967)

Purpose: Prohibits discrimination against employees who are age forty or older. This law originally covered employees until age sixty-five, was amended to age seventy, and then had the age completely removed. Also see the upcoming section on the Older Workers Benefit Protection Act.

Application: All private sector employers with twenty or more people who work twenty or more weeks per year. Also covers labor unions (twenty-five or more members), employment agencies, and state and local governments.

Rehabilitation Act (1973 and 1998)

Purpose: Protects disabled persons from discrimination. A **disabled person** is defined as any person who has a physical or mental impairment which substantially limits one or more major life activities. In 1998, Congress amended the act to require federal agencies to make their electronic and information technology accessible to people with disabilities.

Application: Employers with federal contracts and subcontracts worth more than $2,500.

Special requirements: Requires written affirmative action programs from employers of fifty or more people and with federal contracts worth more than $50,000.

Pregnancy Discrimination Act (1978)

Purpose: Requires employers to regard pregnancy as a "medical condition" and not to exclude pregnant employees from same benefits and medical leave policies.

Application: Employers with fifteen or more employees who work twenty or more weeks a year.

COBRA: Consolidated Omnibus Budget Reconciliation Act (1985)

Purpose: Provides certain former employees, retirees, spouses, former spouses, and children the right to temporary continuation of health coverage at group rates.

Application: Companies with 20 or more employees.

IRCA: Immigration Reform and Control Act (1986, 1990, and 1996)

Purpose: Bans employers from hiring illegal aliens—and establishes penalties for such behavior.

Application: Any individual or company.

Keep in mind: Determining the legality of the employee's status is the employer's responsibility. Matters related to immigration and security are even more important since 2001, when the Department of Homeland Security was established and the Patriot Act (later in this chapter) was passed.

WARN: Worker Adjustment and Retraining Notification Act (1988)

Purpose: Offers protection to workers, families, and communities, requiring employers to provide sixty days' notice of mass layoffs or plant closings.

Application: Companies with one hundred or more employees.

OWBA: Older Workers Benefit Protection Act (1990)

Purpose: Prohibits age-based discrimination in early retirement and other benefit plans of employees who are age forty or older.

Application: All private-sector employers with twenty or more people who work twenty or more weeks per year.

Additional details: One provision of this law gives employees a time frame (at least twenty-one days) to consider a company's offer that includes a promise not to sue the company for age discrimination. It also gives employees seven days to change their minds.

ADA: Americans with Disabilities Act (1990)

Purpose: Gives people with physical or mental disabilities greatly increased access to public services and requires employers to provide reasonable accommodation for applicants and employees with disabilities.

Application: All private-sector employers with fifteen or more employees.

Additional details: Employers in recent years have taken major steps to accommodate otherwise qualified disabled employees by outfitting the workplace with certain features (such as wheelchair ramps, for example) specially designed for disabled people or modifying schedules or training programs.

FMLA: Family and Medical Leave Act (1993)

Purpose: Gives qualified employees the right to unpaid leave for specified family or health-related reasons without the fear of losing their jobs. Employees who are seriously ill or who have seriously ill immediate family members are eligible for up to a total of twelve work weeks of unpaid leave during any twelve-month period. This act also applies to the birth and care of a newborn child of the employee and the placement with the employee of a child for adoption or foster care.

Application: Private employers with fifteen or more employees.

FOR EXAMPLE

Disabilities and Discrimination

The EEOC settled a disability discrimination lawsuit in 2003 against a Nebraska-based distributor of commercial lighting products. A court awarded more than $91,000 to a former worker, charging the company violated the Americans with Disabilities Act of 1990 (ADA) by terminating the long-time employee who needed in-patient care due to bipolar disorder, a psychiatric disability. Rather than allow the employee the additional time off recommended by his physicians, the company fired him by taping a termination letter to the front door of his home. Although the company argued that, at the time of his termination, the former employee was unable to perform the essential functions of his job, the court ruled that a jury should determine whether the employee was entitled to a reasonable medical leave to enable him to recover sufficiently to return to his former position.

HIPAA: Health Insurance Portability and Accountability Act (1996)

Purpose: Establishes guidelines for protecting private, personal information. Covered entities, such as an employer's health plan, healthcare providers, and healthcare clearinghouses, must protect identifiable health information. Individuals have control over how their information may be used.

Application: All employers.

AC-21: American Competitiveness in the Twenty-First Century Act (2000)

Purpose: Seeks to help the American economy in both the short and long run by a combination of temporary visa increases issued for highly skilled labor as well as training and education initiatives.

The act benefits both job seekers and employers. It allows individuals whose employers are trying to get them an extension on their visas to stay in the United States until a decision is made on their cases rather than forcing these persons to leave the country. The act also includes training and educational opportunities for American citizens.

Application: Any company.

Patriot Act (2001)

Purpose: Expands the federal government's ability to conduct investigative and surveillance activities.

Application: All employers.

Key implication: Complying with the Patriot Act requires vigilance in two areas. On one hand, you need to maintain your employees' privacy rights. But you also must comply with the government. Meeting these two demands requires thoughtful discussions with attorneys who can help you clarify and articulate the Patriot Act's legal implications for your employees. Computer, telecommunications, and security experts can assist with everything from ensuring safe internal communications to creating secure means for employees to enter and exit your offices.

Sarbanes-Oxley Act (2002)

Purpose: Requires publicly held companies to be more straightforward in reporting their financial results and how they were calculated. Also requires more stringent company controls to ensure the ethical behavior of all employees.

Application: Publicly held companies and private firms that are considering becoming public companies through an initial public offering.

Strong recommendation: Sarbanes-Oxley requires the establishment of a company code of ethics for its senior financial officers. By extension, many companies seek to uphold the spirit of the law by requesting that their HR teams update and communicate the firm's code of conduct for all employees.

SELF-CHECK

1. What is *age-based discrimination?*
2. The Fair Labor Standards Act prohibits any discrepancies in pay between men and women who perform the same job. True or false?
3. Which regulation allows for temporary visa increases issued for highly skilled labor?

2.3 Complying with EEOC Regulations

The best way to fight discrimination is to prevent it from happening in the first place. Court rulings in recent years make clear that companies who aren't taking an aggressive and **proactive** approach to communicating regulatory information to employees may still be held accountable for violations that individual employees commit. The moral is that, in keeping people in your organization informed about employment law, there is no such thing as overkill.

2.3.1 Staying Ahead of the Game: The Proactive Approach

With the legal ins and outs of the human resources function becoming more confusing—and more restrictive—by the day, your challenge is threefold:

▲ You must keep pace with changes in employment law.
▲ You must make sure that you're constantly bringing other key people in your organization up to speed.
▲ Make all your hiring, promotion, and other decisions solely on the basis of ability to perform the job.

EQUAL OPPORTUNITY AND AFFIRMATIVE ACTION

The EEOC requires some employers to file annual reports demonstrating that their employment practices provide equal opportunity to all qualified applicants and employees:

▲ **Affirmative Action Plans (AAP):** Federal contractors must complete an AAP within 120 days of receiving a federal contract. Currently, the information required includes an analysis of the job groups in the organization, an analysis of the percentage of minorities and women in the job groups, and an analysis of the demographics of the labor pool from which employees are recruited for each job group. If the analysis indicates that some protected groups are underrepresented in the job group based on the demographics of availability in the labor pool, placement goals are set to better reflect the availability of that protected class.

▲ **EEO-1 Reports:** The EEOC requires private employers with 100 or more employees to file the EEO-1 report by September 30 of each year. In some cases, employers with fewer than 100 employees might be required to file if, for example, they are owned or controlled by another company and the total workforce of the two companies is 100 or more employees.

2.3.2 Use EEOC Resources

The Equal Employment Opportunity Commission provides information and solutions to individuals and companies alike to identify and solve problems before they escalate. Check out the EEOC website (www.eeoc.gov) for a number of useful resources:

▲ Reports.
▲ Case examples.
▲ Best practices to encourage learning and understanding among employers and employees.
▲ Outreach activities such as teleconferences and technical assistance visits.
▲ Training opportunities.

The agency is working to "promote healthy workplace practices and to instruct managers in an effort to find the 'cure' for discrimination."

WARNING

Information in this chapter, as well as in other parts of the book, is intended as a legally sound overview. However, it is no substitute for the specific and tailored advice of your own legal counsel.

2.3.3 In the Event of a Complaint

In the event that an employee or group of employees decides to file an equal employment opportunity complaint against your company, it would be helpful to at least have a basic idea of what to expect.

According to the EEOC, employees filed more than 75,000 cases of discrimination in 2005. Though EEOC research indicates that nearly eighty percent of these cases result in no benefit to the individual filing the charge, you should understand the sequence of steps that typically take place after a claim is registered with the EEOC.

1. **The EEOC receives the charges.**
   In nearly every case, the EEOC will accept a charge for filing. The EEOC doesn't investigate and evaluate a charge when it's clear, for example, that the EEOC simply doesn't have jurisdiction. Note that in some states, a complaint must also be filed with a state human rights commission in addition to the EEOC to preserve any claim that a party might have.

2. **The EEOC notifies you of the charges.**
   The EEOC promptly notifies you that a charge has been filed and provides a copy of the charge. The EEOC generally requests information about the allegations, including a statement of the company's position. The EEOC also invites you to participate in mediation/conciliation to try to settle the charge immediately. If you choose not to participate, skip to step 4.

3. **The parties try to hash it out.**
   Someone from your company (probably from human resources) talks with both the person who filed the charge and an EEOC staff member. The plaintiff gets a chance to tell his side of the story—that is, why the person feels that he is the victim of discrimination. Your company's representative then gets to give the company's side of the story. The EEOC staff member tries her best to resolve the issue. (A resolution may involve, for example, giving a dismissed employee another chance or additional severance pay.)

4. **The investigation begins.**
   If step 3 is unsuccessful (or you choose not to participate), the EEOC requests that you provide the information and the position statement requested in step 2. The EEOC may follow up this step with requests for more information, which can include interviews of witnesses and a review of documents at your facility.

5. **The EEOC makes a determination.**
   If, on the basis of the investigation, the EEOC finds **reasonable cause** that your company discriminated against the individual, the EEOC notifies you and, once again, solicits you to participate in a conciliation process (as in steps 2 and 3). If the conciliation process fails (or you choose not to participate), the EEOC then decides whether to take you to court itself or to issue the individual a **right-to-sue notice** so that he (or she) can sue you. (Note that if the EEOC finds no reasonable cause, it will so advise you and the individual but still issue a right-to-sue notice to the individual.)

FOR EXAMPLE

Unlawful Discrimination

The EEOC settled a pregnancy discrimination lawsuit against Walmart for $220,000 for its failure to hire a female applicant due to her pregnancy; the company was also ordered to engage in comprehensive training concerning the Pregnancy Discrimination Act of 1978. The lawsuit alleged that the applicant was refused because she told them she was pregnant—and to "come back after she had the baby." The applicant was not aware that refusing to hire someone because they are pregnant is against the law until she read an article in a magazine in her doctor's office. Under the Pregnancy Discrimination Act of 1978, which amended Title VII of the Civil Rights Act of 1964, employment discrimination on the basis of pregnancy, childbirth, or related medical conditions constitutes unlawful sex discrimination.

2.3.4 EEOC Actions: Corporate Choices

If a complaint leads to an EEOC action, your company will be faced with a difficult choice: You either go along with EEOC proposals or gird yourself for a legal fight that may take years and cost your company millions in court costs, damages, and negative publicity. Even if the EEOC doesn't take the case, the individual claimant can proceed on his own, and you may find yourself in the same predicament.

SELF-CHECK

1. Define *proactive* as it relates to discrimination in the workplace.
2. Give three examples of ways in which the EEOC can offer individuals and businesses assistance.
3. In cases of alleged discrimination the involved parties are given three chances to reach a resolution. True or false?
4. What is the purpose of a right-to-sue notice?

2.4 Legal Matters: The Big Picture

Despite the complex regulations and potential legal landmines surrounding employment practices, companies are surviving and thriving. You can, too, if you use a little common sense. Although this chapter gives you that common-sense guidance, this information is no substitute for legal advice.

2.4.1 Why Legal Fees Are a Good Investment

The legal issues covered in this chapter require careful deliberation and professional review for the following reasons:

▲ **Daily changes:** Every day, new statutes are passed by federal and state governments, new regulations are adopted by federal and state agencies, new ordinances are adopted by local governments, and courts are ruling on existing statutes, regulations, and ordinances.

▲ **Vague definition:** It would be nice if all laws were clearly stated and not subject to interpretation. For example, many laws specifically require you to do what is "reasonable." What is reasonable in a specific situation? The law doesn't say. Just because you think you're acting reasonably doesn't mean that the courts, the administrative agencies, or your employees will agree. If the court or agency eventually decides that you didn't act reasonably, you can be liable for large sums of money.

▲ **Inconsistency:** Laws and regulations are adopted by the federal government, states, counties, cities, air quality districts, water districts, and so on, and they don't consult with one another. Often, the law of one entity contradicts the law of another. In addition, each law is adopted at a different time, and efforts aren't always made to be consistent. In fact, new laws often conflict with old laws without repealing them.

Most laws are defined, refined, and clarified by agency regulations and court rulings that cover areas that the average person wouldn't anticipate. For example, if a law applies only to businesses with twenty-five or more employees, does it apply to your business? That depends on how the law defines "employee." Do part-time employees count? Do temporary or supplemental employees count? Do independent contractors count? What if you never had more than twenty-three people at a time, but, because of turnover, forty different people worked for you at various times during the last year? Each law answers this question differently, and the answer may change often.

2.4.2 Disparate Impact

The laws against discrimination extend not only to intentional acts by you (**disparate treatment**), but may also cover actions that aren't intended to discriminate but have the effect of doing so, which is called **disparate impact**.

For example, assume that you own a grocery store. If you decide that you won't employ people of a certain race, sex, or religion, you're practicing disparate treatment, which is illegal from the standpoint of federal, state, and many local laws.

In other cases you may not intentionally discriminate, but if a certain hiring requirement results in limited hiring of members of a certain race, sex, or religion,

FOR EXAMPLE

Interpreting Disparate Impact

In Griggs vs. Duke Power, the Supreme Court ruled that an employer must show that job requirements are related to job performance. The case was brought by a black man, Willie Griggs, who worked in the Labor Department, the lowest-paid of five departments at a power station in North Carolina. For many years, the company operated without any particular education or testing requirements. In 1955, it began requiring a high school diploma, however; and in 1965, it began to require a passing score on two aptitude tests to move out of the Labor Department. Mr. Griggs was able to show that because many white employees who had transferred out of the Labor Department before these requirements were implemented were performing their duties successfully, neither requirement was related to the ability of an individual to do the work.

you may be guilty of disparate impact. You haven't intentionally adopted a policy against a group, but an apparently neutral policy impacts one group adversely.

If you can then demonstrate that the requirement is a **Bona Fide Occupational Qualification (BFOQ)** for the job, then you will not be guilty of discrimination. A BFOQ is an exception allowed by the EEOC when a business can demonstrate that a practice is necessary to maintain normal business operations. BFOQs are allowed when a position requires that an employee be of a specific religion, sex, national origin, or age. For example, it is reasonable to expect that a synagogue would require a rabbi to be Jewish, or a manufacturer of men's clothing would require that models of its clothing be men.

Keep in mind, however, that your determination of what is a BFOQ will almost certainly be challenged. And the court or administrative agency reviewing the situation doesn't have to agree with you. Therefore, you need legal advice when establishing any job requirements that you think may be open to question.

SELF-CHECK

1. What are three reasons that professional legal review is important for a company dealing with employment laws?
2. Define *bona fide occupational qualification*.
3. Disparate impact refers to a company's intentional acts of discrimination. True or false?

2.5 Sexual Harassment: Keep Your Workplace Free of It

The definition of **sexual harassment,** on the surface, seems straightforward: any form of harassment that has sexual overtones. As with many things in life and business, the reality may not be so simple. According to language originally set forth in 1980 by the EEOC in guidelines under Title VII of the Civil Rights Act of 1964 (see earlier in this chapter), the intent behind the sexual behavior is at issue in identifying what constitutes sexual harassment. Also at issue is the connection between the behavior and the working circumstances and conditions of the person who is being harassed. Sexual harassment is really about power—abuse of power—in the workplace.

2.5.1 EEOC and Sexual Harassment

In its definition of sexual harassment, the EEOC labels the behavior as follows: "Unwelcome sexual advances, requests for sexual favors, and other verbal or physical conduct of a sexual nature." But the law adds some fine print that muddies the waters. It lists three situations in which these unwelcome advances rise to the legal definition of sexual harassment:

▲ Submission to such conduct is made either explicitly or implicitly a term or condition of an individual's employment.

▲ Submission to or rejection of such conduct by an individual is used as the basis for employment decisions affecting such individuals.

▲ Such conduct has the purpose or effect of unreasonably interfering with an individual's work performance or creating an intimidating, hostile, or offensive working environment.

These guidelines are laden with terms that are highly dependent on perceptions and interpretations, which is one of the chief problems that arise when harassment complaints are filed. People (courts included) have varying ideas of what is implicit, and they have different perceptions about what factors make a workplace intimidating or hostile.

No company today can afford to ignore this issue, and no one with HR responsibility can afford to forget that what one person may view as a harmless joke may well be perceived by another as an aggressive and unwelcome sexual advance. Sexual harassment is one area of HR management in which you can never be too careful. To point you in the right direction, the following offer guidelines that may help you develop a proactive—and effective—sexual harassment policy in your own company.

FOR EXAMPLE

Boca and the Beach

A Supreme Court case involving the city of Boca Raton, Florida, proved the importance of aggressively communicating a company's sexual harassment policies. The Court held that the City of Boca Raton was liable for the actions of two male lifeguard supervisors who were alleged to have created a sexually hostile environment for female lifeguards by making offensive and lewd remarks. While the Court conceded that Boca Raton did indeed have a formal antiharassment policy, it concluded that city officials hadn't gone far enough to communicate the policy to employees and didn't inform employees that they had a right to bypass their harassing supervisors in order to file the complaint.

2.5.2 Implementing an Effective Sexual Harassment Policy

It's no longer enough to simply declare in writing your company's commitment to prevent sexual harassment. You need a written sexual harassment policy that spells it out clearly, and you need to state, in no uncertain terms, the penalties for flouting the policy—innocently or otherwise. An effective policy must begin with the support and commitment of the CEO; otherwise, those employees who may have a tendency toward harassing others may not take it seriously.

Your company is responsible for making sure that everyone in the organization—supervisors, managers, and employees—recognizes that sexual harassment is wrong and will not be tolerated. How you communicate and educate people about this policy (by using classes, educational videos, literature, and so on) is up to you.

▲ Publicize your policy on sexual harassment each year. Set a date during the same month each year and send copies of your policies to every employee.

▲ Develop an online sexual harassment policy manual and training course that you can deliver to every employee annually.

2.5.3 Coping with Harassment Complaints

The following sections outline steps an HR department should take to process— and perhaps prevent—sexual harassment in the workplace.

Create a Reporting Process

Employees are not required by law to report sexual harassment to their employer before going to the EEOC or to court. You should, however, encourage employees to report internally so that the company can take care of any problems first. Identify several different sources for employees to use to report harassment, such as their supervisor, an HR representative, or an anonymous, toll-free phone line.

Treat All Complaints Seriously

Regardless of how frivolous you may consider a sexual harassment complaint, you must take it seriously and, at the very least, seek legal council and look into the charge. If an incident ultimately ends up in court and it comes out in testimony that management was aware of the complaint but didn't act on it, you may have to pay more in damages.

Take Decisive Action

Once you've established that sexual harassment is taking place, your company must investigate and take any reasonable action that will end it and prevent it from happening again. Doing nothing or being too lenient can put your firm at great risk and create the impression that you're condoning the behavior. This impression won't do much to help your company recruit or retain good employees and will expose the company to increased monetary damages.

Document Every Complaint

Every sexual harassment complaint should be documented, no matter how trivial it may seem and how quickly or easily it is resolved. Paperwork can be your company's best defense. Documentation of discipline demonstrates that your company is serious about the problem and the solution. Be vigilant about getting detailed statements from the person making the charges, as well as from the accused.

SELF-CHECK

1. Define *sexual harassment* and explain what it has to do with power.
2. By establishing a reporting process, a company may be better able to avoid legal proceedings. True or false?
3. Describe ways in which a company can educate its employees about sexual harassment.

SUMMARY

Regardless of how intimidating the legal minefield of employment regulations may seem, every human resources manager must be accountable for staying up to date with current U.S. law. The Equal Opportunity Employment Commission is responsible for enforcement of federal antidiscrimination regulations; as such it is a valuable source of information on the many equal employment laws. HR professionals should have knowledge of regulations that cover discrimination based on age, race, gender, and disability. Not to be overlooked are regulations that cover layoffs, unemployment, and health care issues. HR programs that are not in compliance with regulations can result in fines, penalties, or lawsuits, none of which help achieve organizational goals. Although a proactive approach is the best way to fight discrimination, sound legal counsel cannot be underestimated in matters of employment law. Such counsel will help an organization navigate through such complex concepts as disparate impact and bona fide occupational qualification. Legal counsel will also be important in cases when sexual harassment occurs. Again, as with other forms of discrimination, a proactive approach—one that includes a clear sexual harassment policy—is the best way to avoid problems in the first place.

KEY TERMS

Age-based discrimination	Unfair treatment against a person because of his/her age.
Bona Fide Occupational Qualification (BFOQ)	Job requirements that are reasonably necessary to meet the normal operations of a business.
Disabled person	Any person who has a physical or mental impairment which substantially limits one or more major life activities
Discrimination	Unfair treatment of a person or group on the basis of prejudice.
Disparate impact	Employer actions that aren't intended to discriminate but have the effect of doing so.
Disparate treatment	Intentional acts by an employer to discriminate.
Equal Opportunity Employment Commission (EEOC)	The federal agency responsible for enforcing federal antidiscrimination laws in employment.
Proactive	Approach of acting in anticipation of future problems, needs, or changes.

Racial bias

A preformed negative opinion or attitude toward a group of persons who posses common physical characteristics (color of skin, facial features; etc.) that distinguish them as a distinct division of humankind, eg, Asians, Blacks, Whites.

Reasonable cause

To have knowledge of facts that would cause a reasonable person, knowing the same facts, to reasonably conclude the same thing.

Right-to-sue notice

Issued by the EEOC when it finds reasonable cause for an individual to file a lawsuit against his or her company.

Sexual harassment

Any form of harassment that has sexual overtones.

ASSESS YOUR UNDERSTANDING

Go to www.wiley.com/college/messmer to assess your knowledge of employment regulations.

Measure your learning by comparing pre-test and post-test results.

Summary Questions

1. Discrimination is unfair treatment based solely on race. True or false?
2. The legislation that had the greatest effect on employment practices is
   (a) The Family and Medical Leave Act of 1993.
   (b) Equal Pay Act.
   (c) Americans with Disabilities Act.
   (d) Civil Rights Act of 1964.
3. The Equal Opportunity Employment Commission enforces federal anti-discrimination employment laws. True or false?
4. The legislation that provides many employees and their families temporary health coverage is known as
   (a) COBRA.
   (b) FMLA.
   (c) HIPAA.
   (d) OWBA.
5. Which two pieces of employment legislation relate to older Americans?
6. WARN protects employees from
   (a) age-based discrimination.
   (b) pregnancy discrimination.
   (c) sudden layoffs.
   (d) unlawful company surveillance.
7. Proactive measures may prevent discrimination from happening in the first place. True or false?
8. To be proactive against discrimination in the workplace, a company needs to both disseminate and enforce anti-discrimination policies. True or false?
9. What is the first step in an EEOC case of alleged discrimination?
   (a) request for mediation
   (b) notification of charge
   (c) EEOC receives charge
   (d) EEOC investigates
10. An EEOC investigation determines reasonable cause. True or false?

11. A company may accept or decline to be involved in discrimination mediation. True or false?

12. Federal, state, and local laws and regulations are consistent with each other. True or false?

13. Disparate impact is
    (a) actions that have the effect of discrimination.
    (b) intentional discriminatory acts.
    (c) a valid job requirement.
    (d) all of the above.

14. Sexual harassment occurs when a female supervisor makes unwanted advances on a male employee? True or false?

15. When a company neglects to investigate a sexual harassment charge, it may
    (a) decrease its liability.
    (b) increase its liability.
    (c) face additional charges.
    (d) file its own charge.

Applying This Chapter

1. As a new HR manager for InfoTeam, an information technology service company throughout the Northeast, what must you do to keep the company EEOC compliant?

2. A tax preparation company is making a move to employ more retired tax accountants to help out during the busy tax season. Which of the EEOC regulations would be most relevant from an HR perspective?

3. You work for a home health care provider that employs twenty women health aides. Two of your employees have recently told you they are pregnant. What must your company do to comply with the Pregnancy Discrimination Act?

4. One of your female employees has filed a charge that the company has violated the Equal Pay Act by paying her male coworker ten percent more than her salary. The coworker does in fact make more money. As director of the company's human resources department, what steps should you take to determine the company's liability?

5. A high-end sports equipment store hires only very physically fit men to sell its exercise equipment. Is the store practicing disparate impact by not hiring physically fit women or less-than-fit men? In what case could this limitation be a bona fide occupational qualification?

6. A female employee reports sexual harassment to a male superior with no results; in fact, the harassment gets worse. What could the company have done to prevent this from happening?

YOU TRY IT

Stopping Sexual Harassment

Write a description of your school or company's sexual harassment policy.

- How is it communicated to its employees?
- When was it last updated?
- What, if any, areas of enforcement or proactiveness are lacking? For example, is there a reporting process in place?
- Propose changes to either the policy or the regulation of it.

Security and Discrimination

Title VII of the Civil Rights Act prohibits national origin discrimination in employment; that is, treating someone less favorably because he or she comes from a particular place, because of his or her ethnicity or accent, or because it is believed that he or she has a particular ethnic background.

- What are the implications of the Patriot Act regaring national origin discrimination?
- Cite a real-world situation involving alleged or proven discrimination based on national origin.

Small Businesses and the ADA

There are many accommodations that even small businesses can make to enable individuals with disabilities to apply for jobs and be productive workers. Using the EEOC website www.eeoc.gov, examine how the ADA affects small businesses. Give examples of reasonable accomadations for the following situations:

- employee in a wheelchair
- employee with impaired vision
- employee in a drug or alcohol recovery progarm

You may also look at the Americans with Disabilities Act Document Center, www.usdoj.gov/crt/ada, which is devoted to information relating to ADA.

3
BUILDING A STRATEGIC STAFFING PLAN
Looking Ahead to the Future

Starting Point

Go to www.wiley.com/college/messmer to assess your knowledge of strategic staffing plans.

Determine where you need to concentrate your effort.

What You'll Learn in This Chapter

▲ Ways in which strategic staffing differs from traditional staffing
▲ The value of outsourcing in today's business environment
▲ The role of job analysis in human resources
▲ How to differentiate between tasks and qualifications in job descriptions
▲ The legal implications of a job title
▲ Types of employee classifications

After Studying This Chapter, You Will Be Able To

▲ Evaluate workflow and staffing needs based on a strategic approach
▲ Judge the immediate and the long-term needs of a company
▲ Complete a task inventory as part of a job analysis
▲ Rewrite general job descriptions, making them clear and specific
▲ Assess the implications of various types of employment classifications

INTRODUCTION

The tasks and responsibilities that make up most people's "jobs" today are a far cry from what they were as recently as ten years ago. In most companies jobs are generally broader in scope than those of the past. As a human resources manager making decisions about work flow and staffing, this means you'll need to focus on what a job should be now and what it may look like in the near future, based on your company's current needs and long-term objectives.

3.1 Strategic-Style Staffing

The traditional hiring notion of "finding the best people to fill job openings" has been replaced by a much more dynamic approach. **Strategic staffing** is putting together a combination of human resources—both internal and external—that are strategically keyed to the needs of the business and the realities of the labor market.

This hiring approach is based on the immediate and long-term needs of the business, as opposed to the specs of a particular job. Of course, setting the strategic direction of your company is primarily the responsibility of senior management and not normally an HR function, but you will be required to look at your company's overall priorities and determine their staffing implications.

3.1.1 Comparing Staffing Approaches

The difference between the traditional approach to hiring and the strategic staffing model is illustrated in Table 3-1.

3.1.2 Taking a Closer Look at Staffing

To bring to your company the skills and attributes it needs to meet the challenges it may face, you must look beyond the purely functional requirements of the various positions in your company and focus on what skills and attributes employees need to perform those functions exceptionally well. You can then begin building a **staffing plan**—the way an organization recruits, hires, retains, promotes, and terminates employees.

Human resources managers can expect to carry out the following staffing functions:

▲ Working with senior management and line managers to identify staffing needs (see Section 3.2).

Table 3-1: Comparing Staffing Methods

Old Staffing Paradigm	Strategic Staffing
Think "job."	Think tasks and responsibilities that are keyed to business goals and enhance a company's ability to compete.
Create a set of job "specs."	Determine which competencies and skills are necessary to produce outstanding performance in any particular function.
Find the person who best "fits" the job.	Determine which combination of resources—internal or external—can get the most mileage out of the tasks and responsibilities that need to be carried out.
Look mainly for technical competence.	Find people who are more than simply "technically" qualified but can carry forward your company's mission and values.
Base the hiring decision primarily on the selection interview.	View the selection interview as only one of a series of tools designed to make the best choice of hiring.
Hire only full-time employees.	Consider a blend of full-time and temporary workers to meet variable workload needs.

▲ Developing staffing strategies that are keyed to your company's short-term operational requirements and long-term strategic needs (see Section 3.2.1).

▲ Overseeing the recruiting process and its many components, such as working with recruiters, placing classified ads, and conducting on-campus recruiting (see Section 4.2).

- Coordinating applicant evaluation and interviewing activities with line managers—and, in many cases, handling these functions yourself (see Sections 4.4, 4.5, as well as Chapter 5).

- Providing the necessary guidance to help managers make the best possible hiring decisions (see Section 5.3).

- Coordinating the new hire **onboarding** process, which includes a logistical, structural, and big-picture orientation to your company; opportunities for peer and senior manager mentoring; a review of job expectations; and other resources to help new employees be successful (see Chapter 6).

FOR EXAMPLE

Strategic Staffing Success

By creating a staffing strategy, the Department of Transportation of a state government was able to move from a workforce with specialized skills to a smaller, more broadly skilled workforce. With more than eighty percent of its staff eligible for retirement by 2010, the DOT was facing the impending loss of much of its highly experienced workers. The agency's response was a proactive approach enabling it to meet DOT and citizens' needs more efficiently, effectively, and with fewer employees. After collecting data on the entire organization, the agency was able to project the number of employees with appropriate skills still available to meet business needs. The DOT then identified gaps between staffing needs and available talent. The result: The DOT looked to alternatives such as outsourcing and temporary workers to address gaps, particularly with seasonal work. Finally, the DOT used a feedback process to evaluate programs and policies.

SELF-CHECK

1. Define *strategic staffing*.
2. Onboarding is a strategic staffing approach geared toward tasks and responsibilities. True or false?
3. List the elements of a *staffing plan*.
4. Describe three staffing functions of a human resources manager.

3.2 Assessing Staffing Needs

Strategic staffing begins with a reassessment of your department's human resources needs in the context of your firm's business priorities. The idea is to begin thinking in terms of need rather than job, long term rather than short term, and big picture rather than immediate opening. This approach ties directly into the changing role of the HR professional from administrator to strategist (see Section 1.4). To be successful with this approach you'll first need to get a firm understanding of your company's major goals and priorities.

3.2.1 Making It a Team Effort

Unless you head an extremely small organization, you can't adopt a strategic staffing approach all by yourself. You'll need to introduce the strategic staffing concept to other managers in your organization. You'll need their input to better understand company and departmental priorities—and they'll need your help in guiding them through the process and adopting this mind-set as well.

As a team, you'll identify everything that may affect the efficiency and prof-itability of your firm's operations—and not just in the short term. To begin, you and other people in your company should answer these key questions before you make your next move:

▲ What are your company's long-term strategic goals or those of depart-ments seeking your assistance in hiring employees?

▲ What are the key competitive trends in your industry? (In other words, what factors have the greatest bearing on competitive success?)

▲ What kind of culture currently exists in your company? And what kind of culture do you ultimately want to create? What are the values you want the company to stand for?

▲ What knowledge, skill sets, and attributes (in general) are required to keep pace with those goals and, at the same time, remain true to your company values?

▲ How does the current level of knowledge, skill sets, and attributes among your present employees match up with what will be necessary in the future?

▲ How reasonable is it for you to expect that with the proper support and training, your current employees will be able to develop the skills they're going to need in order for your company to keep pace with the competition?

▲ What combination of resources (rather than specific people) represents the best strategic approach to the staffing needs you face over the near-term and the long-term?

3.2.2 Choosing between Hiring or Repositioning

Strategic staffing is not just about hiring more employees—it's about making the best staffing choices available. If a manager is thinking of filling an existing position, encourage him to consider how his group's needs have changed since the last time the job was open, rather than immediately searching for a candidate to fill the vacant position.

▲ Is a full-time individual still required in this role?

▲ Should a potential replacement have the same skills and experience as her predecessor?

▲ Does the position need to be refilled at all?

> ### FOR EXAMPLE
>
> **Thinking Outsourcing**
>
> DataNet Ltd. is a new business outside Boston that sells computer hardware from a small store in the center of town. It is a small business, with eight employees who all have specific roles. Business had been slow, with sales not reaching expected figures. The current employees did well with direct sales, but they didn't have experience with other means of selling the products. Though money was not available for a new hire, the company agreed to try a new approach and outsource some sales services—one company to conduct telemarketing sales to other businesses and a mailing company to introduce DataNet's new offers and discounts to the public. Six months later sales figures increased significantly.

▲ Help the manager identify the frequency and timing of workload peaks and valleys and look for predictable patterns.

▲ Discuss the impact of shifts in company priorities and what eventual effect these are likely to have on the work group in question. This discussion allows you to spot any shortfalls in human resources for upcoming initiatives.

3.2.3 Considering a Mix of Resources

How will you bridge any staffing gaps in the event that you do identify shortfalls? By reprioritizing and shifting some duties, can one or more staff members be reassigned to an urgent project when it comes in?

Redeploying full-time staff may partially address rising demands, but this step alone isn't likely to be the answer to all your company's staffing concerns. If core staff are fully occupied and you have new tasks that must be handled on a long-term basis, it may make sense to hire additional permanent staff—full-time and/or temporary. In some cases, **outsourcing**, or turning over an entire function to an outside specialist, may suit your needs best.

By adopting a strategic staffing approach, you gain flexibility. It allows you and other company managers to rapidly expand or contract a well-thought-out mix of talent to meet both current and long-term goals.

3.2.4 Reassessing Goals Annually

Company priorities will certainly shift over time as management seeks ways to keep the business competitive. As a result, you and the managers you support should consider performing your needs assessments on an annual basis to ensure that you're still on track with the assumptions that are guiding your staffing strategy.

SELF-CHECK

1. In most cases, hiring a new employee is more efficient than repositioning an existing employee. True or false?
2. Define *outsourcing*.
3. Explain the value of conducting annual staffing assessments.

3.3 Conducting a Job Analysis

After an organization has determined how many employees will be needed to achieve its goals, it's important to identify which tasks, duties, and responsibilities these employees will perform. To do this, a job analysis is conducted. **Job analysis** is the process of gathering information about various aspects of a job, including reporting relationships, interactions with others, qualifications, work environment, and the knowledge, skills, and abilities needed to perform the job successfully.

3.3.1 Gathering Job Data

The analysis begins with an information-gathering process. To provide the most comprehensive information, you should answer the following questions:

▲ What types of interactions will this job have with other jobs in the work group, the company, customers, vendors, or others?

▲ At what level will the position interact with these individuals?

▲ To which position will this job report?

▲ Is the position exempt from requirements of the Fair Labor Standards Act (FLSA)? See Section 8.2.1 for more on the FLSA.

▲ What are the essential functions of the job? This list is necessary for compliance with the Americans with Disabilities Act (ADA) discussed in Chapter 2. The ADA definition of essential functions includes the following considerations:

• The position exists to perform the function; without it, there is no need for the job.

• There are a limited number of other employees who can perform the function.

- The function is highly specialized, and the person hired will possess expertise of special ability to perform the function.

▲ What are the nonessential functions of the job? How complex are these tasks and how often are they performed?

▲ What is the environment in which the job will be performed? Is it an office or production line? Is it very noisy, hot or cold, or hazardous in some way?

▲ What physical requirements are necessary for successfully completing the essential job functions? Does the job require sitting or standing for extended periods of time? What level of mental capacity is needed to complete the work?

▲ What qualifications are required to successfully complete the essential job functions? This includes the **Knowledge, Skills, and Abilities (KSAs)** that are necessary to successfully perform in a position as well as other more general competencies that employees will need.

▲ How urgent is the need for the KSAs? Will the organization need to hire a new employee who already has the KSAs, or will there be time to train someone internally to acquire the skills needed to do this job?

3.3.2 Employing Methods of Data Collection

There are several methods for collecting information during a job analysis. Some of the most common methods include the following:

▲ **Questionnaires:** Can be completed by a supervisor, manager, or incumbent of a position.

▲ **Interviews:** Can be conducted with an employee who has been doing the job, a supervisor or manager, or coworkers with whom the job will interact. Interviews are more time consuming than questionnaires, but they provide an opportunity for the interviewer to ask followup questions to clarify information.

▲ **Task inventory:** A comprehensive list of tasks that could be performed in a particular job category. A task inventory can also provide information about the level of experience needed in the position. For example, a receptionist may need to have an advanced level of verbal communication skills, but need only an entry-level ability to explain technical information to customers. Table 3-2 provides a sample of a task inventory.

▲ **Observation:** Requires someone (usually from HR) to spend time in the normal work area and observe an incumbent performing the job. The observer makes notes about the tasks and interactions, and then determines the KSAs that are necessary to perform the task.

Table 3-2: Sample Task Inventory								
Task	*1*	*2*	*3*	*4*	*5*	*Entry*	*Int*	*Adv*
	Task Importance					*Training Level Required*		
Communicate verbally at a basic level								
Communicate verbally at a high level								
Communicate in writing at a basic level								
Communicate in writing at a high level								
Explain technical information to customers								
Provide excellent customer service								

3.3.3 Using Competency Modeling

Many firms today are using a process called **competency modeling** to help target the characteristics that distinguish top performers. Companies can then use this information in the hiring process to seek and evaluate prospective employees. Simply put, competency modeling is a way of determining, as accurately as you can, what particular mix of skills, attributes, and attitudes produce superior performance in those operational functions that have the most bearing on your company's competitive strength.

Suppose, for example, that your company is in the business of selling home security systems. One way that you market your service is to solicit potential customers by phone. The basic job of a telemarketer, of course, is to generate leads by calling people on the phone. Some telemarketers, however, are clearly much better at this task than others: They're better at engaging the interest of the people they call, and they don't allow repeated rejections to wear down their spirits. In other words, they possess certain attributes that contribute to superior performance in this job. And these attributes (as opposed to the actual tasks of the job) are the basis of the competency model.

Although you can apply the concept of competency modeling to virtually any function in your company, the basic objective is always the same: To determine as precisely as you can what combination of skills and attributes are required to excel at that function.

You may not always find the perfect match between the skills and attributes that dominate your competency model for a given function and the skills and attributes of the candidates you're considering for that job. But at least you have a frame of reference from which to work. You can now identify with greater precision any skill deficits—gaps between the requirements of the job and the qualifications of the candidate. And if the gaps are not exceptionally wide, you can frequently close them through training and coaching.

The following suggestions can help you gain more insight into the types of skills and attributes that form the basis of your hiring criteria:

▲ **Interview your own "top" performers.** Assuming that you have a group of people who perform the same job—and assuming that one or two of those people are clearly the "stars" of the group—sitting down with your key people to determine what makes them so successful at what they do is certainly worth your time. Try to answer the following questions:

- What special skills, if any, do these star performers possess that the others don't?
- What type of personality traits do they share?
- What common attitudes and values do they bring to their jobs?

▲ **Talk to your customers.** One of the best—and easiest—ways to find out which employees in your company can provide the basis for your competency modeling is to talk to people with whom your staff interact on a regular basis: your customers. Find out which employees your customers enjoy dealing with the most, and more important, what those employees do to routinely win the admiration of these customers.

FOR EXAMPLE

Competency Models at HP

Hewlett-Packard is one of many companies that considers competency modeling an important part of future success. In 2003 Hewlett-Packard used competency modeling to work on improving the overall quality and performance of its sales force. The project started by creating models for various job roles, including role requirements, key competencies for successful performance, as well as learning and career paths. The models were then reviewed and confirmed through interviews with managers and expert performers. The program generated a learning, development, and career planning toolkit. Thousands of employees and managers in sales have completed competency assessments, and the sales teams use the learning and career information to improve performance.

SELF-CHECK

1. Explain the purpose of *job analysis*.
2. Define *KSAs*.
3. With competency modeling, gaps between the requirements of a job and the qualifications of a candidate can eventually be closed through training. True or false?
4. Explain how customers can assist with competency modeling.

3.4 Creating Job Descriptions

By completing a job analysis you've determined the qualities that are most important to specific functions and positions in your company (see Section 3.3). At this point you have what you need to create a job description. A **job description** is a written document that is produced as the result of a job analysis. It contains information that identifies the job, its essential functions, and the job specifications or competencies that enable an individual to be successful in the position.

The job description has long been the bread-and-butter tool of hiring. And, as any hiring professional can tell you, a high percentage of hiring "mistakes" result from job descriptions that fail to accurately capture the essence of the job in question.

Done correctly, a well thought-out job description delivers the following benefits:

▲ Ensures that everyone who has a say in the hiring decision is on the same page with respect to what the job entails.

▲ Serves as the basis for key hiring criteria.

▲ Ensures that candidates have a clear idea of what to expect if, indeed, you hire them.

▲ Serves as a reference tool during the evaluation process.

▲ Is required for ADA compliance (see Section 3.3.1).

▲ Serves as a benchmark for performance after you hire the candidate.

A well-written job description can be considered a "snapshot" of the job. The job description needs to communicate as specifically but concisely as possible what responsibilities and tasks the job entails and to indicate the key qualifications of the job—the basic requirements (specific credentials or skills)—and, if possible, the attributes that underlie superior performance.

3.4.1 Job Description Formats

There are many different formats for job descriptions; a search of the internet will produce many styles and types that can be adapted to your organization. The format selected by an employer must include some basic elements; however it is also important that the format fits the needs of the individual organization. Figure 3-1 shows one possible job description format and the elements it should contain.

3.4.2 Creating a Job Description

The following six guidelines can help you through the important—but often overlooked—stage of creating a job description.

Differentiate Tasks from Qualifications

A **task** is what the person or people you hire actually do: take orders over the phone, deliver pizzas, keep your computer network up and running, and so on. **Qualifications** are the skills, attributes, or credentials a person needs to perform each task, such as possess a driver's license, have an upbeat personality, be familiar with computer networking, and so on.

Do your best to avoid the common pitfall of blurring this distinction. Discipline yourself to clarify the actual tasks and responsibilities before you start to think about what special attributes are needed by the person who will be carrying out those tasks and fulfilling those responsibilities.

Set Priorities

A well-written job description consists of more than simply a list of the tasks and responsibilities that the job entails. It reflects a sense of priorities. In other words, it differentiates those responsibilities and tasks that are primary from those that are secondary. Don't rely solely on a job's history as you're putting together a job description for today.

Key into Credentials

Credentials such as degrees and licenses acknowledge that a candidate has passed a particular test or completed a specific field of study. Credentials are absolute necessities in some jobs. (The person who delivers pizza for you, for example, must have a driver's license; the appropriate medical boards must license the surgeon you hire.) You can often use credentials as a way to eliminate certain candidates from the running if you have far more applicants for a job than you can reasonably handle. (You may decide, for example, to consider only those who have a bachelor's degree or the equivalent.)

It's important to stay flexible, however. Though you prefer certain credentials in a candidate, they may not necessarily be what's required for the position,

Figure 3-1

JOB DESCRIPTION	
Job Title: Receptionist	**Department:** Administration
Reports to: Office Manager	**Exemption Status:** Nonexempt
Salary Grade: 2	**Date Published:** January 12, 2004

Position Summary:
Under general supervision, the receptionist answers the telephone, greets visitors, and logs them onto the security system; and prepares sales packets as directed by members of the sales team.

Supervisory Responsibilities:
Performs duties under only general supervision; determines process and actions to be taken on routine assignments.

| **Essential Functions:**
Using the Nortel T24 KIM Call Director, answers an average of 45 incoming calls per hour within three rings and directs callers to the appropriate person, department, or voice mailbox. | **% Time:**
95% |
|---|---|
| **Nonessential Functions:**
May be required to drive to the post office for mail pickup from time to time. | **% Time:**
5% |

| **Equipment Operated:**
Nortel T24 KIM Call Director, PC, copy machine, postage machine | **Education, Licenses, or Certificates Required:**
Must have a high school diploma or equivalent. Must have a valid driver's license. |
|---|---|

Communication Skills Required:
Must be able to verbally communicate effectively with employees at all levels in the organization, as well as with customers, vendors, callers, and visitors. Basic written communication skills are also necessary.

Experience Required:
1–2 years of experience in an office environment performing entry-level clerical work.

Skills Required:
Basic knowledge of Microsoft Office, including Outlook and Word.

Physical Requirements:
This job requires the ability to sit for approximately 2–3 hours at a time, to listen and talk on the telephone about 95 percent of the time, and to occasionally lift packages weighing 25 pounds.

Mental Requirements:
Requires cognitive skills that allow movement from one task to another, to attend to detail, to process information, and to interpret it as needed.

Work Environment Conditions:
Indoor office environment with controlled temperatures and sealed windows on 44th floor of high rise building.

Approved by:	Title:	Date:

A sample job description.

FOR EXAMPLE

Soft Skills at the Top

When you read about CEOs who build successful companies, you hear far less about their technical skills—be it finance or marketing, engineering or administration—and much more about their strong people skills. The types of people you want in your company are adept at communicating ideas, providing leadership, collaborating with others, and simply making things happen.

---

particularly when you take into account a candidate's various work experiences and accomplishments. This advice is particularly true when hiring for middle and senior-level managers. The thing that you want to make sure of most of all is that the credentials you establish have a direct bearing on a candidate's ability to become a top performer.

Look at Soft Skills

Every job has a set of technical requirements that you typically define in partnership with line managers, but don't overlook the other broad but telling aspects of a candidate. **Soft skills** are skills such as having an aptitude for communicating with people of all levels, skill sets, and backgrounds; the ability to work well in teams (as both leader and team member), and other factors, such as a strong sense of ethics and a talent for efficient and creative problem-solving.

Candidates who are weak in these soft skill areas—even while having solid hard skills and work experience—may prove unable to grow as your company goes through the inevitable changes that are a part of today's business world.

Make the Job Doable

It doesn't matter how good a job description sounds on paper if the person who is hired for the job can't perform the required duties. So the job that you describe must truly be doable. Consider the number of tasks that you may call on a person to perform in a job as well as the compatibility of those tasks. For example, people who are unusually creative don't typically excel at tasks that require considerable attention to detail. By the same token, people who are at their best when they're working by themselves on complex, analytical tasks tend, as a rule, to be more introverted than extroverted. The lesson here is to make sure that when you're putting several tasks into the same job description that you're not creating a job that very few people could fill.

Table 3-3: Good and Bad Task Descriptions

Too general	*Specific*
Handles administrative chores	Receives, sorts, and files monthly personnel action reports
Good communication skills	Ability to communicate technical information to nontechnical audiences
Computer literate	Proficient with Microsoft Word, Excel, and QuickBooks

Be Specific

A solid job description doesn't need to be fine prose, but it should be written in a way that clearly spells out what the job entails. Table 3-3 provides a handful of examples of task descriptions that are far too general, coupled with suggested rewrites.

SELF-CHECK

1. Give two uses for a job description.
2. Which of the following is considered a qualification?
   a. data inputting
   b. carpentry
   c. master's degree
   d. copyediting
3. Define *credentials*.
4. A strong sense of ethical conduct is an example of a soft skill. True or false?

3.5 Choosing Job Titles

Now that the majority of jobs in most companies involve multitasking, job titles are no longer a reliable indicator of the responsibilities of any particular job. Even so, as a human resources manager you need to give some attention to what you're actually calling the job. An inaccurate or overblown job title can create false expectations and lead to resentment, disappointment, or worse.

It's also important to clarify whether the job is exempt or nonexempt **Exempt workers** receive a flat weekly, monthly, or annual salary, regardless of the number of hours they work over a given period. **Nonexempt workers** are paid on an hourly basis (though some receive salaries) and are eligible for overtime pay if they work more than forty hours in a given week.

3.5.1 Legal Implications of Job Titles

A job description is generally regarded as a legal document. As such, any references to race, color, religion, age, sex, national origin or nationality, or physical or mental disability can expose your company to a possible discrimination suit.

In rare cases, an employer can specify a requirement usually considered discriminatory if it's a bona fide occupational qualification or need (see Section 2.4.2). The limiting of recruitment of a live-in counselor in a female residence hall to women is one frequently cited example. You can also find exceptions to the age prohibition. These exceptions are so conditional, however, that the wise employer enlists the assistance of a lawyer.

3.5.2 Considering Employee Classification

The specific arrangements your company has with its employees may not matter to your customers, but they do matter to your accountant, as well as the federal and state agencies that are responsible for collecting payroll taxes. The following sections provide the general classifications, along with a brief description of the main classification criteria

FOR EXAMPLE

Title Troubles

When an HR manager is having trouble coming up with a job title, he or she can go to the website of the U.S. Department of Labor's Dictionary of Occupational Titles (DOT), located at www.wave.net/upg/immigration/dot_index.html. It lists jobs by occupational groups and, within groups, by functions and responsibilities. The DOT assigns each specific job a unique nine-digit code number and defines the principal tasks each job involves. The dictionary is especially useful for describing technical or skilled jobs or if you're trying to translate a veteran's Military Occupational Specialty into a civilian skill.

Full-time Employees

▲ **General definition:** Employees who generally work a full week, regardless of what they do for the company, where they work, or who they work for.

▲ **Major implications:** Employers are required to pay whatever payroll taxes are required by law and must also withhold applicable state, federal, and local taxes. Full-time employees enjoy full protection under all the federal and state laws and statutes that govern HR administration.

Regular Part-Time Employees

▲ **General definition:** Employees who generally work less than a full week, but nonetheless have a regular schedule, perform a prescribed set of tasks, and have a fixed place where they do their work.

▲ **Major implications:** Enjoy many of the same benefits (usually on a prorated scale) and the same federal and state protections as full-time employees.

Temporary Workers and Contract Employees

▲ **General definition:** Individuals who work on an as-needed (that is, contingency) basis, with no set schedule.

▲ **Major implications:** Temporary or contract workers, often referred to as **contingent workers**, represent the fastest growing segment of the workforce, and the tasks they perform are no longer primarily administrative or clerical. Indeed, the world of temporary professionals now includes doctors, teachers, and lawyers—even CEOs.

Although businesses can hire temporary workers directly, an outside staffing source commonly provides temporary workers. The company pays a fee to the staffing agency, which takes responsibility for the temporary worker's compensation, payroll taxes, and, in many cases, benefits.

Temporary and contract employees also receive the same legal protection against discrimination and sexual harassment as do the full-time workers.

Independent Contractors

▲ **General definition:** Individuals such as accountants, lawyers, trainers, graphic artists, and so on who perform services for a company on a project basis and then bill the company for those services and related expenses.

▲ **Major implications:** Strictly defined, an independent contractor controls the methods and means of performing the tasks and is responsible to the employer only for the results. Employers have no tax liability and almost no other administrative responsibility other than paying the invoice and reporting payments on 1099 forms.

The IRS may not agree with your interpretation of an independent contractor and may classify the worker as an employee. Be sure that you understand the specific distinctions. Two significant risks should be considered:

▲ The IRS has a subjective, multifactor test it applies to independent contractor relationships. If an arrangement fails the IRS test, the relationship is recharacterized, and the individual is deemed to be an employee. The employer then becomes liable for back pay, tax withholding, and other statutory payments and penalties that should have been paid on behalf of the employee, which may add up to a lot of money.

▲ Under some Employee Retirement Income Security Act (ERISA) plans, independent contractors who work substantially full time for much of the year may be counted as part of the workforce in determining whether the plan meets ERISA requirements. This classification may result in your plan being disqualified for tax benefits afforded to ERISA plans.

Leased Workers

▲ **General definition: Leased workers,** like temporary workers, are employees who are provided by an outside agency, known as **Professional Employment Organizations (PEOs)**. The main difference: Leased employees work on a full-time basis.

▲ **Major implications:** The basic working arrangement—where employees work, what they do, who supervises them, how much they're paid—stays virtually the same. The only difference is that the PEO assumes financial and administrative responsibility for the employees' salaries and benefits. Because PEOs are administering the benefits for very large groups of employees, they can generally offer the same basic salary and benefits package to employees, charge the client company less than the company would otherwise have to pay, and still walk away with a profit.

SELF-CHECK

1. Explain the difference between an exempt worker and a non-exempt worker.

2. Define *contingent worker.*

3. Both leased workers and temporary workers are often provided to a company by a professional employment organization. True or false?

SUMMARY

Companies that meet their staffing needs in the most effective and strategically sound manner aren't locked into any one philosophy or any one staffing option. The idea is to put together the most strategic mix. As part of this, HR managers must look at a company's long-term goals. The first step of building an effective staffing plan is to assess an organization's staffing needs, keeping in mind options such as outsourcing or repositioning current staff. Next, an organization needs to conduct a job analysis, which gathers useful information about various aspects of a job. This information, which can be collected using a number of common methods, helps to identify the skills and attributes required for a position. Once completed, this analysis can be used to create a well-written job description. Accepted formats for job descriptions may vary, but any effective description will consider tasks, qualifications, and credentials— always in a clear and specific manner, Finally, human resource managers must take into consideration the legal implications of job titles and employee classifications, including the ramifications of whether a job is exempt or nonexempt.

KEY TERMS

Competency modeling	Determining the mix of skills, attributes, and attitudes that produce superior performance in the operational functions of a company.
Contingent workers	Temporary or contract workers.
Credentials	Degrees and licenses acknowledging that a candidate has passed a particular test or completed a specific field of study.
Exempt workers	Employees that receive a flat weekly, monthly, or annual salary, regardless of the number of hours they work over a given period.
Job analysis	Process of gathering information about various aspects of a job, including reporting relationships, interactions with others, qualifications, work environment, and the knowledge, skills, and attributes (KSAs) needed to perform the job successfully.
Job description	A written document that is produced as the result of a job analysis. It contains information that identifies the job, its essential functions, and the job specifications or competencies

	that enable an individual to be successful in the position.
Knowledge, Skills, Abilities (KSAs)	The qualifications that are needed by an individual in order to perform successfully in a position.
Leased workers	Temporary employees that work on a full-time basis; provided by an outside employment agency.
Nonexempt workers	Employees paid on an hourly basis (though some receive salaries) and are eligible for overtime pay if they work more than forty hours in a given week.
Onboarding	Coordination of a new hire process; includes orientation, review of job expectations, and other resources to help new employees.
Outsourcing	Turning over an entire function to an outside specialist when it suits a company's needs.
Professional Employment Organizations (PEOs)	Outside agency that provides temporary workers or other employees to a company.
Qualifications	The skills, attributes, or credentials a person needs to perform a task.
Soft skills	Such skills as an aptitude for communicating with people of all levels, skill sets, and backgrounds; the ability to work well in teams; and other factors, such as a talent for efficient and creative problem-solving.
Staffing plan	The way an organization recruits, hires, retains, promotes, and terminates employees.
Strategic staffing	The process of putting together a combination of human resources—internal and external— that are strategically keyed to the needs of the business and the realities of the labor market.
Task	What an employee does in a job position— from computing taxes to baking the donuts.

ASSESS YOUR UNDERSTANDING

Go to www.wiley.com/college/messmer to assess your knowledge of job analysis and design.

Measure your learning by comparing pre-test and post-test results.

Summary Questions

1. Strategic staffing is
   (a) a traditional approach.
   (b) a contingency plan.
   (c) updated approach to human resources.
   (d) all of the above.

2. Staffs made up of full-time employees are slowly being replaced by a mix of full-time and temporary employees. True or false?

3. What is the name of the process by which new hires are introduced to a company?
   (a) recruitment
   (b) training
   (c) onboarding
   (d) outsourcing

4. A company's immediate needs should be a human resource manager's first priority. True or false?

5. Outsourcing is an alternative to hiring a full-time employee? True or false?

6. What is one question that should be considered when deciding between rehiring or repositioning staff?

7. Which comes first, a job analysis or a job description?

8. A job analysis identifies the skills and attributes required for a job. True or false?

9. Competency modeling is based on the tasks of a job. True or false?

10. Competency modeling can be used as the basis for
    (a) hiring decisions.
    (b) training strategies.
    (c) development strategies.
    (d) all of the above.

11. A high percentage of hiring mistakes are the result of poorly written _____?
    (a) employee manuals
    (b) job descriptions

    (c) employee classifications

    (d) training programs

12. A job description must follow a federal format. True or false?

13. Which of the following is an example of a credential?

    (a) team player

    (b) broker's license

    (c) computer networking

    (d) photography

14. Word processing is an example of a soft skill. True or false?

15. When they work more than 40 hours a week, non-exempt workers are

    (a) paid an annual salary.

    (b) paid a flat weekly rate.

    (c) paid on an hourly basis.

    (d) eligible for overtime.

16. Full-time employees represent the fastest-growing segment of today's workforce. True or false?

Applying This Chapter

1. As the human resources manager of a regional natural food store chain, you need to convince your CEO that it's time to switch over to a more strategic approach to staffing. Why might this be a good move for the company?

2. Your office-cleaning company employs one hundred people and is doing well in your area. Though you'd like to expand the business into the next county, you're hoping to keep office staff to a minimum, and instead focus on continuing to hire good people to work for the clients. What areas of your business could be outsourced or staffed by employees other than those who work full-time?

3. Evaluate how you would conduct a job analysis of employees of a coffee and dessert café that features musical performances on the weekends? List the possible job titles that might be required for such a business, then choose one and indicate any qualifications that would apply to that position.

4. As part of the same coffee shop scenario, create a job description for one of the jobs required to run the shop—at any level.

5. Like many businesses, it makes more sense for Quality Catering Company to use a mix of different types of employees to get the work done. Create a staff that uses at least one of each of the five different employee classifications. Provide brief details for each—title, classification, hours worked, etc.

YOU TRY IT

Stacking Strategies

Question someone who works in human resources or management to assess their staffing approach.

- How much of what they do fits into the strategic staffing model?
- Are some of the traditional concepts and methods still applicable? If so, which ones and why?
- How might the methods vary from industry to industry?

Selling Competency

The basic objective of competency modeling is always the same: to determine what combination of skills and attributes are required to excel at a function. Prepare a proposal for your company, organization, or school that would convince management of the need for competency modeling. What would it require? What would be the benefits?

Winning Job Descriptions

A well-written job description can be considered a "snapshot" of the job. Pick using the internet or other means of research. Fnd three different examples of job descriptions for a position at a neighborhood bookstore. Then, using the three descriptions and the guidelines from the chapter, write your own job desciption.

4

RECRUITING AND EVALUATING PROSPECTIVE EMPLOYEES

Finding and Reviewing Potential Job Candidates

Starting Point

Go to www.wiley.com/college/messmer to assess your knowledge of employee recruitment and evaluation.
Determine where you need to concentrate your effort.

What You'll Learn in This Chapter

▲ The advantages and disadvantages of hiring from within a company
▲ The various ways in which a company can recruit potential new employees
▲ Types of employment recruiters and their specialties
▲ How the job application can be used as an evaluation tool
▲ The guidelines for pre-employment testing

After Studying This Chapter, You Will Be Able To

▲ Evaluate whether or not outsourcing is a viable staffing option for a company
▲ Prepare a well-written and effective job advertisement
▲ Choose the right type of recruiter to fill different types of job openings
▲ Evaluate a resume for any trouble spots or gaps in information
▲ Assess a company's need to use various pre-employment tests

INTRODUCTION

Recruiting and hiring good employees is arguably the most critical of all the areas you're responsible for overseeing in your company. If you're making good hiring decisions, you have the right people to support your work and you can concentrate on the big picture, create new initiatives, and institute new practices that reflect your company's mission and values. A bad hiring decision produces just the opposite result. But most bad hiring decisions are avoidable, assuming that you and others in your company approach the process with respect, understanding, and discipline.

4.1 Finding New Employees

You can look for new employees in two general places: inside or outside your organization. Looking inside your company is the easier of the two approaches, simply because it's a smaller field. But before you get into the specifics of your hiring strategy, you should have a general idea of what you stand to gain—or lose—when you focus your staffing efforts inside your organization or look outside for new talent.

4.1.1 Filling Jobs from Within

The rule in successful staffing has always been to do your best to fill new job openings from within before looking for outside candidates. Here are the key reasons:

▲ **Increased efficiency:** Hiring from within usually takes less time and is generally less costly than hiring from the outside. In addition, you know what type of performance you can expect from existing employees.

▲ **Increased morale:** Hiring from within sends a message to employees at all levels of your organization that good performance gets rewarded and that employees have a reason to work hard, be reliable, and focus on quality.

▲ **Shorter period of adjustment:** An existing employee takes a lot less time to acclimate to the new job than an employee who's never been with your company. Existing employees are also already familiar with company policies.

So what are the drawbacks? The most obvious is that by limiting your search to internal candidates limits the candidates to choose from, you may end up hiring someone who's not up to the challenge of the job. The second drawback is that, whenever you recruit from within, you always run a risk that other valuable employees who don't get the job become resentful and even eventually quit.

Your defense against these problems is to go out of your way to ensure that everyone is aware of the opportunity and understands the scope and basic duties of the job plus the hiring criteria you're using. The following are the key procedures that you need to initiate in setting up a successful internal hiring process:

▲ **Get it out there.** Communicate internal job opportunities using a system that everyone knows—whether it's a bulletin board or an email about the position.

▲ **Spell it out.** Wherever it appears, any notice about a job needs to set specific requirements for the job—length of time in current position, the level of seniority needed, and so on. Include the basic rules in every posting notice.

▲ **Set it up.** Make sure that you establish a procedure for how employees can apply for a position. Some companies require workers to apply through their department heads; others enable employees to apply directly to the HR office.

4.1.2 Looking for Staff Outside the Company

Hiring from within has its virtues, but the following are the basic arguments for looking outside the company to fill certain positions:

▲ **A broader selection of talent:** If your search is confined solely to your current employees, the pool of likely candidates is going to be a lot smaller than if you're looking outside the company. This constraint may not be a problem for certain jobs, but for critical positions, you may not want to limit your options.

▲ **The "new blood" factor:** Bringing in outside talent can go a long way toward diminishing the "We've always done it that way syndrome," generally known as **organizational inbreeding**. Recruiting from outside the company is usually helpful for companies that have held on to the status quo for too long.

▲ **The diversity factor: Workforce diversity** (or the effort to allow and encourage diversity in the workplace) enables a business to draw on the resources, expertise, and creativity of people from the widest possible range of backgrounds: gender, age, color, national origin, ethnicity, and other factors. And filling jobs from the outside may turn out to be the only way you can keep your company within EEOC compliance (Sections 2.2. and 2.3). But remember, having a diverse workforce is not just a matter of satisfying the law. It also makes good business sense (see "Benefiting from a Diverse Workforce").

BENEFITING FROM A DIVERSE WORKFORCE

Although the laws enacted to bar discrimination in hiring practices often can make your HR job more complicated, diversity has a very positive impact on the business environment. If everyone in your company thinks alike, you miss the opportunity for innovative ideas that often come from individuals from diverse cultures and backgrounds—ideas that can help you improve your products and level of customer service.

Ensuring that you have a wide spectrum of job applicants to choose from requires making outreach efforts to various community groups or running classified ads in newspapers read by specific ethnic groups. Beyond hiring, the term **diversity training** may entail conducting training sessions among employees that teach them to increase sensitivity toward others. When people feel accepted and valued by their colleagues, subordinates, and supervisors, their loyalty and morale increases, and this in turn greatly increases productivity.

THE CHANGING FACE OF THE AMERICAN WORKPLACE

As nearly everyone knows, the American workplace is a far cry from what it looked like fifty years ago, when more than half the American workforce consisted of white males who were the sole breadwinners in the household. Consider this fact alone: The Bureau of Labor Statistics predicts that in 2008, women and minorities will make up seventy percent of all new entrants to the workforce.

4.1.3 Outsourcing: The Role of HR

Outsourcing is when a company turns over an entire function (shipping, payroll, benefits administration, security, computer networking) to an outside specialist. In many cases, the outside firm's employees or consultants work side by side with a company's regular employees. In some cases, a function may be moved to a remote location miles away from your office—even out of the country. This latter approach, often referred to as **offshoring**, has generated much debate in recent years.

In HR you need to grasp the implications of outsourcing so that you can help provide strategic counsel throughout any hiring process—and contribute to decisions about whether to use this alternative in the first place. After all, your input about how to conduct an effective search for skilled contractors or consultants is extremely valuable.

FOR EXAMPLE

The Tax Man Goes Offshore

Ernst & Young, the fourth largest public accounting firm in the world, prepared 15,000 of 100,000 mostly corporate tax returns abroad in 2004. About 4,000 were for U.S. citizens living abroad, and about 1,000 for U.S. residents. The average accountant in India makes $250–$300 per month, compared with $3,000–$4,000 in the United States. The company, which already has plans to double its Indian operations, can then use the savings to undercut competitors or add premium services.

In fact, the outsourcing trend affects the HR function itself: Companies are increasingly outsourcing some of their HR services. But no matter which business process is involved, your ability to apply hiring principles can play a major role in ensuring that any outsourcing effort is implemented as efficiently as possible.

SELF-CHECK

1. Explain three advantages of hiring from within a company.
2. A human resources workshop on ethnic sensitivity is one example of diversity training. True or false?
3. Define *offshoring*.

4.2 Help Wanted: The Recruiting Process

Think of the recruiting stage of the hiring process like fishing—your success depends not only on how well you do it, but on where you do it and on what bait you're using. You can go fishing for qualified candidates in any number of ways. You also discover that no one fishing expedition meets the needs of every company in every situation. Some strategies involve more time and cost than others, but in your quest to attract the best possible employees the extra effort is usually worth it. Most of all, the key to effective recruiting is to make sure that whatever options you select are logically and strategically aligned with your priorities.

The obvious objective of a recruiting effort is to attract as large a pool of qualified candidates as possible. But successful recruiting is also about quality. Keep in mind that everything you do as a recruiter—from seeking candidates on the internet to placing an ad in your local paper—is making a statement about your company, and, in the process, shaping your company's reputation. So to recruit the best talent, you need to represent your company as professionally as possible.

4.2.1 Getting Started

Recruiting is probably the most challenging stage of the hiring process. There are no tried and true formulas for getting the most mileage out of your recruiting efforts, but the following list covers some of the general guidelines to keep in mind.

▲ **Make recruitment an ongoing process.** Companies known for their ability to attract and hire good employees are always recruiting—even if they have no current openings. If you're the person in your company responsible for recruiting talent, you're always on the lookout for people who can contribute to your organization's success. At the very least, keep an active database of the names and resumes of talented people whom you've met or who have sent in letters or contacted you online expressing interest in your firm.

▲ **Create a plan.** You should always have a general idea before you start any recruiting effort of how you intend to conduct the process. For starters, you need some idea of the various candidate sources you're going to seek out. A good way to start is to set a deadline for when, ideally, you want to see the position filled. You can then establish a sequence of steps, each with its own deadline. You may decide, for example, that you're going to look inside your company for two weeks and, if unsuccessful, post the opening on the internet, run a classified ad, or seek the services of an outside staffing firm.

▲ **Be systematic.** Before you start the search, set up a protocol—a systematic procedure—for how you intend to process applications, resumes, and cover letters. Try to set aside a certain amount of time each day to focus on the recruiting effort and track your progress.

▲ **Be flexible.** If the initial response to your recruiting efforts is poor, you need to have a contingency plan on hand. Be prepared to revisit the job description or even explore the possibility of restructuring the job—breaking it into two part-time jobs, perhaps—in an effort to attract more (or better) candidates.

4.2.2 What Makes a Good Job Ad?

Whether you plan to post a job ad in the newspaper, on your company website, or on a job board, writing a good ad is a critical step in the hiring process. The task is more difficult than most people think. Keep in mind the following two considerations:

▲ The goal of a job ad is not only to generate responses from qualified applicants, but also to prevent candidates who are clearly unqualified from applying for the position. You're better off getting only five responses from deserving applicants than 100 responses from people you'd never consider hiring.

▲ Think "sell." You're advertising a product—your company. Every aspect of your ad must seek to foster a favorable impression of the organization.

Composing the Ad

If you've done a good job of writing the job description (see Section 3.4), then you've done most of the work. In fact, you actually want to think of the ad as a synopsis of the existing job description.

As for the ad itself, the following list describes the elements you need to think about as you compose the ad:

▲ **Headline:** The headline almost always is the job title.

▲ **Job information:** A line or two about the general duties and responsibilities.

▲ **Company information:** Include a few words on what your company does.

▲ **Qualifications and hiring criteria:** Specify the level of education and experience and relevant attributes and skills (per your competency model; see Section 3.3) required to do the job.

▲ **Respond method:** Let applicants know the best way to respond: email, regular mail, fax, or phone. Include any ground rules, such as whether you prefer to receive online resumes as an attachment or embedded in the email.

These key points will also help you create an effective job ad:

▲ Convey some sense of your organizational culture and values with a few phrases (fast-paced, results-oriented, and client-centered).

▲ Use active voice and action words throughout the ad.

▲ Create a buzz, a sense of enthusiasm; arouse applicants' interest. A dull ad assuredly draws dull candidates.

▲ Keep in mind that an advertisement, regardless of whether it's on the internet or in a newspaper, needs to look as good as it reads. The headline, type size, placement, and graphic element can influence the responses as much as the wording.

▲ Spell out anything that's special about a job or company ("WebWidget is the largest widget store on the Net").

▲ State responsibilities and qualifications accurately. Include sufficient hiring criteria to discourage the obviously unqualified.

Example of an Effective Ad

The following ad was written using the criteria above:

> Busy, growing law office specializing in entertainment and intellectual property seeks well-organized individual to support staff of five lawyers and two paralegals. Responsibilities include processing correspondence, maintaining attorney schedules and client files, and updating publications. High school diploma or GED required; AA (associate of arts) degree preferred. Must be familiar with Microsoft Office. Competitive salary and benefits.
> AAjob@lawfirm.com or Hollywood Law, P.O. Box 999, Los Angeles, CA 99999.

4.2.3 Using the Internet

The internet has created countless new opportunities for employers and job seekers alike. Job boards abound, and today even the smallest of companies frequently have a website describing what they do and, often, the advantages of working for them. In fact, a 2005 study by the Society of Human Resource Management found that 92.4 percent of candidates will visit a company's website at some point during a job search.

FOR EXAMPLE

Quality In, Quality Out

As with other mediums, your internet ad should stand out and attract the best and brightest candidates. Think carefully about how any job posting you write and design is packaged. For example, does the posting explain what makes your company an exciting place to work? Does it make the job attractive, showcasing its growth potential, the chance to use certain skills or other compelling opportunities such as travel? If you write the ad generically—"Real estate firm seeking administrative assistant"—you'll attract generic, undistinguished candidates. But if you make it dynamic—"Orange County's leading mortgage broker seeks administrative assistant to help senior executives manage new opportunities"—then you're likely to get more people enthused about working for your organization.

Highway Hazards

Along with the opportunities the internet creates come a number of significant implications—both practical and legal—that you need to understand and in order to maximize the effectiveness of this powerful tool.

▲ For starters, the internet has the potential of dramatically increasing the number of responses to your job ads. Many HR managers report they have great difficulty even keeping track of submissions. If your budget allows, you can reduce this volume by creating computer protocols that flag certain qualifications to help you narrow down resumes. You can set a filter for an accounting position, for example, to eliminate candidates who lack a CPA credential.

▲ Sometimes emailed resumes or applications include attachments that you can't read or, worse, contain computer viruses. You can sidestep these issues by including a request in your job ad asking applicants to cut and paste resumes directly into the message field instead of sending as an attachment.

▲ You must also consider the laws affecting the handling of online job ads and candidate responses. Any time you post a job opening, you must be sure not to imply that candidates can apply for the job electronically only. Title VII of the Civil Rights Act of 1964, the Americans with Disabilities Act (ADA), and the Age Discrimination in Employment Act (ADEA) stipulate that employers can't discriminate in any aspect of the employment process. In other words, you must make sure that you offer avenues to candidates who do not own computers or have access to email to apply for an open job. And you must spend as much time reviewing these resumes as you do those that come in electronically.

▲ To avoid any problems with responding to all of these inquiries, create a template of automated, carefully worded, neutral email replies that merely let each candidate know that you've received his application or resume and that you will be in touch as the search progresses.

▲ To get the most out of web-based application sites, be certain to keep all information current and up to date.

Website Matters

The internet has dramatically changed the way applicants research a company. Your website is a great place to communicate your unique culture and most appealing characteristics. Well executed, your site can give job seekers a glimpse into the employee experience—what it's like to work in your company. A website that's outdated, difficult to read, or lacking relevant information can reduce your chances of luring top-notch candidates.

4.2.4 Classified Ads

At one time, classified ads were the most widely used recruiting method in business. Despite the opportunity created by the internet, classified ads still have their advantages.

▲ They're legally sound. Anyone can have access to a newspaper.

▲ They attract potential candidates who may not be necessarily focused on searching for a job, but may well find themselves intrigued should they come across your ad while reading the Sunday paper.

▲ Classified ads also help keep your firm visible and let people know that since your company is hiring, it's also probably thriving.

▲ Advertising in newspapers may be your only way of ensuring that you reach all minorities and age groups, a key aim of your diversity efforts.

The downside, of course, is that classified ads cost money and also can attract hundreds of unqualified candidates or even just random job seekers whose resumes you have to sort out. Still, they have their place and remain a useful tool.

> **SEEING THROUGH BLIND ADS**
>
> Some companies choose to place **blind ads**—an online posting or classified ad that doesn't identify the company and typically directs replies to a P.O. box number or blind email address. A company may not want anyone to know—for competitive or internal morale reasons—that it has an opening for a critical job. Or perhaps the company has an image problem that may discourage candidates. But blind ads are a turnoff to many potential candidates—particularly those who are already employed, but looking. Because the company isn't identified, they worry that their response to a blind ad could cause them to inadvertently apply at their current employer, who they may not want to know they're job hunting. So unless you have a compelling reason to do otherwise, avoid blind ads.

4.2.5 Other Recruiting Routes

Aside from some of the traditional recruiting options discussed earlier in this chapter, the following resources may help you in your search for qualified candidates.

Recruiting on Campus

College campuses have long been a fertile hunting ground for companies in search of entry-level talent. However, smaller firms without well-organized college recruiting programs have always been at something of a disadvantage. A little extra footwork—building a good relationship with those that run a school's placement office—can help get you in the door. Consider inviting placement officers to your company to see what you have to offer.

Employee Referrals

Employee referrals were formerly considered a somewhat risky practice—an invitation to nepotism and favoritism. But, in reality, employee referrals may represent one of the most reliable recruiting sources: Most employees would never recommend a friend or relative who may turn out to be a source of embarrassment.

No surprise, then, that more and more companies today have instituted employee referral programs, with rewards (extra vacation days, trips, cash bonuses, and so on) for employees who recommend a person whom you eventually hire and who stays with the company for a specific period of time.

Job Fairs

Job fairs are recruiting events that bring together employers and job-seekers in one location. They're generally sponsored by professional associations, community organizations, or educational institutions. Most job fairs focus on a particular industry or professional group—computer engineers, teachers, or perhaps recent college graduates. Properly run job fairs resemble trade shows or conventions and have the same lively atmosphere and buzz.

Because job fairs are usually regional and industry-specific, however, you may end up with your company's booth located just down the aisle from your main local competitor. This means that potential job applicants can directly compare your company with your nearest competitors simply by walking across the room. It also means that you have to make the strongest impression possible.

Professional Associations and Unions

Most professional associations and unions have some sort of job referral service, publish a newsletter listing available positions, or maintain a resume bank. Advertising your opening on these services is usually free. These associations also give you a chance to meet potential candidates, formally or informally, at meetings and conventions, where you can circulate or, perhaps, host a hospitality suite or information booth.

Direct Applications (Walk-ins)

Some view walk-in applicants as a nuisance; others view someone who has the nerve to make a cold, face-to-face call a person whose resume probably deserves a review. At the very least, have a policy in place to deal with such applicants. Invite the person to either leave behind or send you a cover letter and resume.

State Employment Services

Each state has an agency dedicated to providing services to job seekers, including job counseling and training opportunities. There is no charge for employers to list job openings with the agency, which then screens, test, and refers appropriate candidates.

SELF-CHECK

1. List three hazards of using the internet to advertise a job opening.
2. A classified newspaper ad is no longer a worthwhile recruitment method for a company. True or false?
3. Explain why a company might choose to run a blind job ad.
4. Name the three federal laws that stipulate that employers can't discriminate in any aspect of the employment process.

4.3 Using Recruiters to Get the Job Done

Most companies that rely on outside recruiters to fill positions do so for one of two reasons:

▲ They don't have the time or the expertise to recruit effectively on their own.

▲ The recruiting efforts they've put forward to date have yet to yield results.

Using an outside recruiter involves an extra cost, but keep in mind that if you handle recruiting yourself, you're still paying for such out-of-pocket expenses as classified ads, as well as diverting your employees' time and resources from their core expertise. Composing an internet posting or classified ad may be a routine task for somebody with a background in human resources, but it can be an onerous and timely task for somebody who has never written one before. The same principle holds true for other basic recruiting functions, such as reviewing resumes, which has become exceptionally labor intensive because of the internet.

4.3.1 The Recruitment Players

If you've ever wondered what makes a **headhunter** different from an employment agency or a search firm, you're not alone. The names can be confusing. All these sources fulfill the same basic function: They find job candidates for client firms for a fee. The difference between the various specialists in this large and growing industry is primarily how they charge and on which segment of the labor market they focus.

▲ **Employment agencies**, **staffing firms**, and **contingency search firms** are companies you engage to find job candidates for specific positions. What they all have in common is that you pay them a fee—but only after they find you someone you eventually hire. These firms recruit candidates in virtually every industry, and companies call on them to fill positions at all levels of the corporate ladder. They typically charge you a percentage (typically fifteen to thirty percent) of the new employee's first year's salary.

These search firms typically differ in the types of positions they help you fill. In most cases, employment agencies are generalists and focus on entry- and mid-level jobs in a range of industries, whereas staffing or contingency search firms focus on mid- to upper-level positions usually in a particular field or profession—finance or marketing, for example.

▲ **Executive search firms**, or **headhunters**, focus on higher level executives, up to and including CEOs. Most search firms charge a retainer whether they produce results or not. You can also expect to pay, in addition to expenses, a commission of twenty-five percent—or even a third— of the executive's annual salary if the firm's successful in its search. The main value comes into play if you're seeking someone for a high-level job that's most likely to be filled by an executive who's already working for another company.

4.3.2 Finding the "Right" Recruiter

Like you would with any professional services specialist, you choose a recruiter by asking colleagues for recommendations and meeting with different recruiters. In the end, you want a recruiter whom you feel confident will be able to articulate your company's mission, values, and culture to job prospects effectively. The following list provides some reminders that can help you make a wise choice:

▲ **Be explicit about your needs.** Make sure that the firm understands your business, your company culture, and exactly what you're looking for.
▲ **Clarify fee arrangements.** Have a clear understanding—before you enter into a business agreement—of how your recruiter charges and make sure that any arrangement you make is in writing.
▲ **Ask about replacement guarantees.** Many recruitment firms today offer a replacement guarantee if a new employee doesn't work out after a reasonable period of time. Make sure that you understand the conditions of the guarantee.

FOR EXAMPLE

Recruiting Sleuth

Sheila Stap, a top headhunter who specializes in placing executive talent in senior management functions found a candidate who was a very experienced CEO and a great candidate for the high-level position she was working on. The executive's resume said that he had received a degree in marketing from a prestigious university, but when Stap did her research to verify his degree and other information, she found a discrepancy: his major was actually in music. When questioned, the candidate dismissed the matter as trivial, saying that he had minored in marketing and had simply changed the music major many years earlier because it sounded more professional. Of course, Stap's client was not interested in hiring someone who isn't truthful, so that small issue turned into a very big deal-breaker.

SELF-CHECK

1. Explain why a company would use a recruitment company.
2. A *headhunter* focuses on entry- and mid-level jobs in a range of industries. True or false?
3. What is the value of a replacement guarantee?

4.4 Evaluating Candidates: Applications and Resumes

Most people agree that the job interview is the most important element of the hiring process. But what many otherwise savvy business people often forget is that one of the keys to effective interviewing is effectively evaluating candidates.

If you don't have an efficient process in place for evaluating candidates, you may inadvertently eliminate candidates who clearly deserve a second look. Your process may also fail to accomplish its fundamental purpose: Making sure that you're not wasting your time and effort on candidates who are clearly unqualified for the position you're seeking to fill. This chapter can help you avoid this common—but very avoidable—staffing pitfall.

4.4.1 Job Applications: Are They Obsolete?

Job applications were at one time the primary method of evaluating candidates in most companies. Thanks to the resume, however, applications no longer figure as prominently in the hiring process. One reason is that the typical resume today contains most of, if not all, the information normally asked for on a typical job application.

A bigger issue, however, is Equal Employment Opportunity (EEO) legislation (see Chapter 2). EEO legislation now prohibits many questions that routinely appeared on traditional job applications years ago—items relating to gender, age, marital status, and even birthplace. Some states also have specific regulations regarding what you can or cannot ask.

Application Benefits

A major advantage of a job application form over a resume is that if you design the application form to match your business needs, it generally works better than a resume does as a candidate evaluation tool, because the same information appears in the same place, regardless of the candidate. The application also provides a standardized format that addresses some of the EEO issues mentioned above. And because job applications force candidates to supply you with certain information (along with dates), they don't leave the candidate room to skip key questions.

Setting Up an Application

Although you can purchase inexpensive preprinted application forms, you may decide to create your own. If you do, give yourself some time to think about how much information you really need. As a general rule, less is more.

Second general rule: Make certain that the questions you ask are not discriminatory and are in line with federal and state laws. Be careful to seek legal counsel to review your company's job applications. And don't include questions in the application that relate to any of the following areas:

▲ Race.

▲ Religion.

▲ Sex or sexual orientation.

▲ Age.

▲ Ancestry or national origin (but you can ask whether a candidate is eligible to work in the United States).

▲ Marital status.

▲ Arrests.

▲ Military service.

▲ Height or weight (unless directly related to job performance).

▲ Political preference or membership in social organizations.

▲ Handicaps or disabilities.

The following list describes other things you shouldn't do during the preliminary stages of the hiring process:

▲ You can't request the applicant to provide a photograph before employment.

▲ You can ask an applicant's name but not a maiden name or a spouse's maiden name because such a question may be interpreted as another way of asking about the candidate's marital status.

▲ You can ask for an applicant's address but not whether the applicant owns or rents the residence or how long the applicant has lived there.

▲ Most education qualifications are fair game, but some states prohibit you from asking for high school or college graduation dates. It's a dead tip-off for age.

You always need to require applicants to sign the application and affirm the accuracy of the information they furnish. This step doesn't necessarily guarantee that the information is true, but it gives you some protection if, after you hire an applicant, he doesn't work out and you discover that he made misrepresentations on his job application.

Using the Application as an Evaluation Tool

Some application forms are **weighted**, meaning that you give each element in the form a certain value, putting more emphasis, or weight, on qualifications you feel may more heavily influence later performance on the job.

▲ Weighting the application questions can help you figure out how likely a person with a certain type of experience or skill is to turn out to be the right employee for this particular job.

You can usually recognize a weighted application form if you see a section on the side that reads, "Do not write in this section," along with some mysteriously numbered boxes.

The trick, of course, is figuring out how to weigh the criteria. The basic idea is to determine how accurately a specific criterion might predict superior job performance. The problem, however, is that no one has developed any sort of weighting scale flexible enough to cover everything that can affect job performance. Educational levels, for example, may closely link to success in a certain job in a company filled with people with advanced degrees, in which case you would assign it a higher weighting value relative to other criteria. But education credentials may not be as important in a company with less educated employees. And if you assign values to work experience, licenses held, and so on, you have to be careful that the criteria you're using relate to actual job

---

FOR EXAMPLE

Applications Go Online

Many organizations take a high-tech approach to job applications by allowing candidates to complete forms online. Yale University's application (found at https://apps.business.yale.edu/oja/index.jsp) includes sections on personal information, position information, salary requirements, as well as a section of voluntary affirmative action questions. Applicants are also provided with sections that address resumes and cover letters, in addition to links to a list of current job opportunities and Frequently Asked Questions.

---

performance. Again, if you don't really need the skill, you shouldn't list it as a criterion.

A weighted system isn't scientific but it can weed out obviously unqualified employees and give you at least a preliminary idea of who the top candidates are for the job.

4.4.2 Getting the Most Out of Resumes

If you based your judgment on resumes alone, you'd think that all candidates are outstanding prospects. And no wonder, anyone who does any research at all into how to look for a job knows how to write a resume that puts him in the best light. And those who don't know how to write a great resume can now hire people who do know.

Why, then, take resumes seriously? Because resumes, regardless of how "professional" they are, can still reveal a wealth of information about the candidate.

Resume Basics

Here's what you probably know already, job candidates submit only two types of resumes:

- ▲ **Chronological,** where all the work-related information appears in a timeline sequence.
- ▲ **Functional,** where the information appears in various categories (skills, achievements, qualifications, and so on).

Some applicants use a combination of the two formats, presenting a capsule of what they believe are their most important qualifications and accomplishments, together with a chronological work history.

GETTING A GRIP ON GAPS

In the past, the general rule was that candidates wrote functional resumes because they were trying to hide something, such as gaps in their work history. But because a well-rounded background (in conjunction with one's specialty area) can prove an asset in today's job market, the functional resume is now more acceptable. The key point to keep in mind: Don't automatically turn off to either type of resume.

Before diving into that pile of resumes, consider the following observations:

▲ Many resumes are professionally prepared, designed to create a winning, but not necessarily accurate, impression.

▲ Reviewing resumes is tedious, no matter what. You may need to sift through the stack several times.

▲ If you don't review resumes yourself or delegate it to the wrong person, you're likely to miss that diamond-in-the-rough, that ideal employee who unfortunately has poor resume-drafting skills.

CURRICULUM VITAE

A curriculum vitae is a written description of your work experience, educational background, and skills; also called a CV, or simply a vitae. A CV is more detailed than a resume and is often used by those looking for work outside the United States. A curriculum vitae is also used by those looking for an academic job, i.e., in a college or university.

Reading Between the Lines

With more and more people using specialists or software packages to prepare their resumes, getting an accurate reading of a candidate's strengths from a resume is more difficult than ever. Even so, here are some of the resume characteristics that generally describe a candidate worth interviewing:

▲ **Lots of details:** Though applicants are generally advised to avoid wordiness, the more detailed they are in their descriptions of what they did and accomplished in previous jobs, the more reliable (as a rule) the information is.

▲ **Key words:** In terms of company websites and other online recruitment methods, many times these systems are programmed to hone in on key phrases, terms, or words in a resume. These resumes can then be flagged for additional consideration.

▲ **A history of stability and advancement:** The applicant's work history should show a steady progression into greater responsibility and more important positions. But don't go by job titles alone; look at what the candidate did. Be wary of candidates who have bounced from one company to the next, although people do have good reasons for career moves.

▲ **A strong, well-written cover letter:** Assuming that the candidate wrote the letter, the cover letter is generally a good indication of his overall communication skills.

Watching Out for Red Flags

Sometimes mistakes or omissions can reveal quite a bit about a candidate. Following are some things to watch out for:

▲ **Sloppy overall appearance:** This is a fairly reliable sign that the candidate is lacking in professionalism and business experience.

▲ **Unexplained chronological gaps:** Such gaps in an employment history may mean one of two things: The candidate was unemployed during these gaps, or the candidate is deliberately concealing certain information. But before jumping to conclusions, check to see whether periods of schooling or military service cover the gap. A well-designed application form or probing interview questions can uncover "hidden" work history gaps.

▲ **Static career pattern:** A sequence of jobs that doesn't indicate increasing responsibility may indicate a problem—the person wasn't deemed fit for a promotion or demonstrated a lack of ambition. Exceptions occur, however, especially for those types of workers in highly specialized fields.

▲ **Typos and misspellings:** Generally speaking, typos in cover letters and resumes may signify carelessness or a cavalier attitude. In a Robert Half International survey, seventy-six percent of U.S. executives said that they wouldn't hire a candidate with even one or two typographical errors in his resume.

▲ **Vaguely worded job descriptions:** Perhaps the applicant didn't quite understand what his job was. Before you go any further, find out what a "coordinator of special projects" actually does.

▲ **Weak wording:** Phrasing such as "participated in," and "familiar with" can indicate that the applicant may not have the actual experience he's claiming. A sentence doesn't need to be untruthful to be misleading.

▲ **Job hopping:** A series of many jobs held for short periods of time may signal an unstable or problem employee. Be sure to look at the whole employment history. People do leave jobs for good reasons and should be prepared—and willing—to tell you about it.

▲ **Overemphasis on hobbies or interests outside of work:** This kind of emphasis may indicate an applicant who's unwilling to work extra hours or put in an extra effort.

Figure 4-1 is an example of an acknowledgement of receipt of a resume and/or job application. Some companies use postcards, although most applicants prefer the privacy of a letter.

Figure 4-1

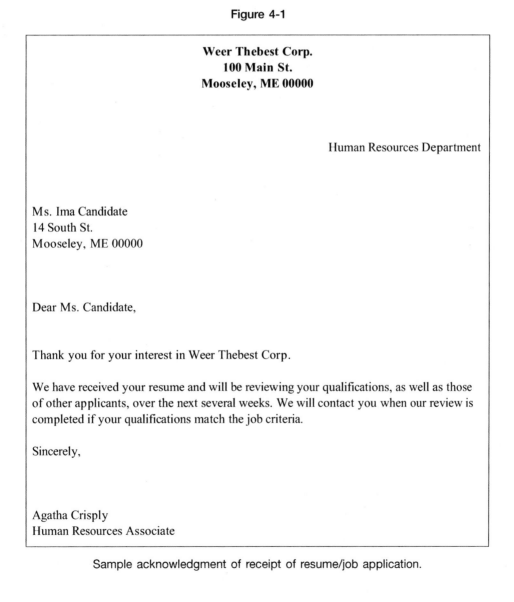

Sample acknowledgment of receipt of resume/job application.

4.4.3 Setting Up a System for Evaluating Candidates

It's a good idea to have some kind of system or protocol in place to review candidates. No matter who is in charge of the process—an HR specialist, line manager, or owner—it should include a set of hard criteria to use as the basis of your decisions. Otherwise, there's a good chance you'll end up making choices based on factors that may have no bearing on desired work performance, such as courses taken at a university you admire or an impressive skill that would be virtually useless in your job opening. Keep in mind the following three key questions at all times:

▲ **What are the prerequisites for the position?** These should track with the qualifications listed in the job description, as long as your description is targeted and carefully thought through (see Section 3.4).

▲ **What are the special requirements in your organization, such as certifications or special education?** If you own a public accounting firm, for example, you would most likely consider only applicants with a valid CPA credential.

▲ **What qualifications and attributes are critical to high performance in this particular position?** Think of the competency models discussed in Section 3.3. If your business depends on telemarketing, for instance, some people will be better than others at engaging the interest of the people they call. What attributes make them better? Identify those attributes that you feel will produce superior performance in functions critical to your company's competitive strength and look for these attributes in prospective employees.

The Evaluation Process

The following is an overview of the evaluation process:

1. **Scan applications or resumes first for basic qualifications.**
   If you do a good job of communicating the job's qualifications to your recruiter or in the ad you write, you shouldn't get too many replies or resumes from unqualified candidates. Keep in mind, however, that some applicants apply to virtually any job opening, whether they're qualified or not. For example, if you're seeking to hire a medical technician who will be working on equipment that requires a license, eliminate applicants without this license.

2. **Look for key criteria.**
   After you eliminate unqualified candidates, you can focus on more specific hiring criteria, such as good organizational skills, supervisory experience, or good driving record. Here again, your task is considerably easier if you do a thorough job of identifying these requirements at the time you put together the job description.
   Begin the evaluation process by setting a high standard (for example, the resume must meet a certain high percentage of the criteria), but if

your reject pile is growing and you haven't "cleared" anyone, you may need to lower the bar somewhat.

3. **Set up a process to flag and identify your top candidates.**

At this point, you should establish a separate file for each of the applicants who pass the initial review. Some HR professionals like to develop a **flow sheet**—a document that you attach to the outside of a folder that lists the steps in the evaluation process with spaces for the date and initials of the person completing the step. Nothing's really complicated about such a sheet. It's simply a form that enables you to tell at a glance what stage of the process the candidate has reached.

Instead of this manual method, many HR organizations use an **applicant tracking system** or a **candidate management system**, which are software applications that can post job openings on various websites, automate resume scanning, generate letters, and perform other functions.

SELF-CHECK

1. Job applications have no value in today's staffing strategies. True or false?
2. Explain the value of an applicant tracking system.
3. Name three problems to look out for on a resume.

4.5 Testing as Part of the Evaluation Process

Pre-employment testing is probably the most controversial of all of today's candidate evaluation options. Everybody agrees with the basic idea that test results can often alert you to attributes and potential problems that you can't infer from a resume and that don't necessarily surface during an interview. No one, however, has proven that testing leads to foolproof or even better hires. In addition, many types of tests are subject to legal restrictions.

So why do testing? Because if you use them correctly and in the right situations, many tests can help you evaluate job candidates, typically prior to the interview stage.

4.5.1 Following the Testing Rules

No matter what type of test you select, all tests must meet, at a minimum, the following requirements:

▲ They must assess the skills a candidate must possess to perform the job functions.

▲ They must show a positive correlation with job performance.

▲ They must be free of **disparate impact** (actions you take not intending to discriminate but which have the effect of doing so anyway). (See Section 2.4.2.)

▲ They must not present an unfair barrier to the disabled.

Tests that fail these requirements may violate the antidiscrimination laws and regulations governing your company.

TESTING ONE AND ALL

If you do test your candidates, keep in mind that individuals can't be singled out to be tested. Tests must be job-related and applied consistently to all candidates for a position or, in some cases, for all positions within a particular department or business unit. You can require a forklift ability test, for example, of anyone applying for a position as a forklift operator, but all applicants must take the same test.

4.5.2 Finding the Right Test

Tests are simply tools meant to measure specific aspects or qualities of applicants' skills, knowledge, experience, intellect or—more controversially—personality (or

FOR EXAMPLE

Putting Skills to the Test

Mark Smithers, a senior manager of operations for a maker of communications software company, uses sales skills testing to help him screen candidates. He starts the hiring process by interviewing each candidate by phone from the company's headquarters, evaluating conversational and investigative skills. To get a real idea of a candidate's technical sales ability, he takes the testing a step further, particularly if someone seems weak in one area. For example, if a candidate received a low score on negotiating price, Smithers might ask the person how he would respond if a customer said he could get the product for $6 less from a competitor. The best response would be something like "Have you looked at our company's history of service?" However, if the candidate only comes up with "Well, eight dollars isn't a lot of money," he probably doesn't have the skills to handle the daily negotiations required of the job.

psychological makeup). Figure out what you want to find out about a candidate and then choose the appropriate test.

Dozens of commercial test publishers collectively produce more than 2,000 different tests in all sizes and shapes, so the following sections provide a run-down of what they are, what they do, and how to use them.

Proficiency Tests

What do they do? Measure how skillful an applicant is at a particular task (word processing, for example) or how knowledgeable he is in a particular field.

Why would you use them? Proficiency tests measure skills that applicants need for successful job performance and are useful if a baseline of particular (usually trade-related) skills is essential.

How reliable are they? Generally quite good. This sort of testing has a good track record of validity in the business and industrial world.

Aptitude and Ability Tests

What do they do? Measure an applicant's capability to learn and perform a par-ticular job and his capability to learn or potential to acquire job-related skills or tasks. These tests fall into the following three basic categories:

▲ **Mental abilities:** Tests of intelligence, verbal reasoning, perceptual speed, and so on, and are sometimes called cognitive tests. Classic example: the SAT.

▲ **Mechanical abilities:** Tests that measure the ability to recognize and visualize a mechanical relationship—to distinguish between pulley and lever systems, for example

▲ **Psychomotor abilities:** These varieties test an individual's skill and/or ability to make certain body movements or use certain senses. The U.S. Navy, for example, tests every recruit's ability to hear differences between tones. High scorers are urged to apply for sonar school.

Why would you use them? Whether you use them alone or in batteries of tests, aptitude and ability tests help many organizations, including governments, select the most likely applicants for specific jobs.

How reliable are they? Generally excellent to adequate, as long as they don't violate antidiscrimination laws.

Personality and Psychological Tests

What do they do? Measure certain personality characteristics, such as assertive-ness, resiliency, temperament, or stability. This group of tests also includes inter-est inventories, which claim to show how close an individual's interests match those of a particular occupational group.

Why would you use them? This sort of testing is designed to uncover personality traits that make good employees—or those that make bad employees. Personality is a component of job performance, so looking into an applicant's personality can help predict his performance.

How reliable are they? That depends. A main problem is that the results aren't always crystal-clear and sometimes need professional interpretation.

Physical Tests

What do they do? Measure an individual's health and physical condition or the ability to perform a certain task.

Why would you use them? To establish fitness to perform job-related tasks. Be forewarned, however, that requiring a physical or medical examination before employment is illegal under federal law. You can't ask about an applicant's height or weight because you may use this information to discriminate unless height (or weight) is a bona fide occupational requirement. You can test for physical agility or ability if it's a legitimate job requirement, but you must administer exactly the same test to every applicant for the same position. (An example is testing for the ability to lift packages of a certain weight if lifting such weights is vital to job performance.)

How reliable are they? Depends on who does the exam but usually quite good.

Drug Tests

What do they do? Measure the presence of illegal drugs or controlled substances in an applicant's urine. (For more uses of drug tests see Appendix C.)

Why would you use them? Substance abuse costs money in lost time, impaired performance, and potential employee theft. Drug tests to check candidates for current substance abuse are legal and can help eliminate applicants with these problems from the running. For some positions, pre-employment drug tests are mandatory. Certain classes of employees—school bus drivers, for example—must submit to testing for drugs and alcohol under the law. In fact, pre-employment drug testing has become so common in some industries that it causes hardly a ripple. Keep in mind, however, that you must give all applicants advance written notice that you intend to test for drugs. You can't observe the test itself, and you must hold test results confidential. You must give applicants notice of a positive result. You can also test only for what you say you're testing for. Privacy concerns make this a legal minefield, however. Talk with a lawyer before you start testing.

How reliable are they? If conducted by a competent, reputable lab, very accurate. However, shrewd and/or experienced abusers can sometimes slip by.

Integrity Tests

What do they do? Measure an individual's personal honesty and sense of integrity. These tests generally include questions on situations of ethical choice—an employee sees a coworker steal company property; what should he do? Or they include questions that can reveal personal standards of behavior—whether the candidate can follow simple procedures and keep company information confidential.

Why would you use them? An employer needs to determine how an applicant may behave in a position of trust—handling cash or safeguarding property, for example. As is the case with personality and psychological testing, these tests are very risky legally, with many privacy issues to consider. Talk to a lawyer first.

How reliable are they? Research has shown that some of these tests can produce reliable, unbiased information, while others aren't very accurate at all.

Polygraph (Lie-detector) Tests

What do they do? Measure stress-related physiological changes, such as blood pressure, sweating, temperature, and so on, to detect untrue statements.

Why would you use them? Employers need to ensure that people who are being hired for jobs with critical security implications are telling the truth about their backgrounds.

How reliable are they? Most experts agree that a competent polygraph operator can usually detect falsehoods from the average individual. However, people mistrust polygraphs enough that their results are inadmissible as evidence in any U.S. court. Be aware that the passage of the Employee Polygraph Protection Act of 1988 prohibits private employers—except under certain conditions—from conducting polygraph tests either on employees or on job applicants.

4.5.3 Staying Out of Test Trouble

The following tips may keep your tests trouble-free:

▲ Establish what traits or information the test is to evaluate and make sure that a relationship exists between these traits and the hiring criteria.
▲ Check carefully into the credentials and reputation of any test vendor.
▲ Double-check that the test isn't biased, even unintentionally, against any group.
▲ Verify that the test is certified by an established reputable group.
▲ Talk to others conducting testing to determine their levels of success.
▲ Federal, state, and local laws limit testing. Get legal advice first.

SELF-CHECK

1. Pre-employment tests are a scientifically proven means of evaluating job candidates. True or false?
2. To avoid problems with the EEOC guidelines, a company must be able to demonstrate how any test you use is job-related and necessary for business operations. True or false?
3. Explain the value of using an integrity test on a job applicant.

SUMMARY

In the long run, it's more difficult for a company to accommodate a poor performer than it is to invest in finding and hiring quality candidates. A savvy recruitment strategy is your best defense in preventing staffing difficulties, whether you opt to fill jobs from within an organization or go to outside sources. In today's business world, current options such as outsourcing and offshoring often serve an organization's needs better than traditional approaches. Any hiring approach should be guided by a plan and a protocol for how the process will be managed. Job advertisements, regardless of whether they are posted in a newspaper or on the internet, should be crafted to draw in the most qualified applicants. Organizations should not overlook the benefits of recruiting from college campuses, job fairs, and professional associations and unions. In many cases, outside recruiters have an edge over in-house recruitment methods, and employers should consider options such as employment agencies and headhunters. Once gathered, candidates can be evaluated with applications and resumes as part of a thoughtful resume review process, which will help spotlight the best candidates—and weed out the rest. Finally, fairly administered pre-employment tests—of proficiency, ability, personality, etc.—can further contribute to an effective evaluation process. However, in all cases such tests must be applied consistently and without any discriminatory effects.

KEY TERMS

Applicant tracking system	Software application that can post job openings on various websites, automate resume scanning, generate letters, and perform other functions.
Blind ads	An online posting or classified ad that doesn't identify the company and typically directs replies to a post office box number.

Candidate management system	Software application that can post job openings on various websites, automate resume scanning, generate letters, and perform other functions.
Contingency search firms	Recruiting focus is on mid- to upper-level positions usually in a particular field or profession.
Disparate impact	Employer actions that aren't intended to discriminate but have the effect of doing so.
Diversity training	Employee guidance that teaches them to increase sensitivity toward others.
Employment agencies	Typically recruiting generalists that focus on entry- and mid-level jobs in a range of industries.
Executive search firms	Recruiting focus is on high level executives, up to and including CEOs.
Flow sheet	A document that lists the steps in the evaluation process with spaces for the date and initials of the person completing the step.
Headhunters	Recruiting focus is on high level executives, up to and including CEOs.
Offshoring	When a function may be moved to a remote location out of the country.
Organizational inbreeding	The effects of recruiting from within a company for too long.
Outsourcing	When a company turns over an entire function (payroll, for example) to an outside specialist.
Staffing firm	Fee-based recruiting company that focuses on mid- to upper-level positions, usually in a particular field or profession.
Weighted	The process of giving elements in an application form certain value, putting more emphasis on qualifications that may influence job performance.
Workforce diversity	The effort to allow and encourage diversity in the workplace.

ASSESS YOUR UNDERSTANDING

Go to www.wiley.com/college/messmer to assess your knowledge of employee recruitment and evaluation.

Measure your learning by comparing pre-test and post-test results.

Summary Questions

1. What are three benefits of hiring new employees from outside a company?

2. Organizational inbreeding occurs when
   (a) a function may be moved to a remote location out of the country.
   (b) a systematic procedure is used to process applications from within a company.
   (c) a company recruits new employees from within for an extended period of time.
   (d) a company turns over its payroll to an outside specialist.

3. With outsourcing, a company loses money by hiring other companies to fill certain functions. True or false?

4. An effective job advertisement should be based on a well-written job description. True or false?

5. Name one disadvantage of attending a job fair (from an employer's perspective).

6. Which of the following is another name for staffing firm?
   (a) headhunter
   (b) executive search firm
   (c) contingency firm
   (d) HR manager

7. A replacement guarantee applies to a company when it chooses to switch to another recruiting company. True or false?

8. Which recruitment service focuses on entry- and mid-level jobs?
   (a) contingency search firm
   (b) employment service
   (c) college placement officer
   (d) headhunter

9. A resume contains much of the same information as
   (a) a job description.
   (b) an internet ad.

(c) a job application.

(d) a cover letter.

10. An employer may not request a photograph before employment; however, an employer can ask how long a candidate has lived at an address. True or false?

11. A weighted application

    (a) is reviewed before all others.

    (b) is illegal.

    (c) gives employers a reason to conduct tests.

    (d) gives extra emphasis to certain qualifications.

12. A chronological gap in a resume is a valid reason to take a job applicant out of the running for a position. True or false?

13. A flow sheet is a software application that can automate resume scanning and generate letters. True or false?

14. Pre-employment tests may do which of the following?

    (a) test an applicant's ability to learn

    (b) be used on selected candidates

    (c) determine the presence of prescription drugs

    (d) present an unfair barrier to the disabled

15. Polygraph tests are a foolproof way to measure a candidate's truthfulness. True or false?

16. An employer may test for physical agility only when

    (a) the test is completed before a candidate is hired.

    (b) the test is different for all applicants.

    (c) the quality is a legitimate requirement for the job.

    (d) the test is a case of disparate impact.

Applying This Chapter

1. The accounting firm that you work for needs to replace a senior manager who is retiring. As with other hiring situations, the company would like to hire from within, but the previous in-house hire didn't work out. Write a memo to the firm's president, in which you justify hiring from within, indicating how you could prevent a bad hire from happening again.

2. You and your best friend have built a successful party planning business called Party Pals. Most of your summer parties revolve around children, and many of the parents want magicians to entertain their young guests.

Compose a job advertisement for a part-time magician that you would employ for the busy summer party season.

3. County Hospital needs to hire eight pediatric nurses to staff a new children's outpatient service. What type of recruiter is best suited to the search and why? How would you choose this recruiter?

4. Given the same hiring need at County Hospital, management has decided to have the hospital's HR department find the candidates and narrow the selection down to twenty-five nurses. Map out the evaluation process that you would use to screen out those applicants not qualified for the job.

5. Personality tests measure characteristics such as assertiveness, temperament, and resiliency. This type of testing is designed to uncover personality traits that make good employees. For each of the characteristics mentioned—assertiveness, temperament, and resiliency—think of a job that would benefit from such testing.

CBO Search Strategies

In 2006, Sheraton's Four Points Hotels launched a clever executive search for a new position—Chief Beer Officer (CBO). Although it sounds somewhat outrageous, the position does have real responsibilities. The person chosen will act as a part-time consultant for Sheraton's newly-launched Best Brews program. As part of the highly publicized search, ads were taken out in the Wall Street Journal, HotJobs.com, and Monster.com. With more than 6,000 applicants, the company got some great attention—as well as some highly motivated applicants for other positions at Sheraton. Using this search as a model, formulate a similar strategy for the following scenario:

Target is launching a line of paint products to rival those of Benjamin Moore, but with competitive prices and a very youthful style approach. How could the company use the internet to build an innovative campaign for their products?

America's Staffing Resources

Your baked goods company is looking to expand and you need to staff a new production center in Newark, New Jersey. The Department of Labor, working with state agencies, has an online resume and job listing service, America's Job Bank. Determine what resources are available to help you fill ten positions, ranging from supervisor to baker to shipping manager. Prepare a recruitment strategy based on those resources.

Strategic Testing

As the human resources director of a regional sporting goods retailer, you've been asked to help combat the company's growing problem of employee theft. For your part, you'll produce a plan based on pre-employment testing.

- What types of tests woud apply in this situation?
- What legal issues must you address?

Research specific tests available and propose as many as you think will be required. You can find out about these tests by using the internet, as well as by looking in two reference books—*Tests in Print*, Volume Two, and *The Mental Measurement Yearbook*, both published by the Buros Institute, University of Nebraska-Lincoln.

5

INTERVIEWING AND MAKING SELECTION DECISIONS
Carrying Out a Hiring Strategy

Starting Point

Go to www.wiley.com/college/messmer to assess your knowledge of the basics of interviewing and selecting job candidates.
Determine where you need to concentrate your effort.

What You'll Learn in This Chapter

▲ Ways in which interviewing methods have changed in recent years
▲ The steps to take to prepare for an interview
▲ The value of setting up a system for applicant evaluation
▲ How to determine the usefulness of reference checks and background checks
▲ The steps in making an official job offer to a candidate

After Studying This Chapter, You Will Be Able To

▲ Set up guidelines for avoiding common interviewing mistakes
▲ Evaluate interview questions as they relate to anti-discrimination laws
▲ Calculate a candidate's weighted rating for a particular skill or attribute
▲ Argue for or against using background checks on a job applicant
▲ Assess an employer's need to negotiate salary based on a particular situation

INTRODUCTION

Hiring is no longer a simple matter of filling job openings. The big challenge today is for you and the hiring managers in your organization to keep the long-term view of your business needs in mind as you conduct interviews and evaluate job candidates. Preparation and planning are key when dealing with today's job applicants; in particular, be aware of the legal issues associated with nondiscriminatory questioning. Finally, stick to your strategy throughout the final selection stage, then make an offer that benefits both the candidate and your company.

5.1 Interviewing: The Basics

Conducting a job interview looks easier than it is. And that's the problem. The vast majority of managers and small business owners who conduct job interviews appear to be under the impression that they can manage this critical and often mishandled component of the staffing process. As a result, most managers take interviewing for granted. They don't invest the time, effort, and concentration that effective job interviewing requires. And, above all, they don't prepare enough for interviews.

The following sections look at interviewing, with a focus on the things you need to know and do to get the most out of the interviewing process.

5.1.1 Keeping Up with the Times

The biggest mistake you can make when you're in the market for new employees is to assume that you can rely on the same methods that you've been using for years. Keep the following in mind as you plan your interviewing strategy:

▲ **Higher stakes:** Gone are the days when you could minimize the consequences of a bad hiring decision by "finding a place" for that newly hired person who isn't working out.

▲ **Qualifications count:** With fewer layers of management in most companies, today's line employees must do their jobs with less supervision than in the past, and not every employee can flourish in this kind of environment.

▲ **Faster pace:** Business tasks have to be done faster than ever, so companies are relying on technological advances to streamline day-to-day operating procedures. Companies can't afford to have employees who can't keep up.

5.1.2 Getting Results

Job interviews enable you to perform the following four tasks that, combined with other steps you take, are essential to making a sound hiring decision:

▲ Obtain firsthand information about the candidate's background, work experience, and skill level that clarifies what you need to confirm or further explore from the resume or previous interviews.

▲ Get a general sense of the candidate's overall intelligence, aptitude, enthusiasm, and attitudes, with particular respect to how those attributes match up to the requirements of the job.

▲ Gain insight into the candidate's basic personality traits and her motivation to tackle the responsibilities of the job and become a part of the company.

▲ Estimate the candidate's ability to adapt to your company's work environment.

However, what occurs during a job interview doesn't tell you—not directly, at least—how effectively candidates may perform on the job if, indeed, you hire them. Nor does the image of the candidate that emerges during the interview necessarily represent an accurate image of who the candidate really is and how he's likely to react in actual job situations.

5.1.3 Interviewing: What to Avoid

The following list takes a look at some of the all-too-common interview practices that create a surefire recipe for hiring mistakes.

▲ **Time constraints:** Failing to give the interviewing process the time and effort it deserves is the main reason that interviews produce mediocre results. Busy managers frequently neglect to prepare for interviews, conduct them diligently, and evaluate the results in a thoughtful manner.

▲ **Lost direction:** Skillful interviewers think through the process and tend to follow that same method each time—albeit with variations that they tailor to individual situations. Unsuccessful interviewers tend to "wing it," creating a different routine for each interview. The hidden danger of winging it: You deprive yourself of the one thing you need the most as you're comparing candidates—an objective standard on which to base your conclusions.

▲ **Too chatty:** If you're talking more than twenty percent of the time during a job interview, you're talking too much. Savvy candidates are usually adept at getting their interviewers to do most of the talking. They've figured out that the more interviewers talk, the easier they, the candidates, can determine what answers are going to carry the most weight.

FOR EXAMPLE

Seeing Halos

A large New York radio station needed to hire an entry-level employee to work with the on-air personalities. The hiring manager, who had filled the position twice in the past year, had to find someone quickly. Of the three final applicants, two had degrees from Hunter College and one had a degree from New York University, the manager's alma mater. Though the three candidates appeared equally qualified, the NYU grad and the manager had so much to talk to about school and campus and so on, that the manager offered her the job, without even checking references.

▲ **Seeing halos:** The **halo effect** is the phrase managers generally use to describe a common phenomenon in hiring. You may become so enraptured by one particular aspect of the candidate—appearance, credentials (see Section 3.4.3, "Creating a Job Description"), interests, and so on—that it colors all your other judgments.

SELF-CHECK

1. List three common interviewing mistakes to avoid.
2. Anti-discrimination laws apply after an employee has been hired. True or false?
3. Define *halo effect*.

5.2 Preparing for an Interview

Your ability to get the most out of the interviews you conduct invariably depends on how well prepared you are. Here's a checklist of things that you should do before you ask the first interview question:

▲ Thoroughly familiarize yourself with the job description, especially its hiring criteria. Do so even if you drew up the criteria yourself.

▲ Review everything the candidate has submitted to date: resume, job description, cover letter, etc. Note any areas needing clarification or explanation, such as quirky job titles or gaps in work history.

▲ An HR person may conduct the initial interview alone. In such cases it may be helpful to speak to the hiring manager or the person in charge of hiring in the department. He or she may have certain questions that should be asked.

▲ Set up a general structure for the interview. Create a basic schedule so that you have enough time to cover all the key areas. Adhering to a rough schedule will help you begin and end the session on time, allowing you to be more efficient and showing that you respect the candidate's time.

▲ Write the questions you intend to ask and keep it with you. Base your questions on the areas of the candidate's background that deserve the most attention (based on the job description and your hiring criteria).

▲ Make arrangements to hold the interview in a private room. A conference room is best, but if your office is your only option, clear your desk, close the door, and either set your phone so all calls go to voice mail or have your calls forwarded somewhere else.

MULTIPLE AND PANEL INTERVIEWS

It's not unusual for more than one company employee to interview a candidate to provide a variety of opinions on the individual, especially if he or she will play a key role in the organization. In fact, sometimes these meetings are carried out simultaneously through the use of an interviewing panel made up of the hiring manager plus other members of the management team or work group, usually no more than three to five people.

Panel interviews are beneficial when you want to quickly get a promising hire through multiple interviews in a timely manner. It's best for the hiring manager to conduct one-on-one interviews with applicants first, however, choosing only a few finalists for panel interviews. This saves panelists' time and ensures that the hiring manager is presenting only those candidates he or she may ultimately hire.

5.2.1 Warming Up: The Introduction

Your priority in meeting a candidate for the first time is to put him or her at ease. If you're seated at your desk as the candidate walks in, a common courtesy is to stand and meet the individual halfway, shake hands, and let him or her know that you're happy to meet him or her. Skilled job interviewers usually begin with small talk—a general comment about the weather or transportation difficulties—but they keep it to a minimum.

Your next step is to give the candidate a very basic overview of what you're expecting to get from the interview and how long you estimate it to last. Be careful not to give too much information, though. Saying too much about the skills and characteristics you're looking for turns a savvy interviewee into a "parrot" who can repeat the same key words he or she just heard.

5.2.2 Mastering the Art of Q&A

The question and answer period is the main part of the interview. How you phrase questions, when you ask them, how you follow up—each of these aspects of interviewing can go a long way toward affecting the quality and usability of the answers you get. The following describe the key practices that differentiate people who've mastered the art of questioning from those who haven't.

▲ **Have a focus:** Even before you start to ask questions, you should have a reasonably specific idea of what information or insights you're expecting to gain from the interview. You may uncover two or three items on the candidate's resume that can use clarification. Or you may have a specific question about one particular aspect of the candidate's personality. Whatever it is, decide ahead of time and build your interview strategy around that goal.

▲ **Make every question count:** Every question you ask during a job interview must have a specific purpose. That purpose may be to elicit specific information, produce some insight into the candidate's personality, or simply put the candidate at ease.

▲ **Pay attention:** Listening attentively is a challenge because your tendency in a job interview is to draw conclusions before the candidate has completed the answer. Another tendency is to begin rehearsing in your mind the next question you intend to ask while the candidate is still answering the earlier question. Fight that tendency. Write down your questions before the interview begins and then concentrate on the candidate and what he or she is saying.

▲ **Don't hesitate to probe:** Whenever a candidate offers an answer that doesn't address the specific information you're seeking, nothing's wrong with asking additional questions to draw out more specific answers. If a candidate talks about the money he or she saved his or her department, ask how much and how, specifically, the savings were realized. Too many interviewers let candidates "off the hook" in the interest of being "nice."

▲ **Give candidates ample time to respond:** Just because you don't get an immediate answer to a question doesn't mean that you need to rush in with another question to fill the silence. Give the candidate time to come up with a thoughtful answer. If the silence persists for more than, say, ten seconds, ask the candidate if he or she wants you to clarify the question. Remember that the interview is a time for you to listen, not talk.

▲ **Suspend judgments:** Reserving judgment isn't easy, but try to keep your attention on the answers you're getting instead of making interpretations or judgments. You're going to have plenty of time after the interview to evaluate what you see and hear.

▲ **Take notes:** Memories can do tricky things, leading people to ignore what actually happens during an interview and to rely instead on general impressions. Taking notes helps you avoid this common pitfall. Keep all notes factual and within nondiscriminatory boundaries. Give yourself time after the interview to review your notes and put them into some kind of order.

5.2.3 Q&A: Varying Styles

You can usually divide interview questions into four categories, based on the kinds of answers you're trying to elicit.

Closed-ended

Definition: Questions that call for a simple, informational answer—often yes or no.

Examples: "How many years did you work for the circus?" "Did you enjoy it?" "What cities did you tour?"

When to use them: Closed-ended questions work best if you're trying to elicit specific information or set the stage for more complex questions.

Pitfall to avoid: Asking too many of them in rapid-fire succession and failing to tie them back to the job criteria, making it feel like an interrogation.

Open-ended

Definition: Questions that require thought and oblige the candidate to reveal attitudes or opinions.

Examples: "Describe for me how you handle stress on the job." "Can you give me an illustration of how you improved productivity at your last job?"

When to use them: Most of the time, but interspersed with closed-ended questions. Using **open-ended questions** related to candidates' past experiences on the job is known as **behavioral interviewing.** This approach requires candidates to describe how they've handled real tasks and problems, so it can be very useful and revealing.

Pitfalls to avoid: Not being specific enough as you phrase the question and not interceding if the candidate's answer starts to veer off track.

Hypothetical

Definition: Questions that invite the candidate to resolve an imaginary situation or react to a given situation.

Examples: "If you were the purchasing manager, would you institute an automated purchase-order system?" "If you were to take over this department, what's the first thing you'd do to improve productivity?"

When to use them: Hypothetical questions are useful if framed in the context of actual job situations.

Pitfall to avoid: You're usually better off asking questions that force a candidate to use an actual experience as the basis for an answer.

Leading

Definition: Questions asked in a way that the answer you're looking for is obvious.

Examples: "You rarely fought with your last boss, right?" "You know a lot about team-building, don't you?" "You wouldn't dream of falsifying your expense accounts, would you?"

When to use them: Rarely, if ever use **leading questions**. You're not likely to get an honest answer—just the answer you want to hear. And you run the risk of appearing unprofessional.

5.2.4 Staying on Course: Nondiscriminatory Questioning

The questions you or others in your company ask during a job interview can result in legal problems for the company if you fail to follow certain guidelines. Even the most innocent of questions can result in a discrimination suit at some point. Antidiscrimination and consumer-protection legislation restricts the type and scope of pre-employment questions that you can ask. To make matters even more confusing, standards can vary from state to state.

Here are some current areas of concern:

▲ **Be sensitive to age discrimination issues.** Remember that any question that may indicate the candidate's age may be interpreted as discriminatory. In other words, don't ask a question such as "When did you graduate high school?"

▲ **Beware of double-edged questions.** Caution all the interviewers in your company to keep their innocent curiosity (such as "What kind of a name is that?") from exposing your company to charges of discrimination.

▲ **Don't confuse before and after.** Questions considered illegal before hiring may be acceptable after the individual is on the payroll. Age is a good example. You can't ask a person's age before hiring, but you may do so after hiring when the information will be needed for health insurance and pension purposes.

The following sections provide a rundown of which questions are permitted before hiring and which are not. Check with your attorney for any local restrictions or new rulings and keep in mind that all questions must directly relate to a bona fide job requirement.

National Origin

Permissible: No questions are permissible, unless given as part of an optional affirmative action form.

Risky ground: Questions related to the candidate's national origin, ancestry, native language or that of family members, or place of birth of applicant or her parents.

Discriminatory: What sort of an accent is that? Where were you born? Where were your parents born?

Citizenship Status

Permissible: If hired, will you be able to prove that you have the right to remain and work in the U.S.?

Risky ground: Questions that may oblige a candidate to indicate national origin.

Discriminatory: Are you a U.S. citizen?

Address

Permissible: Where do you live? How long have you lived here?

Risky ground: Questions about housing aimed at revealing financial status. (May be considered discriminatory against minorities.)

Discriminatory: Are you renting, or do you own?

Age

Permissible: None.

Risky ground: Questions regarding age when age is not a bona fide job requirement.

Discriminatory: How old are you? What year were you born? When did you graduate high school?

Family Status

Permissible: Can you relocate? (If relevant to the job.)

Risky ground: All questions regarding marital or family status.

Discriminatory: Are you pregnant? (Even if the candidate is obviously pregnant.)

Religion

Permissible: Can you work overtime on days other than Monday through Friday?

Risky ground: Any question whose answers may indicate religious beliefs or affiliation.

Discriminatory: In college, what fraternity (or sorority) were you in? What religious holidays do you observe?

Health and Physical Condition

Permissible: Here are the expected functions of the job. Can you perform them with or without reasonable accommodation?
Risky ground: Questions that aren't directly related to a bona fide job requirement and, in addition, aren't being asked of all candidates.
Discriminatory: Do you have a hearing impairment? Have you ever filed a workers' compensation claim?

Name

Permissible: Have you ever used another name or nickname?
Risky ground: Whether the applicant has ever changed her name; maiden name.
Discriminatory: What kind of name is that?

Language

Permissible: What language do you speak, read, and/or write? (Permissible if relevant to the job.)
Risky ground: Questions that reveal the applicant's national origin or ancestry.
Discriminatory: What language do you speak at home? Is English your first language?

5.2.5 Closing on the Right Note

With only a few minutes to go, you can bring the session to a graceful close by following these steps:

1. **Summarize the interview.** Sum up what the candidate has said about his or her fit for the position, reasons for wanting the job, etc. This demonstrates that you were a sincere listener and it leaves a good impression. It also gives the candidate an opportunity to clarify any misunderstandings.

FOR EXAMPLE

Married with Children?

Ron, 45, is being interviewed for a great job in website consulting The meeting has been going well, but as the interview is winding down, the interviewer casually asks: "Will your family mind the amount of travel you may have to do for the job?" Ron—a single father—isn't sure how to handle the question, but he's certain that could be tricky. Instead of launching into a complicated explanation of his family situation, he sticks to the business matter at hand and replies "I'm used to traveling for business. In fact, I find being on the road invigorating, and my track record has been very consistent under these conditions."

2. **Let the candidate ask questions.** Provide an opportunity for the individual to ask any questions he or she may have on his or her mind after the interview.

3. **Let the candidate know what comes next.** Advise the candidate how and when you're going to contact him or her and whether any further steps need to be taken—forms, tests, and so on.

4. **End the interview on a formal, but sincere note.** Thank the candidate for his or her time and repeat your commitment to follow up. By standing or shaking hands again, you formally end the session. Walk the applicant out.

SELF-CHECK

1. Why should you write down questions before an interview begins?
2. Under no circumstances may an interviewer ask a candidate about health or physical condition. True or false?
3. Explain what a leading question is and when it should be used.

5.3 Making Selection Decisions

Because hiring mistakes can be costly, a great deal is riding on your ability to select the best people for your available positions. If you find yourself constantly second-guessing your hiring decisions, you may want to take a close look at the process you're using in making your final choices. This section can help get you started.

As with other aspects of human resources this phase of the hiring process is rife with sensitive legal matters. Don't be your own lawyer. Legally complex (and potentially costly) issues require a case-by-case evaluation by your own attorney.

5.3.1 Seeking Success

Many people differ in their basic approaches to the challenge of making hiring decisions. Some tend to base decisions on intuition or "a gut feeling." Others are highly systematic. Some people rely entirely on their own judgment and assessments. Still others seek outside guidance.

You can never be absolutely certain that the decision you make is going to yield the desired result, but following certain steps along the way can help you improve your chances significantly.

▲ Do a thorough job early on in the hiring process of identifying your needs and drawing up an accurate job description.

▲ Gather enough information about each candidate—through interviewing, testing, and observation—so that you have a reasonably good idea of the candidates' capabilities, personalities, strengths, and weaknesses.

▲ Remain objective in evaluating candidates. Your personal biases don't steer your focus away from your hiring criteria (see Chapter 3).

▲ Develop methods to evaluate your strategies so that, the next time around, you can repeat practices that produce good results.

5.3.2 Utilizing the "Tools" of the Trade

Your available resources in making hiring decisions are usually fairly limited. The following list takes a brief look at the information sources that serve as your evaluation tools and what you need to keep in mind as you're tapping each one.

▲ **Past experience:** If a candidate was hard working, highly motivated, and team-oriented in his or her last job, the same is likely to hold true in the new job. Similarly, the candidate who didn't excel in his or her last position isn't likely to in his or her next one.

▲ **Interview impressions:** Impressions you pick up during an interview usually carry a great deal of weight in hiring decisions. The problem with interview impressions is that they're just that—impressions. Keep them in proper perspective with test results, references, and other information you gather.

▲ **Test results:** Some people regard test results as the only truly reliable predictor of future success because they are quantifiable. However, some candidates simply don't test well. Other candidates may be clever enough to figure out what most tests are actually testing for and tailor their responses accordingly.

▲ **First-hand observation:** More companies are, as part of their hiring procedure, asking candidates to complete some sort of project (usually for pay) to help determine whether they can handle the job. Another trend is starting out an applicant as an interim employee, with the idea that it could become full time.

5.3.3 Putting a Selection System to Work

The easiest way to make a hiring decision is to weigh the options and simply go with what your intuition tells you to do. But decision-makers in companies with good track records of making successful hires don't give themselves the luxury of relying solely on intuition. They use their intuition, but not as the sole basis for their judgments. The following list describes what such decision makers rely on:

▲ **They have in place some sort of** *system*—a protocol for assessing the strengths and weaknesses of candidates and applying those assessments to the hiring criteria.

▲ **The system is weighted**—it presupposes that certain skills and attributes bear more on job performance than do others and takes those differences into account (see related material in Section 4.4.1).

▲ **They constantly monitor and evaluate the effectiveness of the system**— sharpening their own ability and the ability of others to link any data they obtain during the recruiting and interviewing process to the on-the-job performance of new hires.

5.3.4 Setting Up Your Own Protocol

Some companies invest millions of dollars in developing elaborate selection procedures. However you do it, the following sections describe the fundamental steps you must go through with all such processes.

1. **Isolate key hiring criteria.** By this point in the hiring process, you should know what combination of skills and attributes a candidate needs to perform the job well and fit your company's pace and culture.

2. **Set priorities.** You can safely assume that some of your hiring criteria are more important than others. To take these differences into account, set up a scale that reflects the relative importance of any particular skill or attribute.

3. **Evaluate candidates on the basis of the weighted scale** you established in step 2. Take note: Instead of simply looking at the candidate as a whole, you look at each of the criteria you set down, and you rate the candidate on the basis of how he or she measures up in that particular category.

The Weighted System

This weighted system of evaluation takes into account the performance priorities unique to each of the key hiring criteria. Say, for example, that one of the candidate's strengths is the ability to work as part of a team. The candidate's rating on that particular attribute may be a five, but the relative importance of teamwork to the task at hand may be anywhere from 1 to 5, which means that the overall ranking may end up as low as 5 (5 times 1) or as high as 25 (5 times 5).

All in all, a weighted system gives you an opportunity to see how well candidates measure up against one another and how closely their skills and attributes match the job requirements. However, the effectiveness of this system depends on two crucial factors: the validity of your hiring criteria and the objectivity of the judgments that underlie any ratings you assign to each candidate in each area.

Table 5-1: Candidate No. 1 Evaluation

Performance Category	Weighted	Candidate rating (1–5)	Score importance (1–5)
Previous customer service experience	3	1	3
Computer skills	2	3	6
Communication skills	5	4	20
Reliability/work ethic	5	4	20
Ability to cope with stress	4	4	16
Empathy	4	4	16
Total			**81**

The Weighted System in Action

Tables 5-1 and 5-2 demonstrate how a weighted evaluation system works. Notice that the candidate under evaluation in Table 5-1 is relatively weak in two hiring criteria—previous experience and computer skills—but is much stronger in the criteria that carry more weight. The candidate's aggregate score, therefore, is higher than that of a candidate who meets the technical requirements of the job alone.

5.3.5 Factoring in the Intangibles

The difficult part of any evaluation procedure is attaching numerical ratings to the "intangibles"—those attributes that you can measure only through your

Table 5-2: Candidate No. 2 Evaluation

Performance Category	Weighted	Candidate rating (1–5)	Score importance (1–5)
Previous customer service experience	3	5	15
Computer skills	2	5	10
Communication skills	5	2	10
Reliability/work ethic	5	3	15
Ability to cope with stress	4	4	16
Empathy	4	1	4
Total			**70**

HIRING HINDSIGHT

Bad hiring decisions rarely happen by accident. The hiring criteria that you establish from the beginning should serve as your guiding force throughout the evaluation process. If you decide to change the criteria, fine. Just make sure that you're not changing criteria simply because you're enamored with one particular candidate and decide to change the ground rules to accommodate that candidate. Keep in mind three of the most common pitfalls in hiring:

▲ The **halo effect** (becoming so enraptured by one particular aspect of the candidate that you let that aspect influence all your other judgments). (See Section 5.1.3.)

▲ The **cloning effect** (hiring someone in your image even though someone with your particular mix of skills and attributes clearly isn't qualified for that particular job).

▲ How much you "like" a candidate.

observations. The following sections cover the relevant intangible factors, along with suggestions on how to tell whether the candidate measures up.

Industriousness and Motivation

Definition: Candidates' work ethic—how hard they're willing to work and how important they feel it is to perform to the best of their ability.

How to measure: Verifiable accomplishments in their last jobs. Evaluation of past employers and coworkers. Track record of successful jobs.

FOR EXAMPLE

Enforcing a System

To meet the challenge of the city's population growth, the Las Vegas Metropolitan Police Department recruits and selects hundreds of qualified candidates to fill positions. The department is looking for a variety of skills and work characteristics: cognitive skills, language skills, and interactive style, as well as cooperation, teamwork, and accurate interpersonal perception. The selection process adopted by the LVMPD evaluates these skills and characteristics through a series of tests, including a written exam, physical fitness test, oral board, and background interview. Both the written exam and the oral board are weighted and calculated as a percentage of the applicant's overall test score.

Intelligence

Definition: Mental alertness; capability to process abstract information.
How to measure: Evidence of good decision-making ability in previous jobs. Also through testing.

Temperament and Ability to Cope with Stress

Definition: General demeanor—whether the candidate is calm and level-headed or hyper and hot-headed.
How to measure: Personality testing can sometimes prove reliable, but the best way to measure these criteria is to ask during the interview about stress levels in candidates' previous jobs and how they feel they performed.

Creativity and Resourcefulness

Definition: The ability to think "outside the box"—to come up with innovative solutions to problems.
How to measure: Examples of previous work (graphic-design work, writing samples, and so on). Specific examples of situations in which the candidate has come up with an innovative solution to a problem.

Teamwork Abilities

Definition: The ability to work harmoniously with others and share responsibility for achieving the same goal.
How to measure: Previous work experience. Team successes mentioned during the interview. Evidence of ability to work within project team rules, protocols, and work practices. Support for coworkers. Willingness to ask for help.

SELF-CHECK

1. List the four resources employers have to evaluate job candidates.
2. Which of the following is an intangible attribute?
   a. temperament
   b. computer skills
   c. previous experience
   d. college degree
3. Define *cloning effect*.

5.4 Checking Out Applicants

References and other third-party observations are necessary components of the hiring process. Although obtaining useful references and background checks may be time-consuming, not taking these steps can increase your risk of making a hiring mistake.

5.4.1 Checking References

Getting a candid reference from an employer is tougher than ever these days. Employers know that both saying too much and saying too little can have legal consequences, so they are increasingly wary of being specific about past employees and their work histories.

Because of this, rushing through the reference checking process—or bypassing it altogether—in order to make a quick hire may be tempting. While it's important not to delay this step and risk losing the candidate to someone else, getting reliable information from a former supervisor is an important step to take before selecting someone as an employee of your company. Consider the following tips:

▲ **Let the candidate know you check references.** Informing applicants that you're checking usually helps ensure that the answers they give you during the interview are truthful.

▲ **Don't delegate it.** If the employee will report directly to you, you—not a delegate or assistant—should check the references. In particular, calling someone at your same level may establish greater camaraderie that will prompt a more honest and detailed reference.

▲ **Use responses from the interview.** Asking candidates during the interview what their former employers are likely to say about them can provide you with a good starting point if you can actually get the former employer to talk openly. Start out by saying something like, "Joe tells me that you think he's the greatest thing since sliced bread" and have the employer take it from there. You may not get a totally frank answer, but you can get valuable comments and insights.

Contacting Potential References

The best way to communicate with references is via the telephone. Calling gives you an opportunity to ask spontaneous questions based upon what was said in response to one of your primary questions. You can often detect enthusiasm, or lack of it, if you pay attention to the tone of the voice.

Other methods are not as fruitful:

▲ Written references presented to you by candidates are of limited value— how many bad letters of reference have you ever seen?

▲ Sending email is usually ineffective as well. References aren't likely to be as candid in writing as they would be verbally, if they respond at all.

Proceeding with Caution: Online Reference Checks

Advances in technology and more sophisticated online search capabilities have increased the popularity of reference checking via the internet. The practice will undoubtedly grow as more record holders create databases that employers can easily access. As internet-based checks become more standardized, this integration is likely to make turnaround time even faster.

Some employers access blogs or "Google" a person's name to see what comes up. While this approach can reduce costs and sometimes yield faster results, you must also understand that much of the information on a candidate you discover can be either erroneous or irrelevant. Online reference checking should be viewed as a complement, not a replacement, for traditional methods.

5.4.2 Going with Background Checks

Background checks take reference checks a step further, and businesses use them because they feel they're a way to gain more assurance that the people they hire are what these candidates represent themselves to be. In other words, where reference checks allow you to verify with former employers a potential hire's accomplishments and personal attributes, background checks attempt to delve into additional aspects of a candidate's activities and behavior.

Background checks can take many forms—from criminal background checks and academic degree verification to credit checks and workers' compensation report—depending on the position and what the employer considers most important in evaluating job candidates.

FOR EXAMPLE

Checking on a Nanny

GoNannies, Inc. is a company that helps families find and hire domestic personnel such as nannies, housekeepers, and personal assistants. As part of its commitment to quality, GoNannies, Inc. strongly recommends that clients run a pre-employment verification (background check) and check all references of a final applicant. The company offers several types of background checks and "strongly discourages families from relying on online background check services which rely strictly on database searches for their information, as they can often be incomplete, outdated and/or may contain errors." The company also offers a comprehensive criminal background check to clients.

Conducting background checks is frequently not a simple matter. But that doesn't mean that they're not useful tools when pursued appropriately. Whether to conduct a background check depends most on the nature of your business and the position for which you're hiring. In limited cases, you don't have a choice because federal and state laws require background checks for certain jobs. But for most positions, the employer determines the need for investigation.

SELF-CHECK

1. Which of the following is the most useful means of obtaining a reference check?

   a. email request

   b. written employer reference

   c. academic verification

   d. phone call

2. By using the internet for applicant references, employees can efficiently and effectively replace other means of obtaining references. True or false?

5.5 Making Job Offers

Once you've made your final choice for a job, you must make the offer official. Keep in mind that if you fail to handle this phase of the hiring process carefully, one of two things can happen: You can lose the candidate, or, even if the candidate comes aboard, you can start the relationship off on a bumpy note.

In many states employment relationships are subject to the common law concept of employment at will, meaning the relationship can be ended at any time by either party with or without a reason (see Section 11.11.1). As a result, few employees today work under employment contracts. In most cases, the relationship is defined in an offer letter that is composed after negotiations are complete.

▲ **Making and negotiating offers.** One of the goals of the selection process is to gather information from applicants about their expectations for compensation, benefits, and other terms of employment. When it is time to make an offer, these expectations are factored into the process of crafting the offer. Before making an offer, any required approvals should be obtained, along with approval for any "wiggle room" should the candidate come back with a request for a higher salary or increased benefits. Once the verbal negotiations are complete, the written agreement can be completed.

▲ **Offer letters.** The offer letter should be prepared upon acceptance of the verbal offer. The letter should be approved by an organization's attorney. Be certain that any promises of benefits or special conditions made by the hiring manager are included in the offer so that there is no ambiguity about the complete offer.

The following items are worth considering when planning a job offer:

▲ **Don't delay:** After you make up your mind about a candidate, make the offer immediately, especially if you're in a tight labor market.

▲ **Make your offer:** At this stage in the process, you have no reason to be coy. Call the person you want to hire and give him or her all the details about pay, benefits, and anything extra; follow up with an official letter.

▲ **Set a deadline:** Give candidates a reasonable amount of time to decide whether to accept the offer. The time frame for an entry-level job may be a few days, but for a middle or senior-level candidate, a week isn't excessive.

▲ **Stay connected:** While a candidate is considering an offer, you or the hiring manager should stay in touch with him or her to reinforce your excitement.

▲ **Prepare to negotiate salary:** After receiving a response to your offer, you must be prepared to negotiate. Thanks to an abundance of information on salary negotiation through websites and books, most job seekers will be knowledgeable on the topic. To prepare, ask yourself these questions:

  • Are other, equally qualified candidates available if the applicant says no? If the answer is yes, the leverage rests with the company.

  • Has the job been particularly hard to fill? If the answer is yes, the leverage rests with the candidate.

  • Will a stronger offer be out of line with pay levels for comparable positions in your company or hiring manager's department? The lack of internal equity in compensation levels diminishes the spirit of fairness.

FOR EXAMPLE

Attention to Deal Details

Liz received the written job offer for a mid-level position in marketing for an online shoe distributor two days after she verbally accepted the offer. Because this was her first position at this level, she was surprised at the detail with which the letter went into. The offer covered everything from salary and vacation time to phone expenses and travel allowance. Though it included a small signing bonus, the offer did not include any provisions for severance pay. After two additional phone calls—one with the marketing manager and one with the company's hiring manager—the offer was modified and Liz accepted.

- Would the applicant be willing to compromise? Consider making concessions in other areas such as flexible scheduling or a signing bonus.

5.5.1 Proceeding After the Offer

If a promising candidate accepts your final offer, congratulations! You're helping build a strong team for your business. Keep the following items in mind as you move ahead:

▲ **Clarify acceptance details.** Some companies are now asking candidates to sign a duplicate copy of the job-offer letter as an indication of acceptance. If you're making a job offer contingent on reference checking or a physical examination, drug or alcohol testing, or background checks, make sure that the candidate understands and accepts this restriction.

▲ **Stay in touch.** Even after a candidate accepts your offer and you agree on a starting date, keeping in touch with the new employee is still a good idea. Two to three weeks is the customary time between an acceptance and start date. Use the transition period to mail off all those informational brochures and employment forms and to schedule a lunch or two, if appropriate.

▲ **Notify others.** After a selection has been made, it is appropriate to contact the applicants who were not selected to thank them for their time and let them know another candidate was selected.

Figure 5-1 is an example of "thanks, but no thanks" letter to an unsuccessful applicant. Note that the letter gets right to the point, leaves no room for mistake or debate, and is firm but polite.

Figure 5-1

Weer Thebest Corp.
100 Main St.
Mooseley, ME 00000

Human Resources Department

Mr. Ned Nicetry
14 South St.
Mooseley, ME 00000

Dear Mr. Nicetry,

Thank you for interest in our company. We have reviewed our needs for the position of Administrative Assistant, and I regret to advise you that we cannot offer you a position at this time.

We will retain your resume on file for six months and will contact you should another opportunity arise for which you are qualified.

Please accept our best wishes for your future endeavors.

Sincerely,

Agatha Crisply
Human Resources Associate

A sample rejection letter.

SELF-CHECK

1. How much time should an employer allow a candidate to accept—or decline—an offer?

a. one hour
b. one day
c. four to five days
d. two weeks

2. What two things should an employer do after a candidate accepts an offer?

SUMMARY

A well-planned and carefully executed interview is one of the most important aspects of the hiring process. There is too much at stake in today's competitive business world to waste time and resources on hiring individuals who can't keep up. To begin, you'll need to prepare for an interview with the best—and legally appropriate—questions for the job for which you are hiring, all the while keeping in mind your businesses' long-term needs. Depending on the kinds of answers you're trying to elicit, you can use varying styles of questions. Keep your organization's goals close as you further narrow the field, using a fair and consistent system to evaluate the candidates. Consider a candidate's past experience, impressions from the interview, and any test results as part of the decision-making process. In many situations, a weighted evaluation system may guarantee better results than simply an evaluator's own decision, but such systems can be costly and time consuming. Stay vigilant in your evaluation by conducting the necessary reference and background checks; the extra effort will help ensure sound hiring decisions. Finally, carefully negotiate an offer that works for both your company and your potential future employee.

KEY TERMS

Background checks	Employee evaluation tools such as criminal checks, academic degree verifications, and workers' compensation reports.
Behavioral interviewing	Questioning technique using open-ended questions related to candidates' past experiences on the job.
Cloning effect	Hiring someone in your image even though someone with your particular mix of skills and attributes isn't qualified for that particular job.
Closed-ended question	Question that calls for a simple, informational answer.
Halo effect	A phrase used to describe a common phenomenon in hiring in which the interviewer becomes so enraptured by one particular aspect of the candidate—that it colors all your other judgments.
Hypothetical question	Question that invites the candidate to resolve an imaginary situation or react to a given situation.
Leading question	Question asked in such a way that the answer you're looking for is obvious.
Open-ended question	Question that requires thought and oblige the candidate to reveal attitudes or opinions.

ASSESS YOUR UNDERSTANDING

Go to www.wiley.com/college/messmer to assess your knowledge of the basics of interviewing and selecting job candidates.
Measure your learning by comparing pre-test and post-test results.

Summary Questions

1. Which situation is an example of the halo effect?

   (a) an interviewer does more talking than the applicant

   (b) a candidate's resume looks professional but is not accurate

   (c) a candidate answers questions truthfully

   (d) an interviewer is impressed by a Yale degree but overlooks resume gaps

2. An interview gives an accurate reading of how effective a candidate will be in a job. True or false?

3. Which of the following can be explored in an interview?

   (a) marital status

   (b) personality traits

   (c) health history

   (d) religious beliefs

4. "What would you do if you discovered an employee stealing supplies?" is an example of which type of questioning?

   (a) close-ended

   (b) open-ended

   (c) hypothetical

   (d) leading

5. In what kind of situation would it be acceptable to ask a candidate about his or her language skills?

6. What is wrong with asking whether or not a candidate owns her own home?

7. Behavioral interviewing require candidates to

   (a) describe how they've handled real tasks and problems.

   (b) describe a related but hypothetical situation.

   (c) answer with a simple yes or no.

   (d) answer with another question.

8. What is one drawback of testing in an evaluation system?

9. A weighted evaluation system places equal emphasis on all the requirements of a job. True or false?

10. In what ways can a job applicant's teamwork abilities be measured?

11. What is the benefit of informing an applicant that you'll be checking references?

12. Name three types of background checks used by employers.

13. A criminal check is a form of

    (a) employee test.

    (b) background check.

    (c) employer reference.

    (d) job verification.

14. Describe a situation in which an employer should consider making concessions as far as salary negotiation.

15. When an employee signs off on a job-offer letter, she is indicating her acceptance of the offer and any restrictions within. True or false?

Applying This Chapter

1. You've been asked to fill in for a hiring manager to interview three candidates for an accounting position for a large clothing retailer. It's been more than two years since you've had to conduct a job interview. What will you need to prepare for your day?

2. As the human resources director of an exclusive Las Vegas hotel you need to interview applicants for a security guard position. Create five interview questions for the meeting.

3. List five qualifications required for an elementary school teacher. Assign a weight to each of them (1 to 5, with 5 being the most important).

4. For the same school teacher position, assess what level of reference and/ or background check should be required. Give reasons for your answers.

5. You're nearing the end of your negotiations with a landscape architect that you'd like to join your engineering staff. She is asking for more, but you've can't go any higher with the salary range because anything higher would exceed the salary being paid to senior staff members. What can you do?

Canine Credentials

Prepare to interview an applicant for a job as a dog walker for your small business—a pet care company in Boston. Out of your current twelve employees, fifty percent are university students, and you've been coping with recent high turnover issues.

- What credentials, skills, and attributes are required for the job?
- What are the six most important open-ended questions to ask?
- What areas of discriminatory questioning must you avoid?
- What form of testing could you use to further evaluate your candidate?
- What level of reference check/background check would be required for the position and why?

I've Been Googled!

Use the internet to investigate yourself from the perspective of a Fortune 500 employer. Start with a Google search and go from there. What kind of information do you find and how accurate is it? What free online resources are available and to what degree are they useful?

Make Me an Offer

Create a job offer for a senior position in human resources. Include all relevant areas of concern. You may use the internet for examples but draw from your own experiences and the information in the chapter.

6

TRAINING EMPLOYEES
Enhancing Productivity and Corporate Viability

Starting Point

Go to www.wiley.com/college/messmer to assess your knowledge of the basics of employee training.
Determine where you need to concentrate your effort.

What You'll Learn in This Chapter

- ▲ Factors that influence the effectiveness of employee training programs
- ▲ The basic steps of an employee training process
- ▲ Familiar approaches to employee training
- ▲ Common employee training topics
- ▲ Ways of measuring the effectiveness of training programs

After Studying This Chapter, You Will Be Able To

- ▲ Evaluate the appropriateness of training for a particular corporate situation
- ▲ Assess the training needs of a situation using a needs assessment worksheet
- ▲ Choose the most effective training approach for a company's needs
- ▲ Defend the use of a communications training program for mid-level managers
- ▲ Test the effectiveness of a training program using any of four accepted practices

INTRODUCTION

Broadly speaking, **employee training** refers to everything your organization does to upgrade the skills and improve the job performance of your employees, both in the short term and long term. Training encompasses a wide range of learning-based tools, ranging from a live seminar to a DVD instructional session used at their desks. In the HR role for your company, it's your responsibility to not only determine the best training approaches but also to organize and run these programs in a cost-effective way that's in line with your organization's overall culture.

6.1 Determining What Training Can Do For You

No matter what the nature of your business, you won't find it easy to stay on top without a commitment to helping your people stay ahead of emerging trends and changing needs. Increasing the knowledge of your workforce not only enhances your ability as a company to compete but also makes for more satisfied employees. Even in lean times, cutting back on training to reduce expenses can be counterproductive, both in terms of company success and employee retention.

6.1.1 Evaluating Your Training Situation

Now, more than ever, learning is a highly individual process, and because of that you must be wary of taking the "one-size-fits-all" approach. In general, here are some of the factors that most often influence the effectiveness of a program, regardless of which form it takes:

- ▲ **Receptivity level of students:** Consider the extent to which participants are open and receptive to the concepts that are covered in the training. Do your best to communicate to all potential participants the specific learning objectives of the course and how they will benefit.
- ▲ **Applicability of subject matter:** The success of any program will hinge largely on whether participants believe that what they're being taught has direct relevance to the challenges they face in their jobs. Ensure that the workshop focuses on issues that are the most important to participating employees.
- ▲ **The overall learning experience:** Training sessions should be as interactive and participant-oriented as possible. The best courses use a variety of learning tools: lecture, discussion, and exercises.
- ▲ **Quality of instructor:** A big factor in determining the effectiveness of a program is the ability of the trainers (whether they're giving live presentations or are on videotape) to capture and sustain the interest of participants.

▲ **Reinforcement of class concepts:** Devise techniques to reinforce the skills learned in the seminar and apply them to the job or task at hand. Ask seminar participants to create follow-up plans during or at the end of a session.

6.1.2 Assessing Training Needs: Where It All Starts

In today's business environment, you can't afford to let training be an afterthought. Chapter 3 covered the concept of a needs assessment when it comes to staffing. In the case of training, a good needs assessment helps you determine which skills or knowledge your employees require to enable your company to respond to competitive challenges and create new opportunities for the future (see Section 6.2.1).

A growing number of consulting companies and individuals specialize in helping clients identify their training needs. But if you decide to manage this process yourself, consider exploring the following options.

▲ **Employee focus groups:** Generally implemented at larger firms, **employee focus groups** pull together a group of employees from various departments or levels to discuss what a company needs to do to achieve its strategic goals and what skills are required to meet this challenge.

▲ **Surveys and questionnaires:** Surveys may represent the most cost-effective approach to needs assessment. In a typical needs-assessment questionnaire, employees are given a list of statements or questions that focus on a specific skill and asked whether they think improvements in that area will enhance their ability to perform their jobs or advance in the company.

▲ **Observation:** Simply observing how employees are performing on the job and taking note of the problems they're experiencing can often give you insight into their training needs.

▲ **Client feedback:** Depending on the business structure and client base, it may be useful to gather feedback from customers to determine areas where there may be a need for training.

6.1.3 Tying Training Needs to Strategic Goals

Whatever approach (or approaches) you take to evaluate your training requirements, the needs-assessment process should be strategically driven. Any data you gather should be processed within the framework of the following questions:

▲ What are the strategic goals of this business—both long term and short term?

▲ What competencies do employees need to achieve these goals?

▲ What are the current strengths and weaknesses of the workforce relative to those competencies?

FOR EXAMPLE

Intel University

In 2005, as part of a larger effort to improve employee retention, computer giant Intel invested $377 million in employee training and development. The company's website describes how it supports its employees in a variety of ways, including job rotations and training. As part of the process, Intel delivered 2,358 course offerings and trained 765,808 employees in forty-seven countries. On average, the company invested almost $3,775 per employee.

6.1.4 Deciding Whether to Train or Not to Train

Even after you've looked at your needs, how do you determine whether or not to train a group of employees, and how do you determine how much time and money to invest? There are no simple answers, but certain factors can help guide you:

▲ **State of the labor market:** Training decisions are often dictated by the nature of the labor market in your region. The tighter the labor market, the more pressure on you to develop employees rather than replace them.

▲ **Current workload in the company:** Training sessions can be difficult to schedule and run successfully in companies where employees are already under excessive pressure to meet the day-to-day demands of their jobs.

▲ **Internal resources and budget:** Although you can take steps to keep the expenses of training under control, at some point, the lack of a budget may produce training activities that will only worsen rather than remedy the performance problems you're trying to correct.

SELF-CHECK

1. Explain how an employee focus group can identify training needs.
2. Discuss the role of client/customer feedback in determining areas that need training.
3. Surveys and questionnaires represent the most cost-effective approach to needs assessment. True or false?
4. The tighter the labor market, the less likely employees are to pursue training options. True or false?

6.2 Putting the ADDIE Model to Work

The basic steps in a training process are often described by an acronym, ADDIE, which stands for **A**nalysis, **D**esign, **D**evelopment, **I**mplementation, and **E**valuation. The **ADDIE process** is an instructional design model that provides an outline to follow when developing training programs. The following sections take a look at each of these steps in more detail.

6.2.1 Analysis

The analysis or needs assessment phase for a training program in this process is arguably the most important. Beginning the training development process by identifying who will be trained, what information needs to be presented, how it will be delivered, and when it will occur, results in a training program that meets specific organizational needs.

Skipping this step is a common pitfall because people think it's too time-consuming or do not understand its value. The needs assessment is a trainer's best friend because it can tell you what people need to learn and provides answers to many key questions, such as:

▲ Which subjects should be taught?

▲ What type of educational activities do employees prefer?

▲ What resources do we currently have in each department?

▲ Does any training need to be outsourced?

▲ Are there any language or special learning needs?

Using a needs assessment worksheet, as shown in the Figure 6-1, will help you see the big picture and minimize budget and scheduling disasters.

6.2.2 Design

Throughout the design phase of the ADDIE model, the information gathered during the needs assessment is used to create the specifics for the program. There are five steps to be completed during this phase of program development.

▲ **Task inventory:** During this step, the trainer compiles a list of the tasks required by the job by using information gathered during the needs assessment, or by reviewing job descriptions or interviewing supervisors or job incumbents.

▲ **Target audience:** Knowing the target audience is crucial for a successful training program. Are those who will be attending new to the job? Is this program designed to be a refresher course? Or will the information be new to those attending the presentation?

Figure 6-1

Needs Assessment Worksheet
Quick Start

Section 1. General Information	
Date:	Department:
Manager's Name:	Contact Information:
Department Description and Hours of Operations:	
Best Training Days and Times:	

Section 2. Target Audience Assessment	
Number of Employees:	Language & Special Needs:

Types of Learning Activities Employees Prefer (check all that apply)

☐ Videos	☐ Demonstrations	☐ Computer-based	☐ Handouts
☐ Discussion	☐ Mock Scenarios	☐ Lecture	☐ Other:

Section 3. Training Information

Job Position	Job Required Topics	Frequency Needed	Current Training Methods	Resources Available

Section 4. Budget Considerations and Recordkeeping Comments

Needs assessment worksheet.

▲ **Training objective:** Training objectives are used during the development phase to focus the presentation. They also describe for the trainees what they will learn as a result of the program. Finally, they are used during the evaluation stage of the ADDIE process to determine whether or not the training accomplished what it was intended to do. An effective training objective includes four elements:

- Describes the situation.
- Describes a behavior that can be measured.
- Describes the conditions around the behavior.
- Describes the criteria for measuring success.

▲ **Course content:** The course content is developed using the training objectives as a basis for identifying the materials and presentation methods to be used during the training.

▲ **Evaluation criteria:** The design phase establishes the criteria that will be used to determine whether or not the training accomplished its objectives—not only whether the trainees learned the information during training, but also whether they are able to utilize and retain the information when they return to their jobs.

6.2.3 Development

During the development phase, the information acquired in the course of the design phase is converted into the actual program format that will be used. The trainer develops a plan for the presentation, selects and prepares any materials or activities that will be used, and develops a means for testing the trainees to determine whether they absorbed the information.

6.2.4 Implementation

In the implementation phase of the ADDIE model, the training is delivered to the target audience. In this phase, all the work done previously—from gathering information during the needs assessment, to the creation of training objectives and development of the program—come together. If the preparation work has been done well, the training will meet the needs of the audience and provide them with the information or skills that were identified in the needs assessment.

6.2.5 Evaluation

A crucial step in the training process occurs during the training evaluation phase. At this time, the trainees have an opportunity to evaluate the training, and their managers and supervisors have an opportunity to assess the impact of the training on subsequent job performance. There are many different ways to evaluate training programs; some are more effective than others. Section 6.5 of this chapter covers these techniques and their uses.

> **FOR EXAMPLE**
>
> **Needs Analysis**
>
> A health care company that needed to redesign its new hire training program hired a consulting company for the task. The new hires, primarily account managers, were in offices throughout the Northeast, a primary consideration for the training plan. After completing its analysis of the company's training needs, the consultant streamlined the focus and recommended five courses, all of which could be offered through a virtual classroom approach.

SELF-CHECK

1. What are the five steps of the ADDIE process?
2. In which phase of the ADDIE model is the target audience identified?
3. A needs assessment worksheet is used at the completion of training. True or false?
4. A training objective includes a description of a measurable behavior. True or false?

6.3 Weighing the Training Options

Figuring out what programs to offer employees used to be fairly cut and dried. Until recently, most corporate training was delivered the old-fashioned way: through instructor-led, **in-house classroom training**.

Not so today. Classroom training options still abound, but numerous interesting training delivery options are now available. Of course, anytime you're considering a training program, find out more about the credentials of both the organization and, if appropriate, the instructor.

Keep in mind that one size does not fit all with training approaches, simply because everyone learns differently. What follows is a brief look at the options possible today.

6.3.1 Choosing an Instructional Method

There are a variety of instructional methods to choose from when designing a training program, and selecting the appropriate one for a given situation can add to the success of the training.

▲ **Passive Training Methods:** Those methods in which the learner listens to and absorbs information. These methods are instructor focused and require little or no active participation from the learner.

- **Lecture:** Used to inform and to answer questions, often in combination with other training methods such as demonstrations.

- **Presentations:** Provides the same information to a group of people at one time.

- **Conference:** Generally a combination of lecture and presentation with question-and-answer sessions involving the participants.

▲ **Active Training Methods:** Those methods in which the learning experience is focused on the learner.

- **Facilitation:** A moderated learning situation led by a facilitator who leads a group to share ideas and solve problems. Facilitators generally have skills in moderating group discussions and may be experts in the subject of discussion.

- **Case studies:** Reproduces a realistic situation that provides learners with the chance to analyze the circumstances as though it was encountered in the course of business.

- **Simulation:** An interactive training method that provides the learner with opportunities to try out new skills or practice procedures in a setting that does not endanger the inexperienced trainee, coworkers, or the public.

- **Vestibule:** A form of stimulation training that allows inexperienced workers to become familiar with and gain experience using equipment that is either hazardous or requires a level of speed that can only be achieved with practice. Commonly used to train equipment operators in the construction industry and to give retail clerks a chance to improve speed at checkout.

▲ **Experiential Training Methods:** Provide experience in real-time situations.

- **Demonstration:** This method of training can be used as part of an on-the-job training program or combined with a lecture program. The method involves the trainer explaining the process or operation, demonstrating it on the equipment, then having the learner perform it under the trainer's guidance.

- **One-on-one:** With this training, an inexperienced worker is paired with an experienced supervisor or coworker.

- **Performance:** Performance-based-training (PBT) is most often utilized to correct performance problems in highly technical or hazardous professions. The trainee is provided with opportunities to practice until the required level of proficiency is mastered.

6.3.2 Choosing a Delivery Method

Devising suitable delivery methods for training programs is subject to a number of factors, including what information is to be covered, who will be attending, the experience level of the participants, availability of technology, and so on.

▲ **Classroom:** Classroom training provides the same content to a group of employees in a classroom setting. It is effective for small groups when providing the same information to everyone in the group.

▲ **Self-study:** A self-study program is directed entirely by the learner, who determines what, when, and where learning will occur. It may be based on a defined program and involves a trainee or mentor, but it is controlled by the learner.

▲ **E-learning:** E-learning encompasses several types of electronically based training delivery systems that are generally cost-effective, self-directed methods for training employees.

- **Electronic performance support systems:** An electronic performance support system is a training tool integrated in the computer system used by employees on the job. It allows instant access to information that helps them complete tasks more effectively.

- **Computer-based training:** Computer-based training is an interactive training method that combines elements of the lecture, demonstration, one-on-one, and simulation methods, allowing the learner to have real-world learning experience.

- **Distance learning:** Sometimes referred to as virtual classroom, distance learning is similar to lectures and allows simultaneous training to occur in geographically dispersed multiple locations. Distance learning provides participants with the ability to communicate with presenters and participants in other locations.

- **Blended learning:** Blended learning uses multiple delivery methods to enhance the learning experience.

- **Online bulletin boards:** Online bulletin boards allow trainees to post questions and share information with each other. They may be supervised or facilitated by a leader who is knowledgeable in the subject matter and acts as a resource for the participants.

MAKING E-LEARNING WORK

You must monitor and manage **e-learning** if it's to be successful. If you simply upload a slew of training courses for employees don't expect too much. The good news is that e-learning is easy to monitor. In fact, one of the benefits of e-learning is that you can track its usage to make sure that employees are engaged in the learning and are actively participating and completing the required workshops and courses. Encourage—and maybe even offer incentives—to employees who complete training. Set aside specific times for training so that employees feel comfortable temporarily stopping their day-to-day tasks to complete an online course.

6.3.3 Mentoring as a Training Tool

Some skills, such as interpersonal abilities, are not easily taught in the classroom or through online courses. In fact, some skills aren't taught well in groups at all. Enter employee **mentors**—experienced employees chosen to coach less experienced employees. Just as using a mentor for a new hire (see Section 6.4.1) can help that employee acclimate to your work, well-chosen mentors can likewise assist staff with longer term developmental learning. Consider the following examples:

▲ An employee who excels in customer service can help fellow employees discover how to more smoothly interact with customers and colleagues or develop additional skills that require more long-term and individualized attention than a classroom or online course can offer. Employees who are paired with an appropriate manager can pick up such interpersonal skills as persuasiveness and diplomacy.

▲ Mentoring programs are among the most effective ways to transfer tacit knowledge from seasoned leaders to aspiring ones. As firms brace for significant turnover among their most experienced employees due to the retirement of many baby boomers, such arrangements may become increasingly important as a means of passing on valuable know-how to less experienced workers and preparing them take on positions of greater responsibility.

FOR EXAMPLE

Training at Work

At Cisco, a leader in internet networking, employees learn and develop through "education, experience, and exposure." Employees manage their training and development needs through Cisco University, a companywide initiative that provides training, coaching, and mentoring opportunities. Employees can take advantage of a blend of interactive classroom and online courses, allowing them to study at times best suited to their schedules. Cisco offers more than 4,000 courses; on average, about 70,000 course registrations are made each quarter, approximately two per employee.

SELF-CHECK

1. Define *e-learning*.
2. Case studies are an example of passive or active training methods?
3. Give two examples of experiential training methods.
4. Explain why mentoring is particularly relevant in today's workplace.

6.4 Applying Training to Common Topics

While job-specific training programs are unique to each industry, profession, and organization, the need for some types of training programs cross all those lines. These include new hire orientations, diversity training, sexual harassment, and communication training.

6.4.1 New Hire Orientation

An important aspect of new hire orientation is the training that is provided to new employees, which sets the tone for their experience in the organization, helps them to integrate into the culture, and helps them to become productive team members. The training methods that are used should be designed to build on the natural enthusiasm that employees experience on their first day in a new job. In addition to more traditional forms of orientation training (such as videos and group meetings) that take place on the first day or half-day of work, many organizations extend orientation programs with the use of "buddy" or "mentor" programs. The goal of both programs is similar: To assist new employees in their assimilation into the organization.

▲ **Buddy programs:** The main goal of a **buddy program** is to make sure that new employees have a smooth transition into an organization. By pairing a veteran employee with a new employee, the buddy's help establishes an open line of communication and builds rapport so that the new hire feels comfortable asking questions. Buddies might also assist in introducing new employees to coworkers. Buddy assignments generally last from three to six months, or until the new hire feels comfortable with the new work environment.

▲ **Mentoring programs:** The goal of a mentoring program is slightly different from that of the buddy method. In addition to easing the transition of new employees into an organization, a mentor focuses on developing the new employee with an eye toward the longer term. Mentors coach new hires in developing interpersonal or management skills to prepare employees for future responsibilities in the organization. As such, mentoring relationships generally last longer than buddy relationships.

6.4.2 Diversity Training

As the workforce demographic in the United States continues to change, it becomes increasingly important for employers to ensure that all employees are treated fairly and equitably. The role of training in this effort lies in the ability to inform employees about the differences in culture, religion, ethnic origin, and gender of those in the workforce. It is equally important that misconceptions about individuals with physical disabilities be set straight. Providing training that educates employees about the differences between people helps to break down barriers and increase cooperation, and ultimately results in improved productivity for the organization.

6.4.3 Sexual Harassment Training

Although there are few specific legal requirements for trainings designed to prevent sexual harassment (the Equal Employment Opportunity Commission requirement is vague on the specifics), in order to reduce an employer's exposure to sexual harassment claims, three things are important:

▲ Employees must be trained on at least an annual basis as to what constitutes sexual harassment.
▲ Employees must be informed of the organization's policy prohibiting such harassment in the workplace.
▲ Employees must be aware of senior management's commitment to sexual harassment training.

These programs play an important role in reducing instances of harassment and can lead to improvements in productivity because employees feel that they are safe from harassment, know where to turn for help if they believe they are being harassed, and make clear the consequences of harassment that is found to have occurred. (See Section 2.5 for more general information on sexual harassment.)

6.4.4 Communication Training

An ongoing training program that provides information to managers about conducting meetings and communicating effectively with employees on a day-to-day basis reinforces the need for appropriate communications in the organization. Providing employees with training opportunities that teach them the best ways to communicate appropriately within the organization helps them to better exchange information in more productive ways. Communications training concentrates on teaching employees how to build credibility with others, adjust their communication styles so that they are more effective, and learn how to phrase feedback and requests in constructive ways to further understanding within the organization.

Consider the following examples of organizational communication training:

▲ **Email:** Although email is a valuable and time-saving communication method, it lends itself to inappropriate use more often than other types of written communication because of its inherent informality and immediacy. Providing employees with information on the appropriate use of email can reduce misunderstandings and improve productivity.

▲ **Public speaking or presentations:** Many people are intimidated by the thought of speaking in front of a group of people. Training builds confidence and increases the employee's ability to convey information to groups of coworkers, customers, or others—depending on the needs of the organization.

6.4.5 Time Management Training

Time management training is designed to help employees identify ways in which they can improve their personal productivity. This type of training can be delivered in a variety of ways, including books, videos, online web courses, one-on-one coaching, and classroom presentations. The general goal of the training is to help employees develop a personal method to stay organized so that they can

FOR EXAMPLE

Time on Their Side

As Battleship Productions, a travel-heavy consulting group, began to expand, management decided to find an efficient software program to help with time and project management. The consultants often worked on multiple projects and needed a simple, quick course on how to better keep track of their tasks, projects, contacts, resources, and work. The idea of web-enabled calendar options, journal, and organization capabilities, was especially appealing. Because they were so busy—and only at their New Jersey headquarters once a quarter—any training they planned had to be short, yet thorough. A half-day course that trained the consultants to use such programs as Microsoft Outlook fit the bill; most importantly, consultants were given course materials in a quick reference format that could be carried with them to off-site meetings.

accomplish the many tasks that are expected of them. The tools presented in these trainings include such abilities as:

▲ Handling documents so they are dealt with appropriately.

▲ Setting up and maintaining a calendar for appointments.

▲ Keeping track of tasks by utilizing to-do lists or other tools.

The art of delegation is another element of time management that is often difficult for managers to master. Training programs that are designed to assist managers with this key requirement often improve relationships between managers and their employees. As the manager becomes more effective at delegation, employees are better able to produce work that meets the manager's expectations. Managers, knowing that they have communicated their expectations, are better able to allow employees to complete tasks without micromanaging their work.

SELF-CHECK

1. Name three common training topics.
2. Define *buddy program.*
3. What three things are important to remember when dealing with sexual harassment training?
4. Give an example of communication training.

6.5 Measuring Results: Is Training Working?

As the person in your company responsible for the training effort, you can safely assume that you're going to be asked a simple question: Is the money and time being invested in the program paying any real dividends?

Human resources professionals have long wrestled with the problem of quantifying the results of a process that doesn't readily lend itself to quantifiable measures. Most agree, for example, that one of the primary benefits of employee training is that it enhances morale. But how do you measure the bottom-line benefits of morale? Yet another problem with measuring the results of training is that the skills and knowledge that people bring to a task represent only one factor in job performance.

These issues apart, the following sections outline the four generally accepted practices for measuring the results of training.

6.5.1 Initial Employee Reaction

The most common way to gather feedback from participants immediately following a training session is to distribute a questionnaire to each one at the end of the session. The answers give you a general idea of whether your employees thought the training was worthwhile and how impressed (or unimpressed) they were with the instructor and instructional materials. This feedback is useful but limited. Post-training surveys measure initial reactions, but offer little insight into how effective the training was in the long run.

ASKING THE RIGHT QUESTIONS

Employees' answers to the following survey questions can help you gauge the effectiveness of your training sessions.

- ▲ Did the course meet your expectations, based on the course description?
- ▲ Were the topics covered in the course directly relevant to your job?
- ▲ Was the instructor sensitive to the needs of the group?
- ▲ Were the instructional materials easy to follow and logical?
- ▲ Would you recommend this program to other employees?
- ▲ Were the facilities adequate?

6.5.2 Effectiveness of Learning

Your ability to gain an accurate measure of how much people have actually learned in a training session depends in large part on the subject matter. You can measure the learning that takes place during programs that focus on well-defined technical skills (using new software programs, for example) by administering tests before and after the training and comparing the results. Remember, though, that the subject matter of many training programs (leadership skills, for example) doesn't lend itself to measurement. One way around this limitation is to observe the accomplishments or behavior of employees in the weeks and months after soft skills training. Did those who had leadership training, for example, report lower attrition rates for their staff? Do more trainees win promotions than the average employee base? What about staff who joined in team-building exercises? Are they becoming better collaborators?

6.5.3 Impact on Performance

Determining whether training has had a positive impact on actual job performance depends on the nature of the training and the specific tasks. The problem?

Performance in most jobs is influenced by variables that may have little bearing on what was taught in a workshop. It is not at all unusual for participants to bring back to their jobs new skills, but they may run into resistance from supervisors when they try to put their newly acquired skills to practical use. An evaluation (observation, interview, or test) conducted sometime between six weeks and six months after the training course can determine whether the training is being utilized on the job.

MAKING SURE THAT YOU GET FEEDBACK

Email has made it much easier to measure the effectiveness of training in a timely manner. You can quickly send surveys to large groups of employees, asking for responses within a few days or even hours of the session's conclusion, though you may want employees to reflect before providing feedback. You can also record survey responses online, with results organized into databases and available to HR team members and line managers.

6.5.4 Cost/Benefit Analysis

Measuring the bottom-line benefits of training is, by far, the most imposing challenge you face in your efforts to build a business rationale for training. The reason is simple: Training simply doesn't easily lend itself to familiar cost/benefit analysis. The costs are easy enough to quantify. The problem lies with attaching a dollar value to the many indirect benefits that training brings, which may include reduced absenteeism and turnover, reduced employee grievances, a less stressful workplace (with fewer medical problems), and the need for less supervision.

FOR EXAMPLE

Training Report Card

Three months after participating in a certification training program, county employees were asked to complete a short post-training questionnaire. This was in addition to a survey they had completed immediately following the week-long course. The training had been sponsored by a grant, with a stipulation that some follow-up be conducted to determine the value of the course. Questions focused on how the training may have affected individual job performance: Did you receive a pay increase as a result of participating in the training? Did you obtain employment as a result of the training? Did the certification training improve your job performance in your current position? Do you feel that the certification training you participated in will allow you to retain your current position if your organization downsized?

SELF-CHECK

1. Name the most common method of gathering post-training participant feedback.

2. Interviews and tests may be used to determine whether training has had a positive impact on job performance. True or false?

3. The cost/benefit analysis method is based solely on expenses and figures. True or false?

SUMMARY

In a perfect world, all employees would have the necessary skills to function in a job. Fortunately for both employers and employees, training is a way to improve performance, develop careers, and work toward success at all levels. It is up to each organization to evaluate what type of training is required or would be effective for each situation. As part of this process an organization can draw upon focus groups, surveys, observation, and even client feedback to get an idea of where the needs may lie. Throughout the process, an organization should keep in mind its goals as well as factors such as workload and resources. The widely used ADDIE system, with its five phases, begins with a needs analysis—considered by most to be the most important step. By identifying who will be trained, what information needs to be presented, how it will be delivered, and when it will occur, a training analysis will help keep a program on track with the organization's needs. Again, as companies work through the design, development, and implementation steps, it is important to keep the company's long-term strategic goals in mind. Carefully consider the various training methods now available, thanks to advances in technology; the Internet has opened up a whole range of training opportunities. Current areas for training include diversity training, new hire orientation, communication training, and the important area of sexual harassment training. In the final—and sometimes overlooked—step, a company will evaluate the results of the training using a variety of collection approaches, from surveys to performance testing to cost/benefit analysis. By doing so, an organization can make adjustments to a program or justify future training endeavors.

KEY TERMS

ADDIE process

Acronym for **A**nalysis, **D**esign, **D**evelopment, **I**mplementation, and **E**valuation; an instructional design model that provides an outline to follow when developing training programs.

Buddy program

By pairing a veteran employee with a new employee, an employer makes sure that new employees have a smooth transition into an organization.

E-learning

The use of computer and online technology to house and deliver training content.

Employee focus groups

Group of employees who meet to discuss what a company needs to do to achieve its strategic goals and what skills are required to meet this challenge.

Employee training

Everything an organization does to upgrade the skills and improve the overall job performance of employees, both in the short term and long term.

In-house classroom training

A group of employees gathers in a classroom and is led through the program by an instructor; the traditional and most familiar form of training.

Mentors

Experienced employees chosen to coach less experienced employees; generally a long-term relationship.

ASSESS YOUR UNDERSTANDING

Go to www.wiley.com/college/messmer to assess your knowledge of employee training.

Measure your learning by comparing pre-test and post-test results.

Summary Questions

1. Training needs should be evaluated independently from strategic goals. True or false?
2. Which of the following is generally used by large companies to assess training needs?
    (a) focus groups
    (b) surveys
    (c) questionnaires
    (d) observation
3. The best training sessions use one type of learning tool. True or false?
4. Which is the most important step of the ADDIE process?
    (a) evaluation
    (b) development
    (c) design
    (d) analysis
5. Name the five steps of the design phase.
6. During the implementation phase of ADDIE, information is converted into a program format. True or false?
7. Which training approach would be a cost-saving method of training employees based in several geographic regions?
    (a) e-learning
    (b) in-house classroom training
    (c) public seminars
    (d) executive education seminars
8. Explain the role of mentoring in training employees.
9. E-learning is best suited to self-motivated employees. True or false?
10. Time management training focuses on organizational tools and skills. True or false?
11. Which type of training might prevent a case of office email abuse?
    (a) diversity
    (b) sexual harassment

(c) buddy program

(d) communication

12. In general, sexual harassment training should be conducted at least

(a) weekly

(b) monthly

(c) annually

(d) none of the above

13. At what point should an employer do an evaluation to determine whether training is being utilized on the job??

14. Which method of measurement best justifies the expense of a training program?

(a) employee reaction

(b) effectiveness of learning

(c) impact on performance

(d) cost/benefit analysis

15. Which technological advance has simplified the process of asking for and obtaining training feedback?

Applying This Chapter

1. As the human resources director of a specialized clothing catalog company, you realize that competition is fierce in the marketplace. What factors should you consider as you decide whether or not to initiate a training program?

2. Assume that training is warranted for the above-mentioned catalog company. What steps would you take to determine your plan of attack for developing a training program?

3. You've been asked to initiate an e-learning training program for the fifty employees of your design firm. As you prepare to write a memo to your CEO, summarize your recommendations; include any concerns you have about e-learning.

4. Three of the ten latest new employees have left your hospital's nursing staff after only two months. As part of an effort to improve retention, you'd like to improve the hospital's orientation program. Suggest ways in which the buddy program and/or mentoring might help matters.

5. Using the previous example at the hospital, determine how best to evaluate the success and benefits of the new training measures. Consider both short-term and long-term means of evaluation.

YOU TRY IT

Personal Training

Using what you've learned from this chapter, complete a needs analysis of your local movie theater. Consider the following in your analysis:

- What should be taught?
- What is the preferred method of learning?
- What kinds of resources are available?
- Should any training be outsourced?
- Are there any language or special learning needs?

Mistakes of the Past

Interview your peers or coworkers about their employee training experiences, both bad and good.

- What was wrong about or missing from any lackluster training experiences?
- Using the best experience you heard, what could you use to improve your future training efforts?

Reactions and Results

Outside consultants are being brought in to train your software company's upper management in public speaking. Create a short questionnaire to be distributed and completed immedately following the in-house half-day program.

7

ASSESSING AND APPRAISING PERFORMANCE

Evaluating Employee Performance

Starting Point

Go to www.wiley.com/college/messmer to assess your knowledge of the basics of performance appraisal and management.
Determine where you need to concentrate your effort.

What You'll Learn in This Chapter

▲ The benefits of using a performance appraisal system
▲ Guidelines for creating a successful evaluation system
▲ Types of employee appraisal systems
▲ The value of constructive feedback
▲ Methods of following-up after an appraisal meeting

After Studying This Chapter, You Will Be Able To

▲ Evaluate the criteria used as the basis of an employee evaluation
▲ Choose the appropriate review schedule for an appraisal system
▲ Select the most effective appraisal system for a given company's situation
▲ Manage the negative reaction of an employee
▲ Assess the effectiveness of a performance appraisal system

INTRODUCTION

Few management practices are more basic or prevalent than performance appraisals—the mechanism through which managers or supervisors evaluate the job performance of their employees. Yet, as common as the practice may be, many companies, both large and small, experience difficulty in structuring and managing the process. Draw from the successful experiences of others as you plan for the launch of an appraisal system. Take care when choosing the most effective appraisal method for your company's needs. When the time comes for a meeting, careful preparation can go a long way toward ensuring success. Finally, follow-up is an important part of the process and one that should not be overlooked.

7.1 Putting Performance Appraisals to Work

Everybody agrees that **appraisals**—also known as **reviews** or **evaluations**—have their place; they allow managers to monitor employee performance, note which areas need to be improved, and then communicate assessments to them in a constructive way. It's the most effective way of determining how people get promoted, if they deserve salary increases, and how much they should be making.

The problem seems to be not with the concept, but with the format and mechanics. In many companies, managers as well as employees aren't convinced of the value of appraisal systems. For many, the appraisal is an unpleasant, even dreaded, experience. But performance appraisals are a vital management function, and it's up to you to help your company implement a systematic program that takes into account the realities of today's workplace—and the nuances of your firm's unique culture.

7.1.1 Facing the Challenge

Creating and implementing a structured performance appraisal process is by no means a modest challenge. So why bother? Simply put, the long-term benefits of an effective performance appraisal process far outweigh the time and effort the process requires. Here are a few ways in which a well-designed, well-implemented performance appraisal system can help your company:

▲ Creates criteria for determining how well employees are truly performing— and makes it clear how their job descriptions and responsibilities fit in with company and departmental priorities.

▲ Provides an objective—and legally defensible—basis for key human resources decisions, including merit pay increases, promotions, and job responsibilities.

▲ Verifies that reward mechanisms are logically tied to outstanding performance (see Chapter 9).

FOR EXAMPLE

A Customized Appraisal System

AFLAC, probably the most recognized name in supplemental insurance (think desperate quacking duck), knows the value of the employee evaluation process, but it tries hard to take the sting out of it. AFLAC's appraisals focus on three parts:

1. Goals and objectives on which an employee will be evaluated.
2. An employee's learning objectives.
3. An employee's future objectives.

The managers are trained in the process and given a guidebook that gives them specific examples of behaviors and verbiage to use in an appraisal. On the other side, AFLAC creates training opportunities so that employees can be successful in achieving their goals. In fact, although other companies often rate productivity at eighty to ninety percent of an evaluation, only fifty percent of AFLAC employee evaluations are based on achieving their goals. The other fifty percent is leadership skills and modeling the company's values.

▲ Motivates employees to improve their job performance.
▲ Irons out difficulties in the supervisor-employee relationship.
▲ Gives underperforming employees guidance that can lead to better performance.
▲ Keeps employees focused on business goals and objectives.
▲ Helps employees clarify career goals.
▲ Assesses training and staff development needs.

7.1.2 Understanding the Legal Aspects of Appraisals

Depending upon how you develop and conduct it, an appraisal system can do one of two things with respect to your company's legal exposure:

▲ Unnecessarily expose your company to the danger of discrimination lawsuits.
▲ Provide your company with a strong defense if you're taken to court by an employee or former employee over an unfavorable personnel action.

The best defense against wrongful dismissal is a carefully documented record of unfavorable performance evaluations, coupled with an employee's inability or refusal to carry out suggestions to correct poor work or on-the-job behavior.

At the same time, you need to be sure that no aspect of your appraisal system violates state or federal antidiscrimination legislation. As is the case with other aspects of HR, consult with an attorney before adopting an official appraisal system.

SELF-CHECK

1. A "review" is another word for "performance appraisal." True or false?
2. Give an example of a management decision that can be based on a performance appraisal.
3. Explain the legal necessity of carefully documenting the appraisal process.

7.2 Launching an Appraisal Program

In setting up a new performance appraisal system, you need to gather input from both senior management and employees and ensure that the program is workable and well communicated throughout the organization. The following sections list guidelines taken from studies of companies with successful performance appraisal systems.

7.2.1 Enlist the Support of Senior Management

Make sure early in your development process that senior management is willing to give the initiative strong support. One way to do so is to explain to top management how the particular approach you're recommending is tailored to the company's business and culture. For example, a retail environment has a heavy emphasis on teamwork and collegiality. In this instance, where on-floor sales personnel, clerks, and cashiers are all highly dependent on one another, a multi-rater assessment can be quite useful (see Section 7.3.7 in this chapter).

GIVE EMPLOYEES A SAY

Bring employees who are going to be evaluated into the developmental process as early as possible. At the very least, invite employees to offer input on what specific skills, attributes, behaviors, and goals should be the basis of the performance criteria.

7.2.2 Choose Performance Measures with Care

The cornerstone of a successful performance appraisal process is the criteria used as the basis of evaluation. Here are some of the key factors you should bear in mind when formulating criteria, along with the questions you should ask yourself with respect to each factor:

▲ **Job-relatedness:** Are the criteria connected to strategic business goals? How are these big-picture goals linked to successful work performance?
▲ **Feasibility:** Do employees have the resources, the training, or the autonomy required to meet the goals?
▲ **Measurability:** Can the behaviors that underlie each performance be observed, measured, and documented?

7.2.3 Develop a Tracking Approach

In small companies, when supervisors and employees are working closely together, keeping track of day-to-day behavior is not much of a problem. In larger companies, though, tracking can become a key issue. Essentially, you need a reliable and fair mechanism (on-the-job observation, for example) to ensure that the results of the appraisal are an accurate reflection of day-to-day employee performance.

7.2.4 Devise an Evaluation Method

There is no one "right" way to determine which specific evaluation method will work best in your company (see Section 7.3). Some methods are more suitable for managers and professionals than for other workers. Keep in mind, too, that some systems require more training than others to implement effectively.

FOR EXAMPLE

Misery Loves Company

The annual review season is a time of great angst for employers and employees alike. Enough people have had unsatisfying and even awful performance reviews to spark the creation of www.worstreview.com, where readers can post their appraisal stories as well as comment on other people's experiences. One of the worst reviews, about an actual and very awkward review that took place at side-by-side urinals, is bad enough to make most employees appreciate their own appraisal process.

7.2.5 Think about Timing

When establishing or revising an appraisal process, a decision must be made on when evaluations will be conducted. There are two standard approaches:

▲ **Anniversary reviews:** As the name implies, anniversary reviews are scheduled on the anniversary of the employee's date of hire. Many organizations that use this schedule will give new employees their first appraisal six months after their hire date, and subsequent appraisals are conducted annually on that date. For many companies, particularly those with a large number of employees, the anniversary schedule is easier to manage because HR departments are not inundated with hundreds or thousands of reviews to process at one time.

▲ **Focal reviews:** In a focal review schedule, all appraisals are given at one time during a review cycle, regardless of individual dates of hire. This schedule allows employers to judge performance based on the achievement of goals during the entire review cycle, so performance can be judged more equitably. It also gives employers the ability to assess varying levels of contribution by different employees more easily. Although a focal review cycle places a significant administrative burden when hundreds of reviews are being done at the same time, it can make it easier to distribute salary increases equitably.

7.2.6 Develop a Communication Game Plan

Most appraisal processes live or die on the basis of how clearly and how openly you communicate the aims and the mechanics of the system to employees. At the very least, everyone involved in the process should be aware of the following information before you launch a program:

▲ The overall goals of the program.
▲ How employees themselves will benefit from the program.
▲ How performance criteria will be developed.
▲ The length of the appraisal periods.
▲ The degree to which appraisal results will be linked to bonuses, merit pay increases, and other HR-related activities.
▲ What recourse employees have in the event they disagree with the results.
▲ What training, if any, will be made available to managers expected to implement the program.

No matter how you communicate your plan, make sure that everyone has a clear understanding of how the program will work and their roles in ensuring the program's success.

OVERCOMING OBSTACLES

Regardless of how much care you take in launching a new performance appraisal system, you may still face objections. When it comes to the potential obstacles encountered by performance appraisal systems, here's what you can expect—and what to do about it (see Section 7.4.4 for more):

▲ **Employee resistance:** Employees often feel threatened, and some employees actively dislike being appraised. *How to respond:* Communicate as clearly and as openly as possible the purpose and mechanics of the new appraisal system and that it was built with their input. Make sure that employees understand what role the appraisal will play in influencing the things they care about: raises, promotions, and so on. Spell out the role they're expected to play in the process.

▲ **Supervisor resistance:** Appraisal systems require extra work by supervisors and managers, as well as create additional paperwork and administrative overhead. *How to respond:* Keep forms and paperwork to a minimum, but provide forms for continuing tasks such as critical incidents reporting. Train evaluators and audit their performance to see whether follow-up training is needed.

SELF-CHECK

1. Employee input should be considered the final stage of the evaluation process. True or false?
2. List the three factors that should be considered when formulating evaluation criteria.
3. The critical incident appraisal method is universally effective. True or false?

7.3 Deciding on a Performance Appraisal System

Once you've decided either to introduce a performance appraisal system in your company or to change your current one, you need to determine which kind of system is best for your company. Although the basics of the systems are much the same—setting performance criteria, developing tracking and documenting procedures, determining which areas should be measured quantitatively, and deciding how the information is to be communicated to employees—the methods vary. The following sections offer a brief description of appraisal methods commonly used today, including advantages and disadvantages of each.

7.3.1 Management By Objectives (MBO)

First created in 1954, **Management By Objectives (MBO)** is still an extremely popular appraisal system because of its focus on results and the activities and skills that truly define an employee's job. Even more recent forms of appraisal, such as the increasingly popular multi-rater assessment (see Section 7.3.7), are in large part based on the principles of MBO.

In a typical MBO scenario, an employee and manager sit down together at the start of an appraisal period and formulate a set of statements that represent specific job goals, targets, or **deliverables**.

What makes MBO so powerful is its direct link to organizational objectives and priorities. In the case of MBO, goals, targets, and deliverables should be as specific and measurable as possible. For example, instead of "improve customer service" (too vague), try something like "reduce the number of customer complaints by five percent." And instead of "increase number of sales calls" (too vague), go with "increase the number of sales calls by five percent without changing current criteria for prospects."

Advantages:

▲ Is familiar: MBO has been used for decades and provides a sharp focus for evaluating employee performance.

▲ Draws the employee into the appraisal process.

▲ Gives employee a blueprint for successful performance.

▲ Emphasizes action and results.

Disadvantages:

▲ Takes time and involves considerable paperwork.

▲ Works effectively only if supervisors are trained in the process.

▲ Can lack sufficient specificity of goals.

7.3.2 Critical Incidents Reporting

The **critical incidents method** of performance appraisal is built around a list of specific behaviors, generally known as **critical behaviors**, deemed necessary to perform a particular job competently. Performance evaluators use a critical incident report to record actual incidents of behavior that illustrate when employees either carried out or didn't carry out these behaviors. You can use these logs to document a wide variety of job behaviors, such as initiative and leadership ability.

Advantages:

▲ Records employee performance as it happens.

▲ Always links employee behavior to job performance.

▲ Provides documented record of behaviors over time.

▲ Offers more insight into job descriptions and core competencies.

Disadvantages:

▲ Requires disciplined and regular attention.

▲ Can often compromise objectivity of recorded incidents because of the evaluator's emotional state when the incident is recorded.

▲ Depends on a clear definition of critical behaviors.

7.3.3 Job Rating Checklist

The **job rating checklist** method of performance appraisal is the simplest method to use and lends itself to a variety of approaches. To implement this approach, you supply each evaluator with a prepared list of statements or questions that relate to specific aspects of job performance. The questions typically require the evaluator to write a simple "yes" or "no" answer or to record a number (or some other notation) that indicates which statement applies to a particular employee's performance.

A more sophisticated variation to this method is to establish a **weighted rating system** in which a number is used to reflect the relative importance of each criterion being evaluated. The weighted variation presents a clearer picture of how employee strengths and weaknesses measure up against the priorities of the job.

Advantages:

▲ Minimizes the amount of paperwork for the evaluator.

▲ Can customize lists in any number of ways.

▲ Can purchase lists commercially.

Downsides:

▲ Unsuited to jobs with evolving or frequently changing requirements.

▲ Offers only a sketchy outline of job performance.

▲ Doesn't encourage evaluators to focus on "improvement" strategies.

7.3.4 Behaviorally Anchored Rating Scale (BARS)

Behaviorally Anchored Rating Scale (BARS) systems are designed to emphasize the behavior, traits, and skills needed to successfully perform a job. A typical BARS form has two columns. The left column has a rating scale, usually in stages from *Very Poor* to *Excellent*. The right column contains behavioral anchors that are the reflections of those ratings.

If the scale were being used, for example, to evaluate a telephone order taker, the statement in one column may read "1-Very Poor," and the statement in the right column may read, "Occasionally rude or abrupt to customer" or "Makes frequent mistakes on order form" (see Table 7-1).

Advantages:

▲ Reduces the potential for biased responses.

▲ Focuses on specific, observable behaviors.

▲ Provides specific and standardized comments on job performance.

Downsides:

▲ Can be time consuming and complicated to develop.

▲ Depends on accuracy and appropriateness of "anchor statements."

▲ Impractical for jobs with frequently changing requirements.

7.3.5 Forced Choice

Forced-choice methods typically come in two forms: paired statements and forced ranking. In the paired statements method, evaluators are presented with two statements and must check the one that best describes the employee; it's

Table 7-1: Sample BARS Anchor Statements

Rating	Anchor Statement
5	Greets customers warmly and makes them feel welcome.
4	Pleasant to customers and answers their questions.
3	Courteous to the customers.
2	Finishes other work before greeting customers.
1	Rude to customers when they approach the desk.

either one or the other. In the forced ranking method, a number of options are listed, allowing the evaluator to select a description that may fall somewhere in between.

The following example illustrates how each version may be used to cover the same aspect of job performance for a field service representative.

▲ Paired statements:

_____ Provides sufficient detail when filling out trip reports.

_____ Doesn't provide sufficient detail when filling out trip reports.

▲ Forced ranking:

_____ Provides sufficient detail when filling out trip reports.

_____ Exceptional.

_____ Above average.

_____ Average.

_____ Needs improvement.

_____ Unsatisfactory.

Advantages:

▲ Minimizes bias.

▲ Is somewhat more objective than other ranking methods.

Downsides:

▲ Requires skill and professional training to develop.

▲ Must be redesigned when job requirements change.

▲ Doesn't lend itself to behaviors that are difficult to quantify.

FOR EXAMPLE

Spotlight on General Electric

Serious change was in order in 1981 when Jack Welch took over as CEO of General Electric. In an effort to get away from an appraisal system in which supervisors often gave all their employees "above average" ratings, Welch broke from tradition. Executives now had to identify the top twenty percent of managers and mark them for advancement. On the flipside, they also had to indicate who was in the bottom ten percent; those employees would then either have to improve or leave. This forced ranking system is now used by one third of all employers on at least some of their staff. In addition, many U.S. companies use forced ranking systems as a factor when deciding which employee will be laid off.

7.3.6 Ranking Methods

Ranking methods compare employees in a group to one another. All involve an evaluator who asks managers to rank employees from the "best" to the "worst" with respect to specific job performance criteria. The three most common variations of this method are as follows:

▲ **Straight ranking:** Employees are simply listed in order of ranking.

▲ **Forced comparison:** Every employee is paired with every other employee in the group, and the manager identifies the better of the two employees in any pairing. Employees are ranked by the number of times they're identified as the best.

▲ **Forced distribution:** Employees are ranked along a standard statistical distribution, the so-called bell curve. This method is suitable only for large groups to be statistically valid, typically thousands of employees.

Advantages:

▲ Can be helpful in presenting an overall picture of employee strengths and weaknesses throughout the company.

▲ Requires little training.

Disadvantages:

▲ Is the most subjective of appraisal methods.

▲ Provides little information on training and development needs.

▲ Focuses on individuals rather than job outcomes or behaviors.

▲ Forces raters to evaluate employees in terms of other employees.

7.3.7 Multi-Rater Assessments

Multi-rater assessments are also called **360-degree assessments**. The employee's supervisors, coworkers, subordinates, and in some cases, customers are asked to complete detailed questionnaires on the employee. The employee completes the same questionnaire. The results are tabulated, and the employee then compares her assessment with the other results.

Advantages:

▲ Draws assessments from a wide variety of sources.

▲ Gives maximum feedback to employee.

Downsides:

▲ Need to have the questionnaires professionally developed.

▲ Relies on people outside the employee's immediate work circle, which may cause resentment.

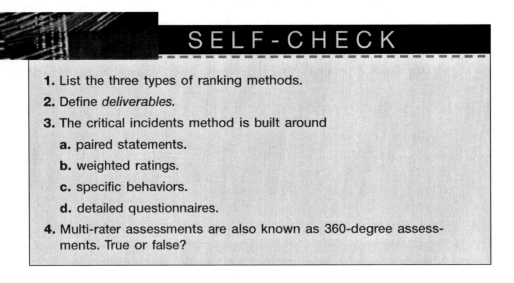

7.4 Getting the Most Out of an Appraisal Meeting

As part of the process of creating a performance appraisal process, you need to address the "people" component—what happens when managers and employees meet to set goals or to discuss work performance during the appraisal period.

You should not assume that this aspect of the process will simply "take care of itself." The simple truth is that very few managers have ever been trained to conduct an effective performance appraisal session. So while your managers may be responsible for what happens during the session, you and others in HR are responsible for making sure that they're prepared for the challenge.

7.4.1 Preparing for the Meeting

Prior to holding a performance appraisal session, managers should be informed about the importance of preparation. Emphasize that they should not wait until the last minute before thinking about how the meeting is going to be handled. Managers should have a clear idea before the meeting begins of what specific behaviors are going to be the focal point of the session. Other points to stress include the following:

▲ Give employees sufficient time to prepare for the session.
▲ Allot sufficient time to conduct a productive session.
▲ Have all documentation ready prior to the meeting.
▲ Have information from the previous appraisal (if applicable), including the resulting goals and objectives.
▲ Choose a suitable place (private, quiet, with no interruptions) for the meeting.

CONSIDERING ISSUES OF FAIRNESS

Employers must base appraisal decisions on job-related criteria, not personal bias. Those conducting appraisals should be aware of the common biases that can affect the appraisal process and avoid them to the extent possible.

- ▲ **Central tendency:** This bias occurs when a supervisor is reluctant to identify those employees who are performing at a very high or very low level. As a result, the performance of all employees is assessed as "average." This creates problems by lowering the morale of high performers; for low performers, an average review does not give them the opportunity to improve, which may lead to later termination.
- ▲ **Halo/horn effect:** This bias occurs when a supervisor evaluates an employee who made a single mistake in an otherwise error-free performance and characterizes him or her as a poor performer. Conversely, the same is true of a supervisor who focuses solely on a single very positive event, overlooks other negative moments, and gives a positive review.
- ▲ **Recency:** This common bias occurs when supervisors use only the most recent performance results as the basis for an evaluation.

7.4.2 Conducting the Session

If more than a handful of managers will be involved in your performance appraisal process, think about setting up training sessions for them on how to conduct an effective appraisal session. Here are the points that should be stressed:

- ▲ The appraisal meeting should be a two-way conversation, not a lecture.
- ▲ Positives should always be emphasized before negatives are discussed.
- ▲ Reinforce positive behaviors to help keep employees on the right track.
- ▲ Keep the emphasis on what needs to be done to improve, not what was done wrong.
- ▲ Encourage employees to comment on any manager observations.
- ▲ Managers should know how to explain to employees the difference between effort (how hard employees are working) and quality results (whether the results of those efforts are contributing significantly to business objectives).

NO SURPRISES

Regardless of what method you use or when you do it, a performance review meeting should not be the first time an employee hears about a performance issue. Ongoing feedback is a critical part of a successful performance management program.

7.4.3 Giving Constructive Feedback

For most managers, the toughest part of the appraisal meeting will be to talk about performance areas in which the employee is lacking. Again, work in advance with your managers so that they're sufficiently prepared to handle this undeniably tricky aspect of the process. Here are the points to emphasize:

▲ **Candor:** In cases when the negative aspects of employee performance need to be discussed, employees can't very well improve if the manager doesn't address the problem. Also, if it becomes necessary to fire an employee, a manager's failure to mention the employee's weakness in a performance appraisal can jeopardize the company's ability to defend the firing decision.

▲ **Documentation:** Be prepared to back up critical comments with specific, job-related examples. The documentation should be gathered prior to the meeting.

▲ **Careful wording:** How a criticism is worded is every bit as important as what behavior is being described. Managers should focus on the behavior itself and not on the personality quality that may have led to the behavior. For example, instead of saying, "You've been irresponsible," describe the specific event that reflects the irresponsibility, as in "For the past few weeks, you've missed these deadlines."

▲ **Employee feedback:** Once managers have issued any piece of criticism, employees should be given the opportunity to comment. Given a chance, employees will often admit to shortcomings and may even ask for help.

▲ **Positive ending:** No matter how negative the feedback may be, appraisal meetings should end on a positive note and with a plan for improvement.

7.4.4 Preparing for a Negative Reaction

In a well-managed company, most employees are probably performing adequately or better, but some people don't take criticism well, no matter how minimal or appropriately delivered. In any performance appraisal meeting, an employee whose work is being criticized has the potential to become agitated, confrontational, verbally abusive, and, in very rare instances, violent. The following advice can give managers a strategy for response:

▲ **Hear them out.** Don't respond, comment on, or challenge the employee while he is agitated or angry. Sometimes a calm demeanor can defuse a situation.

▲ **Don't fake agreement.** The worst thing you can say in this sort of situation is "I can see why you're upset." It can very well set the employee off again.

▲ **When the storm passes, continue the meeting.** A lack of response usually ends most outbursts, and the employee quickly realizes he has made a serious mistake. Accept the apology and move on.

7.4.5 Choosing Areas for Further Development

As part of the appraisal meeting, supervisors should recommend areas for improvement and, together with their employees, build a set of workable performance-development activities. To prepare, supervisors should take time prior to the meeting to create a concise, one-page list of potential developmental activities for the employee. The list can include:

▲ Recommended readings devoted to the topics where development is suggested.

▲ Possible classroom or online courses.

▲ People within the company who may offer useful input. ("John became a supervisor last year, so you can talk with him about managing people.")

Even the very best employees have room to improve and further develop themselves. For any professional, appraisal time is the ideal opportunity to tie a look backward with a look forward.

7.4.6 Concluding the Meeting

At the end of the appraisal meeting, an employee should be asked to sign the review, to indicate that they have received a copy of the document—but

---

FOR EXAMPLE

Appraisal Jitters

Jeff Sparta, a college administrator required to do performance reviews of six staff members, was worried about one of the reviews coming up. Materials given to him by the office of human resources gave him some tips on how to prepare for the negative reaction he was predicting. The first was to not build up the employee with praise or compliments before breaking the bad news. The second was to not react to any strong feelings expressed by the employee by commiserating or communicating any acceptance. Finally, he practiced what he was going to say to the lackluster staffer: "Tim, with this tutoring project, I would have preferred to see things go differently. Here is what I thought did not go as well as it should have. I also have some thoughts on how I would like to see it done differently next time."

not that they necessarily agree with its contents. That signature can be used later to confirm that the employee knew of the key points of performance (positive and negative) and understood what had been achieved and what areas needed improvement. This is particularly useful as documentation for any future termination.

SELF-CHECK

1. Why is it useful for an employer to have an employee sign off on a review?

2. Explain one strategy for handling a negative reaction in an appraisal meeting.

3. If an appraisal is largely focused on poor performance or behaviors, management should end the meeting on a negative note. True or false?

7.5 Following-Up After an Appraisal

Although some managers feel that the performance appraisal meeting is the final step of the appraisal process, the days following this session are in fact extremely important. Adequate follow up, including regular monitoring of employee progress toward performance-development goals, is key to the success of an appraisal process. Without sustained follow up—both formal and informal—any input an employee receives is unlikely to be long-lasting. Some tips to consider:

▲ The employee and supervisor should have both short- and long-term methods to review progress on the improvement areas discussed and schedule specific dates to do so. Many companies advise managers to conduct interim meetings after six months, but the interval can be shorter or longer.

▲ Between these sessions, supervisors should be encouraged to remain easily accessible so that employees can share thoughts, concerns, or suggestions on any of the topics covered during the appraisal.

▲ Managers should understand the benefits of providing input to staff throughout the year: If feedback is ongoing, nothing in the performance appraisal should come as a surprise to employees.

7.5.1 Take a Look at Yourself

Anyone who conducts a performance appraisal should take some time to evaluate his or her own performance.

▲ Were you able to thoroughly explain the evaluation approach?

▲ Did employees feel the session was conducted appropriately, with enough time for discussion?

▲ Did you recommend specific actions to take following the appraisal—courses, reading, or contacts who may offer a different perspective?

Again, the evolution of your job from "personnel administrator" to "business strategist" requires extensive attention to these very human, delicate matters. Though the transition may not be easy, it can be quite rewarding—for the company, for employees and also for your own personal growth.

7.5.2 Evaluating Your Appraisal System

Here's a list of questions to ask yourself about your company's current program. If you can answer "yes" to all the questions, you can probably relax. A "no" answer may indicate an aspect of your program that needs to be reexamined.

▲ Are all performance criteria job-related?

▲ Is the focus on results, as opposed to personal traits?

▲ Do your employees understand how the process works and how appraisals tie into other aspects of their jobs?

▲ Have managers been adequately trained to implement the system?

FOR EXAMPLE

Flexible Follow-Up Schedule

In many cases, particularly when a performance review goes well, a manager will schedule a follow-up meeting for two or three months after the initial appraisal. Heidi, who just had a difficult review with a disgruntled graphics designer in her catalog company, found the employee was simply too angry to continue. In this case she decided to let it pass for the moment. Instead of scheduling a meeting months from now, she gave Suzanne the weekend to think about the situation, then they would meet again on Monday.

▲ Is the program thoroughly understood by employees?

▲ Have all relevant employee behaviors been documented?

▲ Have promises of confidentiality been kept?

▲ Are all subsequent HR decisions consistent with employee evaluations?

▲ Are follow-up plans built into appraisals?

▲ Have you reviewed all elements of your program with legal counsel?

SELF-CHECK

1. The review meeting marks the end of the performance appraisal process. True or false?

2. Explain the purpose of short-term follow up?

3. How does constructive feedback benefit an employee?

SUMMARY

Although they are often dreaded by both managers and employees alike, performance appraisals are a critical part of the management success. By following in the footsteps of companies with successful performance appraisal systems, your company can break the negative cycle of the review process. In launching an appraisal system an organization must have the support of senior management and be in agreement about the criteria that will be used to measure performance. In addition, managers will need to determine the timing of such a system; that is, whether you will use an anniversary or focal review schedule. Which appraisal method (or combination of methods) you choose will affect the results of your system. For example, management by objectives, which has been practiced for decades, is an effective way of setting specific job goals for an employee. Alternatively, behaviorally anchored rating scale systems focus more on the behavior, traits, and skills needed to successfully perform a job. Not to be overlooked is the critical meeting phase of the appraisal system. After careful preparation, employers can conduct an effective appraisal, taking into account logistical details such as timing, setting, and documentation. Although many meetings are focused on the downsides of employee performance, an appraisal meeting is also an important opportunity to offer constructive feedback in an honest and positive manner. Finally, a follow-up plan should be implemented, with a schedule for progress review as well as opportunities for additional discussions throughout the year.

KEY TERMS

Anniversary reviews	Performance appraisals scheduled on the anniversary of the employee's date of hire.
Appraisals	Part of a management process in which managers monitor employee performance, note which areas need to be improved, and then communicate assessments in a constructive way.
Behaviorally Anchored Rating Scale (BARS)	Evaluation system designed to emphasize the behavior, traits, and skills needed to successfully perform a job.
Central tendency	Evaluation bias that occurs when a supervisor does not identify those employees who are performing at a very high or very low level, leaving all employees with an "average" assessed.
Critical behaviors	Specific behaviors deemed necessary to perform a particular job competently.
Critical incidents method	Performance appraisal technique built around a list of specific behaviors deemed necessary to perform a particular job competently.
Deliverables	Specific job goals or targets.
Evaluations	Another word for performance appraisal.
Focal reviews	Performance appraisals given at one time during a review cycle, regardless of individual dates of hire.
Forced-choice methods	Evaluation method with which evaluators choose one of two statements that best describes the employee; alternatively, evaluators select a description that may fall somewhere in between.
Forced comparison	Ranking appraisal method in which employees are compared to other employees and ranked by the number of times they're identified as the best.
Forced distribution	Employees are ranked along a standard statistical distribution, or bell curve.

Halo/horn effect	The tendency for a supervisor to focus on a single event that had either a very positive or very negative result.
Job rating checklist	A prepared list of statements or questions that relate to specific aspects of job performance.
Management By Objectives (MBO)	Appraisal system that focuses on results and the activities and skills that define an employee's job.
Multi-rater assessments	An employee and her supervisors and coworkers are asked to complete detailed questionnaires on the employee.
Ranking methods	Evaluation technique that compares employees in a group to one another; three variations used.
Recency	Bias that occurs when supervisors use only the most recent performance results as the basis for an evaluation.
Reviews	Another word for performance appraisal.
Straight ranking	Appraisal method in which employees are simply listed in order of ranking.
360-degree assessments	Also known as multi-rater assessments.
Weighted rating system	A number is used to reflect the relative importance of each criterion being evaluated.

ASSESS YOUR UNDERSTANDING

Go to www.wiley.com/college/messmer to assess your knowledge of performance appraisal and management.
Measure your learning by comparing pre-test and post-test results.

Summary Questions

1. Pay raises and promotions should not be based on performance reviews. True or false?

2. In what way can a performance appraisal protect a company in a legal case about an employee dismissal?

    (a) Allows management to make the dismissal public knowledge.

    (b) Provides an alibi for management.

    (c) Provides a defense for the company.

    (d) Uncovers a violation of state antidiscrimination laws.

3. A performance appraisal can help an employee work on career goals. True or false?

4. With an anniversary review schedule, a review is held

    (a) three months after a new hire.

    (b) on the anniversary of the company's founding.

    (c) on the anniversary of the date of hire.

    (d) every six months.

5. A focal review is conducted at the beginning of each fiscal year. True or false?

6. Which information should be included in communications regarding appraisals?

    (a) the length of the appraisal periods

    (b) the goals of the appraisal process

    (c) the connection between results and bonuses

    (d) all of the above

7. Which of the appraisal methods is considered the easiest to use?

8. The management by objective evaluation method records employee performance as it happens. True or false?

9. Behaviors that are necessary to perform a job competently are

    (a) weighted rankings.

    (b) critical behaviors.

    (c) deliverables.

    (d) critical objectives.

10. It's best to discuss the negative points of a review before highlighting the positive. True or false?

11. Which statement is the most constructive way of addressing a performance issue?

    (a) You've missed all of your deadlines.

    (b) Your attitude needs work.

    (c) Your co-workers like you but think you're unmotivated.

    (d) You have talent, but we need to channel your energy better.

12. By signing a review, an employee is in legal agreement with its contents. True or false?

13. Ongoing feedback takes the place of an anniversary performance appraisal. True or false?

14. A performance review should focus on

    (a) opinions.

    (b) results.

    (c) bad habits.

    (d) personality.

Applying This Chapter

1. The owner of a twenty-employee window-cleaning company has never gone through a performance review system. Give three reasons she should incorporate such a review into her business.

2. Your law firm is looking to revamp its performance appraisal system. Given that you have one hundred employees—secretaries, file clerks, paralegals, associate lawyers, and partner lawyers—choose an appraisal model that would best serve your firm's needs; explain why.

3. Using the previous example assess which appraisal schedule—anniversary or focal review—would work best for your company and why.

4. Imagine that you are the supervisor of Michael, a new administrative assistant in the human resources department of your company. Michael is an energetic and pleasant employee who gets along with everyone. On several occasions, however, he has made mistakes in employee records that have caused some problems with payroll. Is he careless, rushing, or in need of training? Choose your words carefully and write down how you'll address this in your appraisal meeting.

5. Using the previous scenario, set up a follow-up schedule for Michael, include a plan for two areas of his work that require further development.

YOU TRY IT

Appraisal Makeover

Using the guidelines from this chapter, evaluate the existing appraisal system in use at your company or school. How do employees and managers view the process? Which areas are effective? Write a proposal for any changes in areas that are not working.

Learning from Others

Interview a peer or coworker about his or her experiences, both bad and good, in appraisal meetings.

- In what ways do the negative experiences go against the guidelines taken from successful company appraisals?
- Using the best experience you heard, what piece of advice would you carry on to future appraisal meetings?

Time to Make an Appraisal

You're in charge of creating a performance appraisal plan for a statewide chain of doughnut shops. Consider the followiing as you formulate your plan:

- evaluation method
- timing
- communication plan
- ongoing interaction/followup

If helpful, use the internet to draw from information about existing doughnut companies.

8

COMPENSATION STRATEGIES AND PRACTICES
Creating a Fair and Effective Pay System

Starting Point

Go to www.wiley.com/college/messmer to assess your knowledge of the basics of compensation strategies.
Determine where you need to concentrate your effort.

What You'll Learn in This Chapter

▲ Types of compensation philosophies
▲ The five areas of human resources affected by the Fair Labor Standards Act
▲ The components of a total rewards system
▲ Options for setting pay scale in an organization
▲ The role of incentives in a compensation strategy

After Studying This Chapter, You Will Be Able To

▲ Examine external factors that affect a compensation program
▲ Assess the proper exemption status for a given employee situation
▲ Differentiate between direct and nondirect forms of compensation
▲ Organize employees based on their importance to an organization's mission
▲ Choose the most effective method of additional payment for a situation

INTRODUCTION

Although some employees think of **compensation** as simply the cash compensation they receive in the form of salaries or wages, cash is only part of the story. Compensation includes paychecks and incentives—as well as a wide variety of benefits that will be discussed in Chapter 9. Though individual approaches vary, an organization's compensation strategies must be in line with its strategic goals. Once the appropriate level of compensation is determined for various jobs, it must be properly administered, according to regulations. Employers can use compensation not only as a way to retain employees but as a hiring incentive.

8.1 Building a Compensation Foundation

One of the most important responsibilities of a human resources program is to determine the appropriate amount of compensation for different jobs. Miscalculations can have serious implications for an organization, impacting the morale of employees as well as the organization's ability to hire and retain qualified and motivated employees. Decisions made about compensation affect other areas of a HRM plan as well, including performance management, particularly when **salary** increases are based on an employee's level of performance.

8.1.1 Taking on the HR Role

As you manage your company's human resources function, your goal is not to know everything that anyone can know about employee compensation. However, you do need to keep aware of changes taking place in this critical area.

Consider your role in building a compensation plan. Generally, if you're not the owner of the company, you don't decide how much a particular individual should be paid. Instead, you alert senior management to the options available for building a compensation system. It's also your responsibility to make sure that your compensation package is competitive enough to keep your top employees from being wooed away by other companies.

8.1.2 Forming a Compensation Philosophy

If your company doesn't already have one, you need to formulate a compensation philosophy—a well thought-out, strategically driven set of criteria that becomes the basis for wage and salary decisions. The following are some questions you may want to ask yourself as you formulate this philosophy:

▲ Are you going to make your basic salaries simply competitive with the going rate for employers in your area or higher?
▲ Are you going to establish a structured pay scale for specific jobs in your company, or are you going to set salaries on an individual basis, based on the qualities and potential of the person filling the job?

▲ To what extent are the monetary rewards you offer your employees going to take the form of salary, performance bonuses, or benefits?

▲ Are salaries based on how well people perform or on other factors, such as how long they stay with you or what credentials they bring to the job?

▲ Are you going to award bonuses on the basis of individual performance, tie bonuses to company results, or use a combination of the two?

No specific answers are right or wrong. What's important is that your compensation philosophy takes into account your company's mission. If your goal is to become the dominant company in your industry within five years, you probably need to offer attractive wage-and-benefit packages to attract the people who can fuel your growth. If your goal is to improve productivity, you need to tie compensation to performance and productivity. Start with your goals and work upward.

Choosing a Direction

Although there are probably as many compensation philosophies as there are organizations, for the most part they fall into one of two categories:

▲ **Entitlement philosophy:** Rewards employees based on their length of service; typically found where wage increases are based on seniority (union situations and government). Though this philosophy once prevailed, in recent years many businesses have replaced it with a philosophy that ties performance to pay.

▲ **Performance-based philosophy:** Rewards employees based on the level of contribution they make toward the achievement of individual, departmental, or organizational goals. This philosophy is being used by more and more organizations, driven largely by the need to operate more efficiently.

See Figure 8-1 for an example of a compensation philosophy.

8.1.3 Focusing on Strategy

Creating an effective compensation system requires thinking strategically—that is, with a constant eye toward the long-term needs and goals of your business. Your goal is a well thought-out set of practices that helps to ensure the following results:

▲ Employees receive a fair and equitable wage (from their perspective) for the work that they perform.

▲ Payroll costs are in line with the overall financial health of your company.

▲ The basic philosophy of compensation is clearly understood by your employees and has the strong support of managers and employees alike.

▲ The pay scale for the various jobs in the company reflects the relative importance of the job and the skills that performing those jobs require.

Figure 8-1

XYZ Company Compensation Philosophy

XYZ Company believes that our rewards and recognition programs are essential for communicating performance expectations, for improving productivity, and for recognizing contributions to the company's success.

The objectives of our compensation programs are:

1. To pay our employees fairly based on your role in the organization, the fair market value of your position, and your performance.
2. To attract and retain the best people, we aim to keep our employees properly motivated and directed.
3. To recognize individual performance differences.
4. To offer all of our employees performance rewards based on achieving specific business goals.

A sample compensation philosophy.

▲ Pay scales are competitive enough with those of other employers in your region so that you're not seeing competitors hire your top employees away from you.
▲ Compensation policies are in line with state and federal laws involving minimum wages and job classifications.
▲ Compensation policies are keeping pace with the changing nature of today's labor market—particularly in recruiting and retaining top performers.

8.1.4 Managing External Factors

When developing and administering a compensation program, businesses must cope with a range of outside factors including economics, the labor market, competition in the marketplace, as well as other pressures such as those related to accounting requirements and government regulations.

Economic Factors

The ability of an organization to find qualified employees is affected by factors at the local, national, and global levels:

▲ Economic growth.
▲ Inflation.
▲ Interest rates.
▲ Unemployment.
▲ Comparative cost of living.

These factors impact the **cost of labor**, or the cost to attract and retain individuals with the skills needed by the organization to achieve its goals.

Organizations recruiting employees with a particular skill set create a competitive environment for individuals with those skills, resulting in an increase in the cost of labor. For example, when two large companies in a metropolitan area are hiring large numbers of experienced manufacturing technicians, the supply of individuals with this skill set is in demand and the availability of qualified individuals decreases. This combination of increased demand and decreased availability **raises** the compensation rate, thereby increasing the cost of labor.

Labor Market

Organizations may need to revise their compensation programs to meet the demands of changing labor markets. The **labor market** is comprised of any sources from which an organization recruits new employees. A single organization may find itself recruiting from several different labor markets depending on the availability of skills for different positions. Ultimately, the combination of supply and demand for a certain skill set in the labor market impacts what the employers competing for those skills must pay to individuals who possess them.

The way people look at pay has changed over the years. During the technology boom of the late '90s, job hopping and generous compensation packages were very popular. When the technology bubble burst and the unemployment rate increased, organizations were able to recruit for many positions locally. HR professionals must be aware of changing labor market conditions to ensure

FOR EXAMPLE

Mapping Labor Costs

Labor markets vary by region and industry. In New York and other urban areas, there is a greater pool of candidates with a wider set of skills from which to select. But because there are more businesses in urban areas competing for this pool of candidates, urban environments may be more competitive, leading to an increase in the cost of labor. For an insurance company headquartered in the southeast, this means having to utilize regional pay structures to reflect the market conditions of the different areas in which they have business locations. The company's regional offices in New York and San Francisco, for example, have a different pay scale than the regional offices in Tampa and Tulsa.

compensation programs in their organizations achieve the desired objective of maintaining a competitive edge.

Market Competition

Competition in the marketplace puts financial pressure on an organization and challenges its ability to attract and retain qualified employees. Increased competition creates pressure to do everything faster, better, and cheaper. These added pressures place a strain on the employee population.

In a climate epitomized by strong competition between organizations accompanied by a decrease in demand, issues related to the financial health of an organization will likely surface. For employees this may mean wage freezes, which may result in skipping a merit review process and/or not paying incentives. In a strong economy, increased competition can mean growth for the organization due to increasing demand resulting in increased financial rewards for employees.

Tax and Accounting

The Internal Revenue Service (IRS) affects compensation and benefits issues through its enforcement of federal tax legislation, such as social security and Medicare taxes, pension regulation, and enforcement of rules about some benefit programs (these will be discussed in Chapter 9). When an organization wants to make changes to compensation or benefit programs it may want to find out how the IRS will view the changes for tax purposes before it makes them. Figure 8.2 shows a sample paycheck statement with common deductions indicated.

Government Regulation

Of course, the major government impact on the human resources management comes from legislation that regulates pay and benefit practices. Legislation related to benefits is discussed in Chapter 9.

SELF-CHECK

1. Define *cost of labor.*
2. Name the two types of compensation philosophies.
3. Inflation and unemployment are two factors that affect the ability of a company to find qualified employees. True or false?

Figure 8-2

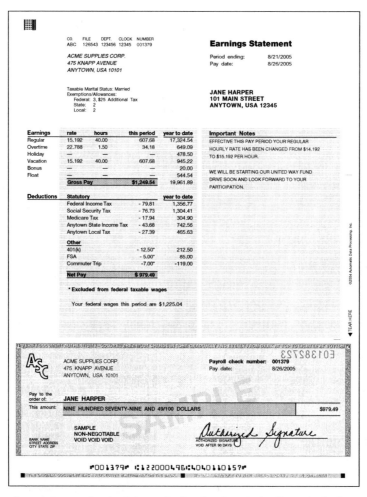

A sample paycheck statement showing tax deductions, including
Medicare and Social Security.

8.2 Looking at Compensation Legal Issues

The federal government first began regulating compensation practices during the
Great Depression. Initially, legislation impacted only those private employers who
did business with the government, but a few years later the Fair Labor Standards
Act expanded coverage to include virtually all employers in the United States (see
Section 8.2.1). These laws were designed to protect workers from unfair pay prac-
tices and other abuses by employers and are administered by the Wage and Hour
Division of the Department of Labor, Employment Standards Administration.

The following list offers a brief look at federal laws that affect how and how much you pay your workers. Of course, you should still seek the sound advice of your own lawyer when dealing with compensation issues. He or she can assist you in setting up policies and wage structures that can help keep you out of legal trouble.

- ▲ **The Equal Pay Act of 1963:** This law prohibits unequal payments to men and women doing the same job, assuming that the jobs require equal skill, effort, and responsibility and that the jobs are performed under similar conditions. The law permits a few exceptions, such as seniority, so check with a lawyer.
- ▲ **Civil Rights Acts of 1964:** Title VII of this law prohibits wage discrimination on the basis of race, sex, color, religion, or national origin. The U.S. Equal Employment Opportunity Commission enforces this law (see Section 2.2).
- ▲ **Service Contract Act (1965):** The Service Contract Act of 1965 requires any federal service contractor with a contract exceeding $2,500 to pay its employees the prevailing wage and fringe benefits for the geographic area in which it operates, provide safe and sanitary working conditions, and notify employees of the minimum allowable wage for each job classification.
- ▲ **Age Discrimination in Employment Act of 1967:** As amended in 1978, this law bans wage discrimination based on age forty or older. One of the most common violations is the denial of pay increases to people nearing retirement to avoid increasing retirement benefits that are based on an employee's salary.
- ▲ **Davis-Bacon Act of 1931, the Copeland Act of 1934, the Walsh-Healey Act of 1936, and the Anti-Kickback Act of 1948:** These four laws focus, in different ways, on the compensation policies of companies with federal contracts. Though each law differs, the basic purpose of each is to ensure that employers pay prevailing wages and overtime and prohibit excessive wage deductions and under-the-table payments by employees to obtain work.
- ▲ **The Wage Garnishment Law:** This law prohibits employers from firing workers whose wages, for whatever reason, are subject to garnishment by creditors or spouse for any one indebtedness and also limits garnishments in most cases to no more than twenty-five percent of an employee's take-home pay.

8.2.1 Fair Labor Standards Act

Enacted in 1938 and amended frequently since then, the Fair Labor Standards Act (FLSA) remains a major influence on basic compensation issues for businesses in the United States. FLSA regulations apply to workers who are not already covered by another law. For example, railroad and airline employers are subject to wage and hour requirements of the Railway Labor Act so the FLSA does not apply.

The FLSA established requirements in five areas relevant to HR professionals:

▲ **Exempt status:** One of the main purposes of the Fair Labor Standards Act is to ensure that employers pay American workers a certain minimum hourly wage and compensate them appropriately if they work more than forty hours a week. Thus were born the two main employee distinctions in the workplace, exempt and nonexempt. The key difference between these two classifications is that **exempt workers** receive a flat weekly, monthly, or yearly salary, independent of the number of hours they work during any given week or month, while you pay **nonexempt workers** on an hourly basis (see Section 8.2.2).

▲ **Minimum wage:** The FLSA sets the federal minimum wage, which at the time of this writing is $5.85 per hour. Some states have set the minimum wage at a higher rate than the federal government; when this is the case, the state requirement supersedes the federal minimum wage. The DOL provides a useful map showing current minimum wage requirements by state at www.dol.gov/esa/minwage/america.htm.

▲ **Overtime:** The FLSA identified the circumstances in which overtime payments are required and set the overtime rate at one and one half times the regular hourly wage. FLSA regulations established that nonexempt employees be paid overtime for all compensable time worked that exceeds forty hours in a work week (commonly known as time-and-a-half). The FLSA does not require or prohibit overtime payment for exempt employees, who can be paid at straight time, time and a half, or as a bonus. Public employees may be compensated with what is known as compensatory time off, or comp time, for overtime.

FOR EXAMPLE

Going Exempt

Erika was delighted when she was promoted from staff engineer, a nonexempt position, to principal engineer. The higher-profile position would give her more prestigious projects, more authority, and room to advance. Now in an exempt position, however, Erika had to give up the lucrative overtime pay she had become accustomed to. In fact, even though she had been given a raise with her promotion to the new position, she brought home less each paycheck for nearly a year.

▲ **Child labor:** The FLSA placed limitations on working conditions for children to protect them from exploitation. In particular, it states that a child must be at least sixteen to work in most nonfarm jobs and eighteen to work in nonfarm jobs that have been identified as hazardous.

▲ **Record keeping:** The FLSA requires the maintenance of accurate records by all employers; records are usually the responsibility of the payroll department.

8.2.2 Classifying Exempt and Nonexempt Workers

The exempt/nonexempt distinction is extremely subjective. But if labor authorities overturn your classification of a long-time employee as exempt, you become responsible for all the overtime pay that employee is due, going back two or three years of the individual's employment. How you choose to classify your workers can be a complicated affair depending on your industry. Consult your attorney if you have any questions at all. Failing to properly compensate your workers can lead to serious repercussions, so bear in mind the following guidelines:

▲ **Don't rely on job titles:** Remember that what people do and not what you call them is what counts the most in complying with the FLSA.

▲ **Correct problems when you find them:** Don't wait for a lawsuit or a government inspector. A person who willfully violates FLSA regulations can be fined as muc h as $10,000 and imprisoned for as long as six months.

▲ **Keep accurate records:** Keep timesheets for all nonexempt employees. If there is a dispute about an employee working overtime, the employee will probably win unless the company can produce an employee-completed time sheet.

8.2.3 Communicating Your Policies

Many companies make the mistake of spending a lot of time and effort designing a compensation system and then leave it to the paycheck alone to communicate their pay philosophy and administration. You need to thoroughly brief managers and supervisors on your company's pay systems so that they can explain, administer, and support your policies. Managers and supervisors should know the following:

▲ Your company's pay philosophy.
▲ How to conduct a performance appraisal, if your company has such a system (see Chapter 6).
▲ How to handle and refer employee pay complaints.
▲ Legal implications of all compensation policies.

You also need to advise employees of the company's pay policies and how these policies affect them individually. Be certain to communicate and explain any changes in these policies. Employees need to possess the following information:

▲ The job's rating system, how it works, and how it affects them.

▲ How the performance-appraisal and incentive systems work.

▲ How they can raise their own income through performance and promotion.

▲ How to voice complaints or concerns.

Along the way, you must keep your compensation system competitive and up-to-date. You'll do so by reviewing competitive data at regular intervals and by reviewing salary systems in terms of your company's financial condition. Figure 8-3 shows a sample pay philosophy.

Figure 8-3

Pay Philosophy

XYZ Company's pay decision guidelines emphasize continued development and expansion of skills, knowledge, performance, and the ability to be flexible. Our goals are three-fold: 1) to compete for qualified staff in an evolving environment, 2) to pay employees equitably and fairly, and 3) to be fiscally responsible.

XYZ Company believes that it is important to consider both internal and external factors as pay decisions are made. Internally, importance should be placed on equity in relation to others in like job/positions, as well as an individual's skills, knowledge, performance, and job/position related experience. Externally, the relevant labor market will be monitored to determine market movement, keeping in mind its effect on employees and their respective pay. The external market consists of similar companies and general industry employers with whom we compete for employees with relative skills and experience.

XYZ Company expects that employees will strive for excellence in their job/position performance and take accountability and ownership for their careers. It is essential that employees, either in doing their current job/positions or in preparing to take on new and different responsibilities, continue to develop and expand their skills to keep pace with change and ready themselves for opportunities as they become available. It is also essential that managers and administrators provide employees with opportunities to grow and learn.

Human Resources, in conjunction with department managers and administrative officers, will watch the job/position market closely. Human Resources tracks the market by participating in annual salary surveys and, wherever possible, obtaining salary information on "industry standard" positions, typically referred to as benchmark job/positions; i.e., those job/positions that are typical in our industry and similar industries and are easily matched and compared to job/positions at XYZ Company. Results of salary surveys give us the range of pay found in the market for job/positions similar to ours. On the basis of these data, Human Resources will review salary levels and ranges annually to determine whether there is a need to adjust them, and will review job/positions within specific job/position families to determine whether we are paying "at market."

Job/Position markets vary for certain job/positions, depending on the recruitment pool, whether certain skill sets are in increasing demand, or whether there is a shortage of individuals with a specific expertise. Therefore, market pay levels for specific job/positions may increase slowly or aggressively.

An example of a pay philosophy.

SELF-CHECK

1. The FSLA covers all employees in the United States. True or false?
2. Exempt employees are paid on an hourly basis. True or false?
3. *Time and a half* is used to describe
   a. minimum wage.
   b. overtime.
   c. disability payment.
   d. pay raises.

8.3 Types of Compensation

Each organization selects components for its compensation package that it believes will achieve the results it desires. In very small organizations, this may be accomplished with the use of only the total compensation component of a reward program: the cash compensation that is paid to employees. Very large organizations, on the other hand, may find it beneficial to develop different compensation packages for different job categories. Consider the examples of sales teams and executives and how different compensation methods best serve each:

▲ **Sales teams:** Because it is easy to track how many sales are produced by each salesperson, the direct relationship between sales made and compensation earned is clear, so establishing incentive pay for increased sales is a proven method of motivating a sales team.

▲ **Executives:** Compensation packages for executives are often tied to company performance, such as increased stock prices, net profits, or other quantifiable measures. Such packages often include a variety of special benefits, known as **perquisites** (also known as executive perks), that are not made available to the general employee population—the use of a company jet or club memberships.

8.3.1 Total Rewards

A **total rewards** program includes all the methods (cash, equity, and benefits) used by employers to pay employees for the work they provide for the organization. An effective total rewards package includes a variety of components that attract and retain employees who have skills needed by the organization. Because people have different needs, based on their individual circumstances, the components included in the package should be sufficiently varied to address the different requirements of people at different stages in their lives. For example, employees with young children may be looking for benefits that help them raise their children, such as day care or time off to attend school activities.

The elements available for inclusion in a total rewards package fall into two basic categories: monetary compensation and nonmonetary compensation. A total rewards program includes elements from both categories.

▲ **Monetary compensation:** Compensation for which an organization expends funds. It includes payments made directly to employees as well as benefits the company pays on behalf of its employees; it is also referred to as remuneration. There are two forms of monetary compensation: direct and indirect.

  • **Direct compensation:** Salaries or wages, incentive awards, bonus payments, and sales commissions.

  • **Indirect compensation:** Benefits provided by organizations, such as medical and dental insurance, workers' compensation, mandated benefits such as Social Security and Medicare, and retirement plans. (See Chapter 9 for a complete discussion of benefits.)

Table 8-1 illustrates the relationship between total cash compensation, total direct compensation, and total rewards.

▲ **Nonmonetary compensation:** Nonmonetary compensation includes aspects of working in a particular organization that are unique and beneficial for employees and can be an important factor in attracting and retaining them.

  • Convenient location that is within walking distance of public transportation.

  • Free parking for employees.

  • Telecommuting or flex-time arrangements.

Because many of these nonmonetary benefits are related to the organization's culture, Chapter 10 will discuss them in greater detail.

Table 8-1: Total Rewards Formula

Pay (wages/salary)
+ Incentives (bonus, commissions, etc.)
+ Benefits (insurance, retirement, etc.)
= Compensation package/Total rewards

Direct Compensation

Most employees are very familiar with some types of direct compensation because they receive paychecks on a regular basis. The various forms of direct pay are described in the following points:

▲ **Base pay:** The basic form of compensation employees receive in exchange for the work they do for the employer. The amount of base pay that specific jobs are worth is based on external factors such as the labor market, and on internal factors such as how much value the employer places on the job in relation to other jobs in the organization. The company's compensation philosophy drives the type of program that is used:

- Performance-based pay programs are based on how well individual employees perform against the company's process for measuring performance.
- Seniority-based compensation systems make pay decisions based on the length of time employees have been in a position and on years of related experience.

▲ **Variable pay:** Compensation that is tied to specific performance goals. Variable pay includes sales commissions, bonuses (one-time payments that are unrelated to base pay), and incentives.

▲ **Equity:** Equity plans provide benefits to employees as well as convey a sense of ownership in the company to individuals; companies do so by incorporating a stock option plan, by awarding stock to employees directly, or by establishing a plan that allows employees to purchase stock at preferred rates.

THE UNION EFFECT

In a union context, long-term and short-term compensation decisions are the result of negotiations between the union and the employer. Because of this, they are not necessarily driven by an organization's compensation philosophy. In a union environment, annual increases are typically determined by seniority. For more on unions, see Chapter 13.

Ability to Pay

An organization's leaders may want to attract employees with the highest levels of skill by paying higher base salaries than other businesses. Doing this requires that the organization have the necessary financial resources. If the resources are not available, alternative methods of paying employees must be developed. For example, the organization can tie part of the total compensation package to performance goals with the use of incentive pay. In this way, the employees who make the greatest contribution to achieving goals receive the largest rewards.

> ## FOR EXAMPLE
>
> ### Total Rewards
>
> The Total Rewards program at Vanguard, one of the world's largest investment management companies, offers "an exceptional combination of cash compensation, benefits, and conveniences." Using a performance-based philosophy, the company is committed to ensuring that the best performers receive the highest rewards. Each November, employees receive a performance and compensation review. On top of that, the company offers its Vanguard Partnership Plan, which ensures that a part of an individual's compensation depends on overall company performance. As far as bonuses, exempt employees are eligible for individual performance-based bonuses, and the company offers an incentive program for non-exempt employees.

SELF-CHECK

1. Define *perquisite*.
2. Nonmonetary and monetary compensation are both parts of a total rewards system. True or false?
3. Name the three types of direct compensation.

8.4 Administering a Compensation Plan

The final element of a compensation strategy is the framework that allows the plan to be administered fairly, equitably, and in the way in which organization leaders designed it. One of the fundamental tasks is to develop a consistent protocol for setting pay levels for each job in your organization. The more essential a job is to the fundamental mission of your company, the higher its pay range is likely to be.

The following procedure can help you determine some preliminary answers to this fundamental question:

1. Make a list of all the jobs in your company, from the most senior to the least senior employee.
2. Group the jobs by major function—management, administrative, production, and so on.
3. Working on your own or with other managers, rank the jobs according to their relationship to your company's mission.

At the end you should have two major categories—those jobs that contribute directly to the mission and those jobs that provide support for those mission-critical jobs. Following are some questions to ask yourself in making this distinction:

▲ How closely does the job relate to our mission?

▲ How indispensable is the job?

▲ How difficult is the job—does it require special skills or training?

▲ Does the position generate revenue or support revenue-producing functions?

▲ Do political or other factors make this job important?

Eventually, you produce a ranking or hierarchy of positions. Keep in mind that you're not rating individuals. You're rating the relative importance of each job with respect to your company's mission and strategic goals. A key element in evaluating job worth is to keep in mind that the process is designed to evaluate the *job*, not the *person in the job*. Job worth is based on two factors:

▲ **Internal equity:** The value of the job to the organization relative to other jobs. The starting point for determining internal equity is the job description, which contains a list of the duties of the position, the knowledge, skills, and abilities necessary to perform the duties, and an assessment of the job's difficulty level.

▲ **External equity:** The value of the job in the marketplace. External equity is used to compare the jobs in an organization to the same or similar jobs in other organizations to find out how much they are worth in the labor market. This is done by collecting salary data about jobs from organizations in similar industries or within defined geographical areas to find out how many specific jobs are worth in the labor market.

8.4.1 Setting Pay Scale

In setting the actual pay scale for specific jobs, you have several options, as the following sections describe.

Job Evaluation and Pay Grading

How this approach works: You look at each job in your company and evaluate it on the basis of several factors, such as relative value to the bottom line, complexity, hazards, required credentials, and so on. A classic example of the traditional job-evaluation and pay-grade system is employed by the Department of Defense's Defense Logistics Information Service (DLIS). Most DLIS jobs fit into one of fifteen numerical grade levels. This system keys the pay scale to the job level, and employees at those levels receive their pay accordingly.

The rationale: In large companies, you must use a reasonably structured approach to deciding what pay range to apply to each job. The more systematic you are as you develop that structure, the more effective the system is likely to be.

The downside: Creating and maintaining a structure of this nature takes a lot of time and effort. Compensation systems that you key primarily to the job (or grade) and not the person or the performance are currently out of fashion.

The Going Rate

How this approach works: Look at what other companies in your industry (and region) pay people for comparable jobs and set up your pay structure accordingly. You can obtain this data from government and industry websites and publications. Robert Half International (www.rhi.com) publishes a variety of salary guides focusing on professional disciplines like accounting and finance, law, technology, advertising and marketing, and the administrative field.

Rationale: The laws of supply and demand directly affect salary levels. But assuming that you're able to rapidly and constantly discover what other companies pay, this system is fairly easy to set up and administer. Benchmarking salaries (and benefits) is an important way to ensure that you're paying people competitively.

The downside: Comparisons can be difficult in today's job market. Many of new jobs that companies are creating today are actually combinations of jobs in the traditional sense of the word and, as such, can prove difficult to price, going only by how the job functions in other companies are paid, but it is a good starting point.

Management Fit

How this approach works: The owner decides arbitrarily how much each employee is paid.

Rationale: The owner of a business has the right to pay people whatever he deems appropriate.

The downside: Inconsistent wage differentials often breed resentment and discontent. Lack of a reasonable degree of internal equity diminishes the spirit of teamwork and fairness.

Collective Bargaining

How this approach works: In unionized companies, formal bargaining between management and labor representatives sets wage levels for specific groups of workers, based on market rate, and the employer's resources available to pay wages.

The rationale: Workers should have a strong say (and agree as a group) on how much the company pays them. This system, of course, is (arguably) the ultimate form of establishing internal equity.

The downside: Acrimony arises if management and labor fail to see eye to eye. In addition, someone else—the union—plays a key role in your business decisions. Also, employees who perform exceptionally well can feel less rewarded because their wages are then the same as less proficient colleagues in similar positions.

8.4.2 Accounting for Individuals

At the most basic level, a business pays people, not positions. So at some point you must program into your salary decisions those factors that relate solely to the individual performing the job. The following list describes the key "people factors" that you may want to consider in defining a pay-scale structure.

▲ **Experience and education:** To a certain extent, you see a fairly reliable correlation between the productivity of employees and their education levels and experiences. However, more experience and more education don't always translate into better work. People who are over-qualified for positions, for example, often prove less productive than others. The key is to make sure there's a logical connection between the employee's education and experience and the basic requirements of the job.

▲ **Job performance:** You should pay more to workers who produce more—in theory, at least. The challenge is putting this simple practice into practice. To do so effectively, you need to address the following questions:

  • What barometers are you using to measure job performance, and how do they tie in to your strategic objectives? If you're evaluating the performance of technical service personnel, for example, are you going to key your pay levels to their technical proficiency or their ability to interact?

  • Who's responsible for measuring performance? Is it an immediate supervisor, or do you use a team-based evaluation approach? And what

---

FOR EXAMPLE

Comparing Salaries

Salaries in Stamford, Connecticut, and Richmond, Virginia, are on average similar for the same job, although the cost of living in Stamford at the same time is thirty to forty percent higher than in Richmond. Although it would seem that employers in Stamford would have to pay more to compensate for the higher cost of living, Stamford has a surplus of white-collar workers not found in Richmond, which keeps salaries low.

recourse are you giving employees who take issue with your evaluations? Can they take their case to someone other than their supervisor?

- Are the performance criteria you're using to reward performance discriminatory in any way? In other words, does any aspect of your company's job performance criteria favor one gender over another, one age group over another, or one ethnic group over another?

▲ **Seniority:** Length of service has long been a factor in the pay scales in most industries—unionized industries in particular. The rationale is that loyalty is valued and should be rewarded. The downside: No strong evidence suggests that seniority and productivity in any way directly correlate.

▲ **Potential:** Some companies justify higher pay for certain individuals because they consistently demonstrate the potential to become exceptional producers or managers. This consideration is generally why comparatively unskilled, inexperienced college graduates may receive extra compensation if you select them for management-trainee programs.

SELF-CHECK

1. In evaluating job worth, you evaluate individual employees rather than jobs. True or false?
2. Name the type of equity that is determined by looking at similar jobs in the marketplace.
3. Seniority is a proven barometer for increased productivity. True or false?

8.5 Using Raises, Bonuses, and Incentives

Offering competitive compensation is key to attracting and keeping top talent. Most companies enhance their compensation through raises, bonuses, and incentives designed to retain their best workers and give them a reason to stay on.

According to several salary surveys, almost two-thirds of U.S. companies include some sort of variable compensation in the pay packages offered to employees. Known as **variable compensation** or **incentive pay**, these programs reward employees for individual and/or organizational results. An effective variable pay program motivates employees to achieve the objectives; this form of compensation can help to shape or change employee behavior or organizational culture by rewarding behaviors that are valued by the organization.

Employers structure effective bonus and incentive programs around the following main principles:

▲ **Results-oriented:** Employees must accomplish something to receive a bonus.
▲ **Fair:** The rules for bonuses are clear, and you enforce them equitably.
▲ **Competitive:** The program rewards extra effort and superior performance.

8.5.1 Designing a Plan

Once an organization determines the type of employee performance or behavior it wants to encourage, an appropriate incentive plan can be selected. Whether the incentive plan is based on individual or group performance, or on some type of special incentive depends on the organization's specific needs.

Individual Incentives

Individual incentives reward employees who achieve set goals and objectives and can be powerful tools for motivating individual performance. Incentives are prospective in that they state specific objectives that need to be achieved over designated periods of time and include payout targets stated either as a percentage of base pay or a flat dollar amount.

Three phases are essential for any successful incentive program:

▲ **Design:** Plans should make it as easy and convenient as possible for employees to understand and recall performance goals (for instance, an employee needs to increase production by ten percent).
▲ **Review:** Typically, bonus review and payment corresponds to the end of the organization's fiscal year. In some cases, incentives may be paid more frequently if employees have a direct influence on revenue generation.
▲ **Communication:** Individual incentive objectives are ideally communicated before or at the beginning of a review period. For example, annual, calendar based plans are usually communicated in January. Some organizations create a plan document that describes the incentive program in detail.

A BIG ENOUGH BONUS?

Research on incentives has found that a minimum target of ten percent is required to influence and change behavior. Bonus targets of less than ten percent of base pay may not provide sufficient motivation for employees to put forward the effort or spend the additional time to achieve the plan objectives and as a result may not produce the desired results.

Group Incentives

Group incentives have many of the same characteristics as individual incentives. These incentives are commonly used to increase productivity, foster teamwork, and share financial rewards with employees. As the name implies, group incentives are not used to reward individual performance.

Two common group incentives are profit sharing and stock ownership, both of which are outlined in detail in Section 8.5.3.

8.5.2 Choosing a Reward Approach

To keep your best and brightest employees, you need to figure out fair—and affordable—ways to augment what you pay them. Most companies use raises and bonuses to some degree as a way to enhance their compensation plans.

Pay Raises

Traditional pay systems often link raises to **tenure** (that is, time spent in that grade or position). Other systems frequently tie raises to performance. The most common types of raises include:

▲ **Seniority step-ups:** These types of raises usually depend solely on an employee's length of service and are pretty much automatic. Such raises are a common feature of union contracts.

▲ **Merit raise:** These raises are increases for superior performance, usually as a formal performance evaluation system measures it, but sometimes driven by other considerations, such as attainment of an educational or training objective.

▲ **Productivity increases:** These raises generally involve increasing pay after employees exceed a certain norm—a production quota, for example. These systems usually apply to workers performing repetitive tasks.

FOR EXAMPLE

Allocating Raises

A regional real estate company has twenty employees in its marketing department. The company allocates the department manager enough money to give each employee a four percent increase, based on the group's current salary dollar total. She decides to give a four percent boost to the majority of the team because that is the general guidance from management. But she also decides to give superior performers more than four percent and underperformers less—and three get no raise at all.

Bonuses

A **bonus** is additional payment for performance above and beyond what was expected and is paid in addition to an employee's base salary or hourly rate. Bonuses are always keyed to results: the company's, the employee's, or those of the employee's department. Bonus plans are different from incentive plans because incentives are communicated prior to the start of the project. In addition to the common examples listed below, bonuses also take the form of referral bonuses, patent awards, employee of the month rewards, and so on.

▲ **Annual and bi-annual bonuses:** These bonuses are one-shot payments to all eligible employees, based on the company's results, individual performance, or a combination thereof.

▲ **Spot bonuses:** Spot bonuses are awarded in direct response to a single instance of superior performance (such as an employee suggestion). Employees receive the bonus at the time of, or soon after, the action that has earned the bonus.

▲ **Retention bonuses:** You make such payments to persuade key people to stay with your company. These bonuses are common in industries that employ hard-to-recruit specialists or to retain top managers or star performers.

▲ **Team bonuses:** These bonuses are awarded to group members for the collective success of their team.

8.5.3 Incentives

Incentives are like bonuses in that they don't increase base pay. The difference is that most incentive programs, unlike bonuses, are often long term in nature to cement employee loyalty or spur productivity. The following sections outline some common incentive programs.

Profit-sharing Plans

Profit-sharing plans enable the company to set aside a percentage of its profits for distribution to employees. If profits go up, the employees get more money. You can focus these programs very sharply by allocating the profit sharing on a department or business-unit basis. Employees who stand to share in the company's profits have an extra incentive to work hard and be more aware of avoiding waste and inefficiency. After all, it's their business, too.

Profit-sharing plans fall into one of two categories:

▲ **Cash plan:** Payments are distributed quarterly or annually.

▲ **Deferred plan:** The company invests the profit-sharing payment in a fund and then pays out an employee's share if he retires or leaves the company.

Deferred plans offer significant tax advantages to both the company and the employees. On the downside, deferred plans can have less effect on productivity: In some cases, the worker doesn't actually see the profit-sharing money, except as a figure on paper, until retirement.

Stock

Stock in the company is an incentive that publicly traded firms (or firms planning to go public) may choose to offer their employees. Stock option plans give employees at publicly held companies the right to purchase shares in the company at a time of their own choosing, but at a price that is set at the time the option is awarded. Employees are under no obligation to exercise that option, but should the stock go up, employees can buy the stock at the cheaper price and either hold on to it or sell it for the current value, thereby earning a profit.

If your company is thinking about offering stock options as part of your overall benefits package, bear in mind that these programs must comply with tax laws and also with the Securities and Exchange Commission (SEC) regulations. Also, stock options must now be counted as a corporate expense, a change in law that has led many companies to offer fewer stock options than they had in previous years. Get thorough legal and tax advice before you put together any sort of stock option plan.

Some other considerations you need to bear in mind:

▲ Most stock option plans include some form of **vesting**, meaning that options may not be exercised until an employee has been with the company for a specified period of time. Vesting is a retention strategy by the company.

▲ Most stock option plans set an expiration date, a point beyond which employees can no longer exercise options.

▲ Most plans require the approval of current shareholders.

▲ The plan you adopt may obligate you to provide periodic financial information and reports to option holders.

Many companies that eliminated stock options are instead offering **restricted stock** to their employees. Restricted stock is ownership in a company with rights to vote and receive dividends without the right to transfer or sell the shares until the shares are vested. Once the vesting conditions have been satisfied, the shares are employees' to hold, transfer or sell as they desire, subject to applicable securities laws and payment of withholding taxes and applicable commissions.

Commissions

Commissions provide incentives to sales employees by paying them a percentage of the sale price for products and services sold to a customer. Commissions may serve as the entire cash compensation package, or they may be used in combination with a base salary. When sales employees receive a base salary, it is usually a portion of their target cash compensation. The incentive or variable component is intended to drive sales objectives. Compensation for sales employees paid on a commission-only basis must meet at least the minimum wage. When performance targets are clearly communicated, commissions are an excellent way to motivate sales employees.

8.5.4 Avoiding Plan Pitfalls

The easiest way to start a mutiny among your employees is to institute a raise or bonus process that people don't clearly understand and that neither managers nor employees support. The following list offers guidelines to avoid any problems:

▲ **Set clear rules:** Regardless of what program you're using, everyone must clearly understand the rules concerning how you give out the rewards: who's eligible for the program, what they must do to receive the reward, who decides on those who benefit, and how much the reward is.

▲ **Set specific targets or goals that you can quantify:** Make sure that you set a specific target for incentives: "125 percent of our annual sales quota," for example. Specific numbers eliminate misunderstandings.

▲ **Make the goal worthwhile:** If the incentives aren't attractive, they're not incentives. Think about setting up different rewards for varying levels of achievement: four percent increase, for example, for an "average" performer and, say, eight percent for a top performer.

▲ **Don't ask for the impossible:** If employees perceive incentive targets as being unattainable, you merely discourage them from striving for the rewards, and you also lose credibility with them.

▲ **Don't make promises you can't keep:** Never promise a bonus or incentive you're not sure that you can afford.

SELF-CHECK

1. Explain the difference between an *incentive* and a *bonus*.
2. Define *spot bonus*.
3. Profit-sharing plans give employees less incentive to increase productivity. True or false?

SUMMARY

The compensation system you establish for employees is one of the main engines that drive your business. The way you compensate people plays a key role in your ability to attract and retain a productive, reliable workforce. How much you pay your employees and the factors you use to establish pay scales and award raises, bonuses, and incentives make up a critical part of a human resources strategy. However, an organization's compensation system must be developed with certain external factors in mind—economics, labor market, government regulation, and market competition among them. Human resource professionals should be familiar with the laws that have been designed to protect workers from unfair pay practices, including the Fair Labor Standards Act (FLSA). The act is important for many reasons: it sets the minimum wage, covers issues related to overtime, and sets standards for working conditions for children. Employers may include two types of compensation, both monetary and non-monetary. The monetary elements are either direct (salary, commission, bonuses) or indirect (medical insurance, retirement plans, workers' compensation). In addition to making decisions about types of compensation, an employer must determine which of several methods will be used to set an employee's pay scale. On top of pay scale are the elements of variable compensation or incentive pay, which can add to the value of a package. The intended end result of these decisions is a system that not only gives your employees equitable compensation, but also focuses on the market realities of your business.

KEY TERMS

Benefits
Items offered to employees in addition to their base wage or salary; examples include health insurance, stock options, and retirement plans.

Bonus
A reward for a job well done; usually financial, but may include rewarding time off, free membership in a local health club, or discounts on merchandise.

Commissions
A percentage of the sales price of a service or product that salespeople receive in addition to (or in lieu of) salary.

Compensation
All the rewards that employees receive in exchange for their work, including base pay, bonuses, and incentives.

Cost of labor	The cost to attract and retain individuals with the skills needed by an organization.
Direct compensation	Salaries or wages, incentive awards, bonus payments, sales commissions, and other monetary compensation paid directly to employees.
Entitlement philosophy	Salary and promotion decisions are based on length of service; this philosophy is exemplified in a union environment.
Equity	Plan that provides benefits to employees in the form of stock option plans, or by awarding stock to employees directly or at preferred rates.
Exempt workers	Classification of employees who perform certain types of duties and receive salaries (as opposed to an hourly basis).
External equity	Compares jobs in the organization to other similar jobs in other organizations to make sure that the organization's wages and salaries are sufficient to attract the qualified employees it needs.
Fair Labor Standards Act (FLSA)	Regulation enacted in 1938 that remains a major influence on basic compensation issues for U.S. businesses.
Group incentives	Programs used to increase productivity, encourage teamwork, and share financial rewards with employees; common group incentives include profit sharing and stock ownership.
Incentive pay	Programs that reward employees for individual and/or organizational results.
Incentives	A tool used to boost productivity; an incentive comes before work is done.
Indirect compensation	A type of monetary compensation that consists of benefits paid by the organization on behalf of employees, such as medical insurance, workers' compensation, or mandated benefits.
Internal equity	The worth of a job to a company; value is based on the content of the job, its level of

	responsibility, and how much impact the decisions in the job have on an organization.
Labor market	Sources from which an organization recruits new employees.
Nonexempt workers	Workers paid an hourly wage.
Performance-based philosophy	Salary increases and promotions are awarded to those employees who contribute to the achievement of organization goals.
Perquisites	Special benefits not made available to the general employee population.
Raises	Increases in base salary or rate of pay, as opposed to one-time or periodic awards.
Restricted stock	Ownership in a company with rights to vote and receive dividends without the right to transfer or sell the shares until the shares are vested.
Salary	Pay arrangements of employees who receive their compensation as a flat amount, regardless of how many hours they work.
Stock option	Program that gives employees at publicly held companies the right to purchase shares in the company at a time of their own choosing, but at a price that is set at the time the option is awarded.
Tenure	Time spent in a job grade or position.
Total compensation	All types of direct cash compensation.
Total rewards	Monetary compensation (direct and indirect) and nonmonetary compensation, unique and beneficial aspects of working for a particular employer.
Variable compensation	Programs that reward employees for individual and/or organizational results.
Variable pay	Pay tied to specific performance goals and includes commissions, bonuses, and incentives.
Vesting	An employee must stay with the company for a specified time before exercising stock options.

ASSESS YOUR UNDERSTANDING

Go to www.wiley.com/college/messmer to assess your knowledge of compensation strategies.

Measure your learning by comparing pre-test and post-test results.

Summary Questions

1. A performance-based philosophy is best utilized in union situations. True or false?

2. A company may draw from a single labor market to meet its staffing needs. True or false?

3. How does an increased demand of skilled labor in a tight market typically affect the cost of labor?

   (a) no effect on it

   (b) increases it

   (c) decreases it

   (d) reverses it

4. Which federal law protects children from unfair labor practices?

   (a) Civil Rights Acts of 1964

   (b) Age Discrimination Act of 1976

   (c) Fair Labor Standards Act

   (d) David-Bacon Act

5. Non-exempt employees who work 50 hours a week are entitled to overtime payments. True or false?

6. A job title is the most accurate way to determine an employee's exempt status. True or false?

7. Variable pay is

   (a) negotiated annually.

   (b) determined by cost of labor.

   (c) based on stock options.

   (d) tied to performance goals.

8. Give three examples of variable pay options.

9. A total rewards system can help achieve a company's strategic goals by

   (a) attracting and retaining highly skilled employees.

   (b) establishing a pecking order for jobs within the company.

   (c) maintaining an entitlement culture.

   (d) enlisting support of upper management.

10. Explain how job worth is determined.
11. Which approach to setting pay scale is used in unionized situations?
    (a) management fit
    (b) collective bargaining
    (c) going rate
    (d) job evaluation
12. Unlike bonuses, incentives increase base pay. True or false?
13. Sales commissions are a form of incentive. True or false?
14. What is the minimum percent to use as incentive for increased employee productivity?
    (a) 5 percent
    (b) 7.5 percent
    (c) 10 percent
    (d) 15 percent
15. Which of the following type of bonus is used to keep employees from leaving for another job?
    (a) spot
    (b) team
    (c) bi-annual
    (d) retention

Applying This Chapter

1. Imagine you've inherited your family's printing business in Texas. It's clear that not a lot has changed as far as staffing and pay since the company was started thirty years ago. Although the company is still profitable, competing office supply mega stores are now a real concern. Determine which, if any, external factors will affect how you develop a new performance-based compensation plan.
2. Using the previous business situation, evaluate the ways in which the Fair Labor Standards Act might impact your compensation plan. Assume that you have fifty employees (including ten part-timers).
3. As the new human resources manager of a hotel and spa, you've been asked to analyze the company's outdated rewards system. Because the system is grounded on a performance-based philosophy, incentives should play a role. Keeping in mind that the range of jobs is wide and varied, differentiate the kinds of compensation elements that would suit the customer service agents versus those that would suit the restaurant staff.

4. Look at the types of jobs required for the hotel and spa example then evaluate which method of setting pay scale would be most effective. Explain your reasoning.

5. You manage a day care facility that is part of a national chain. You've been told that salary increases are on hold for this year, largely due to a large drop in enrollment. However, you've been given a $3,000 budget to put toward an incentive program. Propose a program that would benefit both the employees and the company.

YOU TRY IT

Grading the System

Evaluate the compensation system in place in your organization or in a local company. Call the HR department to find out the following information:

- What type of philosophy is in use?
- What types of compensation are utilized?
- What method is used to set the pay scale?
- How is the plan communicated to employees?

Rate the system on a scale from 1 to 10, with 10 being the most effective.

Top Rewards

Using the internet or other resource, compare the total rewards plans of two different Fortune 500 companies. Choose the most attractive plan of the two and explain your choice.

Using Incentives Wisely

Nearly two-thirds of U.S. companies include some sort of incentive compensation in the pay packages offered to employees. Create an incentive plan for your organization; your plan can include raises, bonuses, profit-sharing, and commissions. Address the five guidelines from Section 8.5.4 of this chapter.

9

DESIGNING AND ADMINISTERING BENEFITS
Completing a Total Rewards Program

Starting Point

Go to www.wiley.com/college/messmer to assess your knowledge of the basics of benefits design and administration.
Determine where you need to concentrate your effort.

What You'll Learn in This Chapter

▲ The role of employee benefits
▲ Types of involuntary employee benefits
▲ Ways in which employees provide health and welfare benefits
▲ Examples of family-friendly voluntary benefits

After Studying This Chapter, You Will Be Able To

▲ Categorize voluntary and mandatory employee benefits
▲ Evaluate how a company adheres to benefits regulations
▲ Assess a company's ability to minimize healthcare costs
▲ Differentiate between several employee retirement benefit options

INTRODUCTION

Employee benefit programs are an integral part of a company's total compensation plan and represent a significant cost to employers. Of equal importance to compensation in the total rewards mix (see Chapter 8), employee benefit programs are varied and designed to meet specific employee needs. In today's market, there is an increased need for creative benefit programs that address the current workforce's family challenges and lifestyle goals. There are two basic types of benefit programs: those that are legally mandated and those that are voluntary. This chapter explores how HR professionals, working with senior management, can determine the mix of benefits that will attract and retain the type of employees needed by the organization to achieve its objectives.

9.1 Identifying the Role of Employee Benefits

Strictly speaking, a **benefit** is any form of indirect compensation that isn't part of an employee's basic pay (that is, direct compensation)—and that isn't tied directly to either the requirements of their jobs or their performance in those jobs.

Specific employee benefits today take a multitude of forms—everything from the basics that you find in every benefits package (Social Security, workers' compensation, and unemployment insurance) to highly specialized offerings ranging from multiple-option healthcare coverage, tuition reimbursement, and childcare and eldercare assistance at one end of the spectrum to in-house concierge services, health club memberships, and on-site auto repair services at the far end of the spectrum. Exactly which benefits you offer and how much of your payroll expense goes to pay for benefits are decisions that your company's financial health and business philosophy must determine. Your job in taking on the HR function is to make sure that both your company and its employees are getting the best deal.

THINKING OUTSIDE THE BENEFIT BOX

When most employees think about their benefit packages, they think of medical and dental insurance, vacation and sick leave, and the retirement plan, but employers provide many other benefits that employees often overlook. These include such things as the location of their facilities and the length of the daily commute for employees, "dress down" days, and salaries that are competitive with the industry and profession. These are all factors taken into consideration by candidates when considering whether or not to accept an offer. However, it's often up to an employer to make employees aware of the value of the benefits provided for them because they rarely consider these costs when they think about their total income.

> Decisions about these facets of the employment relationship in each company can either help or hurt the efforts of the organization to attract and retain employees.

9.1.1 Knowing the Types of Benefits

Though there are many forms of indirect compensation, the most common are known as employee health and welfare benefits. These benefits include various forms of insurance and retirement options that employers provide as part of a total rewards package (see Chapter 8). Some of the benefits employers provide are mandated by federal or state laws or regulations, and include such things as Social Security, unemployment insurance, and workers' compensation. All other benefits are provided voluntarily, which means that individual employers can select benefits that will attract and retain individuals who are most likely to have the skills they need to achieve their goals. Table 9-1 displays some of the more common benefits in each of these categories, along with some common benefits that don't fall into one of these categories. Note: These benefits are voluntary according to the federal Fair Labor Standards Act, but may be mandated by state laws; check with your state employment agency or your employment attorney to find out what is required for your organization.

9.1.2 Following Key Trends in Benefits Management

Managing the benefits side of the HR function today is a far cry from the way it was fifty or so years ago when the typical company benefits package was a one-size-fits-all healthcare and pension plan. You have a lot more to think about these days when you're administering benefits—more administrative details, more pressure to reconcile employee desires with the financial realities of your business, and more government regulation.

Much of this increased complexity is due to the changing face of the workplace. Today's diverse workforce has diverse needs, and this diversity extends to the benefits they want. Add to this a wide range of laws and healthcare and retirement plan options, and you quickly see how complicated it can be to create and implement effective benefits programs.

As challenging as all these factors seem at first glance, you have an opportunity to do a great deal of good for your employees, your company, and yourself. And, best of all, if you know what you're doing in building a competitive benefits package, you can strengthen your company's ability to attract and retain top talent.

Table 9-1: Types of Benefits

Category	Benefit	Mandated or Voluntary
Health care	COBRA benefit continuation	Mandated
	Dental insurance	Voluntary
	HIPAA portability rights	Mandated
	Medical insurance	Voluntary
	Mental health benefits	Voluntary
	Prescription drug coverage	Voluntary
	Vision care	Voluntary
Insurance	Life insurance	Voluntary
	Long-term disability insurance	Voluntary
	Prepaid legal insurance	Voluntary
	Short-term disability insurance	Voluntary
	Unemployment insurance	Mandated
	Workers' compensation	Mandated
Work-life balance	Adoption benefits	Voluntary
	Dependent care assistance	Voluntary
	Employee assistance plans	Voluntary
	Flextime	Voluntary
	Gym memberships	Voluntary
	Onsite child care facilities	Voluntary
	Telecommuting	Voluntary
Time off	Bereavement leave	Voluntary
	Family and Medical Leave Act	Mandated
	Paid holidays	Voluntary
	Paid rest breaks	Voluntary
	Paid sick leave	Voluntary
	Paid vacation leave	Voluntary
Retirement	401(k) plans	Voluntary
	Early retirement programs	Voluntary
	Individual Retirement Accounts (IRAs)	Voluntary
	Pension plans	Voluntary
	Social Security	Mandated
	Medicare	Mandated
Other benefits	Credit union membership	Voluntary
	Educational assistance	Voluntary
	Onsite fitness facilities	Voluntary

Much is going on today in the rapidly changing world of benefits administration. The following list provides you with a quick glimpse at four key trends:

▲ **Changing the definition of employee:** Demographic changes in the American workplace in the past twenty-five years have affected the number and nature of the offerings that you now find in the typical benefits package. Trends such as delayed retirement, second careers, domestic partners, single-parent households, and alternative work arrangements have drastically changed the profile of a typical employee and his expectations of a benefits program.

In response, most large companies offer flexible, or **cafeteria benefits**, which give employees a menu of choices instead of the traditional "one-size-fits all" approach. For example, a parent with young children may select dependent coverage as a benefit to cover day care needs. Once the children no longer require day care, the employee may select another benefit (such as 401(k) matching). Although this trend makes employees happier, the more choices you offer, the more complex your benefits plan becomes to administer.

▲ **Containing costs:** To offset the rising cost of employee benefits, more and more companies these days are asking employees to assume a larger portion of the overall benefits tab. For example, in the all-important realm of healthcare costs, the typical employee's contribution has risen considerably. To ease the sting of increased employee payments, progressive companies have introduced so-called **lifestyle benefits**—relatively inexpensive rewards or services, such as concierge services, that make life a little easier for employees.

▲ **Home-based employees:** As the telecommuter population increases, a new need has surfaced—benefits geared specifically for people who

FOR EXAMPLE

Banking and Balance

More companies are implementing programs designed to entice and retain valued employees who struggle with the balance between work and life. Bank of America is serving its employees with an innovative twist on a flexible work environment. The company opened a facility near its headquarters in Charlotte, N.C., which allows people who live in nearby communities to spend a day or two every week off-site, instead of commuting an hour or more each way into the city. Company representatives say they have seen increases in productivity among employees who use the option.

divide their work time between the office and home. The biggest challenge is how to structure a work-related injury- or illness-insurance program that accounts for the possibility that "on-the-job" injuries can now occur in an employee's home.

▲ **Regulations:** In recent years, Congress and state legislative bodies have taken a more active role than ever in regulating many basic benefits policies, especially health insurance and 401(k) retirement and pension plans. In large part, increasing government involvement is a response to the well-publicized financial misconduct within some companies that triggered the failure of their pension plans.

9.1.3 Getting a Grip on Administration

Benefits administration can get very complex. The good news is that five simple principles, if followed, can make the job of administering benefits in your company much simpler.

▲ **One size doesn't fit all:** You need to constantly evaluate which mix of benefits works best for your company and its broad spectrum of employees. For example, members of various age groups often have different preferences about benefits policies and workplace accommodations. The single most important thing that you can do to win employee support for your program is to involve them as much as possible in all aspects of the plan, particularly as you're deciding which options to offer.

▲ **Know your programs:** You and the people who work with you in benefits administration need to have a thorough knowledge of your benefits package and about the benefits field in general. Otherwise, you can't explain your offerings to employees, help employees sort out problems, or make the best benefits choices for your company.

▲ **Bring benefit education on board:** Education of benefit options should be one of the main priorities of your orientation/onboarding program. Take the time to develop an information package that spells out what you offer but that doesn't overload new employees with overly detailed information.

▲ **Spread the word:** Increase the effectiveness of your program by making sure that each employee is provided with the most up-to-date information about their benefits. Use email, standard mailings, and other means to notify employees of plan changes.

▲ **Monitor your program:** Don't make the mistake of waiting for resentment and dissatisfaction to build before you do something about aspects of your benefits package that aren't working. Stay attuned to employee attitudes.

▲ **Provide feedback and problem-resolution procedures:** Establish formal mechanisms to receive employee comments and complaints and set up a system to resolve problems. Many problems aren't really problems at all but misunderstandings that stem from miscommunication. Try to develop some means of tracking problems through various stages of resolution.

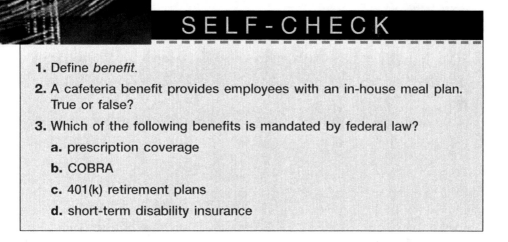

SELF-CHECK

1. Define *benefit*.
2. A cafeteria benefit provides employees with an in-house meal plan. True or false?
3. Which of the following benefits is mandated by federal law?
   a. prescription coverage
   b. COBRA
   c. 401(k) retirement plans
   d. short-term disability insurance

9.2 Administering Benefits Required by Law

Most employee benefits are voluntary: You're under no legal obligation to provide them. The notable exceptions to this rule are **Social Security** and **Medicare**, **workers' compensation**, the **Family Medical Leave Act**, and **unemployment insurance**. The following sections take a brief look at each program.

9.2.1 Social Security and Medicare

The first involuntary, or legally mandated, employee benefits were introduced as part of President Franklin Delano Roosevelt's New Deal programs to aid the millions of Americans who lost their jobs and were unable to find work during the Great Depression. In response to this economic crisis, when FDR was elected in 1932, he set about creating protections for American workers to provide a safety net during economic downturns.

▲ **Social Security:** A key piece of the legislation introduced by FDR that has had an enduring impact on employers was the Social Security Act of 1935 (SSA). The Social Security system was originally designed to provide basic retirement income for all workers who have contributed to the plan and to provide healthcare benefits to Americans who are age sixty-five or older or become disabled. You and your employees may be eligible to begin receiving payments as early as age sixty-two, but keep in mind that the benefit will be reduced permanently. On the other hand, if an individual delays in applying for this benefit past the age of eligibility, the benefit will increase. In 2003, the age of eligibility for full retirement began to increase gradually. People born between 1943 and 1954 must be sixty-six to quality for a complete retirement benefit. By the year 2025, the retirement age for full benefits will be sixty-seven.

▲ **Medicare:** A key part of Social Security is Medicare, a federal health insurance program for people sixty-five and over. In the early 1960s, Presidents John F. Kennedy and Lyndon B. Johnson committed themselves to raising the standard of living among poor and elderly Americans; the resulting Medicare program was created by the Social Security Amendments of 1965 and provided medical and hospital insurance benefits for the elderly. Beginning in 2006, the government passed laws reducing the cost of prescription drugs for those covered by Medicare.

Social Security and Medicare are financed by payroll taxes. Your employees typically surrender 7.65 percent of their gross take-home pay to fund both programs, and federal law obligates your company to match that amount. (Self-employed workers pay 15.3 percent.) The first 6.2 percent of the tax that goes to the Social Security fund is assessed only up to a specific income ceiling—$94,200 in 2006. Any income over that limit isn't subject to Social Security tax. No ceiling exists, at present, on the 1.45 percent Medicare tax. Keep in mind, however, that these rules are subject to change.

9.2.2 Unemployment Insurance

Unemployment insurance provides basic income for workers who become unemployed through no fault of their own. The individual states run the unemployment insurance program, which was established as part of the 1935 Social Security Act, under loose federal guidelines. Except in a handful of states (Alaska, Pennsylvania, and New Jersey) that expect employees to pay a small percentage of the cost, employers pay for their workers' unemployment insurance. The cost to employers is generally based on the company's experience rating—how frequently its former employees receive payments through the program. The more people you lay off, the greater your potential assessment becomes.

9.2.3 Family Medical Leave Act

In 1993, President Bill Clinton signed the Family Medical Leave Act (FMLA), which was created to assist employees in balancing the needs of their families with the demands of their jobs. In creating the FMLA, Congress intended that employees not have to choose between keeping their jobs and attending to seriously ill family members. FMLA provides three benefits for eligible employees of covered organizations:

1. 12 weeks of unpaid leave within a 12-month period.
2. Continuation of health benefits.
3. Reinstatement to the same position or an equivalent position at the end of the leave.

FMLA applies to all public agencies and schools, regardless of their size and to private employers with fifty or more employees working within a seventy-five-mile radius. However, consult your lawyer to determine if the details of these requirements apply to your organization and its employees.

FMLA presents covered employers with a list of circumstances under which FMLA leave must be provided if requested by an eligible employee:

▲ The birth of a child and caring for an infant. FMLA leave is available to both fathers and mothers; however, if both parents work for the same employer, the combined total of the leave may not exceed the twelve-week total. In addition, the leave must be completed within twelve months of the child's birth.

▲ Placement of an adopted or foster child with the employee. The same conditions that apply to the birth of a child apply here as well; in this case, the leave must be completed within twelve months of the child's placement.

▲ To provide care for the employee's spouse, son, daughter, or parent with a serious health condition. For purposes of FMLA leave, a spouse

FOR EXAMPLE

Caretakers and the FMLA

A veteran public school teacher in New Jersey was faced with having to care for his aging parents in Florida. Instead of relocating, however, the teacher received FMLA leave for eight weeks at the beginning of the spring semester. While he was away, his school district hired a substitute, but held his position for his return. In Florida, he was able to care for his mother and father; he also had time to inquire into the possibility of moving them both into an appropriate assisted living residence. He would have found it much more difficult to handle all of this without the FMLA time off.

must be recognized as such by the state in which the employee resides.

▲ When an employee is unable to perform the functions of the job due to a serious health condition. According to FMLA, a serious health condition is an illness, injury, impairment, or physical or mental condition that requires:

- Inpatient care or subsequent treatment related to inpatient care.
- Continuing treatment by a health care provider due to a period of incapacity of more than three consecutive calendar days.
- Incapacity due to pregnancy or prenatal care.
- Treatment for a serious, chronic health condition.

9.2.4 Workers' Compensation

Workers' compensation is an insurance program that provides protection for workers who suffer injuries or become ill on the job regardless of whether the employee or the employer was negligent. It pays medical bills, provides disability payments (income replacement) for permanent injuries, and pays out death benefits.

Depending on the state in which you work, your company contributes to a state fund, a private insurance fund, or a mixture of both. Some states permit private insurance, so if your company can demonstrate financial capability to state authorities, you may choose to be self-insured. Other states require you to contribute to one state-managed fund or permit a mixture of state and private insurance.

Some employers, especially those with large numbers of off-site workers or telecommuters, have integrated workers' compensation programs into health-insurance programs. As with other areas surrounding employees who work away from a specific office, thoroughly explore this option with an attorney.

9.2.5 Health Benefit Continuation

Prior to 1986, employees who were laid off or resigned from their jobs lost any health care benefits that were provided as part of those jobs. While no federal law requires employers to provide health benefits, organizations with twenty or more employees who provide health care benefits are required to continue the benefits for those who leave the company or for their dependents when certain qualifying events occur. The Consolidated Omnibus Budget Reconciliation Act (COBRA) was signed by President Ronald Reagan in 1986 and requires employers to continue health care coverage at the employee's expense.

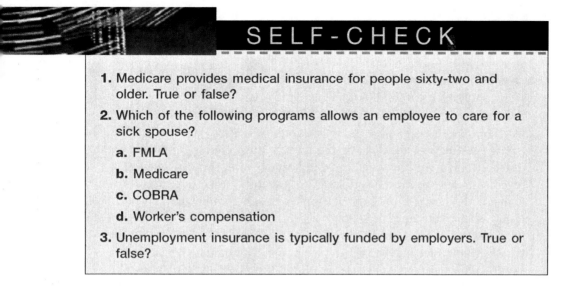

1. Medicare provides medical insurance for people sixty-two and older. True or false?

2. Which of the following programs allows an employee to care for a sick spouse?

   a. FMLA

   b. Medicare

   c. COBRA

   d. Worker's compensation

3. Unemployment insurance is typically funded by employers. True or false?

9.3 Administering Health and Welfare Benefits

Health and welfare benefits have come to be expected by most American workers. Of those benefits, health insurance is an organization's most expensive offering. Without a doubt, it's also the most difficult benefit to administer, not just because of its cost but also because of the many options available and the challenges companies face balancing two seemingly contradictory objectives: Keeping costs down while at the same time meeting employee needs.

9.3.1 Taking on Healthcare Plans

The number of individual healthcare plans available today is enough to fill a book—a book that, given the changing world of healthcare, would no doubt go out of date quite quickly. Following is a bit of information on the three most prevalent healthcare plan options. Bear in mind that these options (in fact, the entire structure of employer-provided healthcare) may change rapidly, given the pressure for companies to control healthcare costs:

▲ **Fee-for-service (indemnity plans):** Fee-for-service plans are insurance programs that reimburse members for defined benefits, regardless of which practitioner or hospital delivers the service. Under some fee-for-service arrangements, members pay the bills themselves and then submit their claims to the carrier for reimbursement. Under other plans, the physicians or hospitals assume the responsibility for filing and collecting on claims.

   Fee-for-service plans have two fundamental parts—the Base Plan and Major Medical. The **Base Plan** covers certain "defined" services, usually in connection with hospitalization—an appendectomy, for example, but not routine mole removal. **Major Medical**—an option—covers such services as routine doctors' visits and certain tests.

▲ **Health Maintenance Organizations (HMOs):** Health Maintenance Organizations (commonly known as HMOs) offer a wide range of medical services but limit your choices (both in medical practitioners and facilities) to those specialists or organizations that are part of the HMO network. Each person that the plan covers must choose a primary physician (sometimes known as the **gatekeeper**), who decides whether a member needs to seek specialty services within the network or services outside the network. As long as employees stay "within the network" (that is, they use only those facilities and medical practitioners who are part of the HMO network), the only additional cost to them if they undergo any procedure that the plan covers is a modest copayment. HMOs differ in their out-of-network policies. Some are highly restrictive. Others allow members to seek care outside the network but only with the approval of the gatekeeper; members who use approved services outside the network may also assume additional costs (up to a predefined deductible) for each out-of-network visit.

▲ **Preferred Provider Organizations (PPOs):** Preferred Provider Organizations (or PPOs) are similar to HMOs but with two key differences: Employees have a wider range of choices as to whom they can see if they experience a medical problem, and PPOs typically require no gatekeeper—members can go outside the network as long as they're willing to assume the costs, up to the agreed-on deductible. Also, the cost to employees for participating in a PPO is usually more than the cost to participate in a comparable HMO plan.

Weighing the Options

In recent years, many companies have altered the options they most favor. The traditional fee-for-service, or indemnity, plans are still available, but most companies today make it most advantageous for employees to elect HMOs and PPOs, which are also known as managed-care programs. HMOs and PPOs provide the same benefits as the traditional fee-for-service plans but set limits on which practitioners and which facilities that employees on the plan can use to receive maximum benefits.

When deciding which type of plan to carry for your employees, you need to take into account the following factors:

▲ **Extent of coverage:** The procedures that health-insurance plans cover can vary widely, but most plans—both indemnity and managed-care plans—offer the same basic coverage. This coverage includes emergency trips to the hospital, illness-related visits to doctors, most routine tests, most surgical procedures (but not cosmetic surgery), and hospitalization. What varies widely, however, are any "extras"—the extent to which coverage includes, for example, chiropractic care or home nursing, or whether it accommodates long-term needs such as hospitalization for mental illness.

▲ **Quality of care:** The quality of medical services that members of managed-care programs receive has become an issue today for an obvious reason: Employees covered by these plans are obliged to use only those physicians or facilities designated by the plan's administrators. Therefore, you must make sure that any managed-care program you choose has high standards and a quality reputation. In addition, check to see whether the National Committee for Quality Assurance (NCQA) certifies that program at http://hprc.ncqa.org/cvoResult.asp.

▲ **Cost:** Keep in mind that you get what you pay for, regardless of the particular option you choose. Insurers generally base their pricing on three factors: the number of people that the plan covers; the demographics of your workforce (average age, number of children, and so on); and the amount of the deductible and copayment for the plan. The higher the deductible and the more money members pay for each doctor's visit, the less expensive the premium.

▲ **Ease of administration:** A key factor in your choice of insurance carriers is the ease with which you can administer the program. The best plans, for example, offer an easy-to-use website and a 24-hour, 800 number that lets individuals swiftly modify benefit plans or levels. Some plans, on the other hand, curtail costs by shifting much of the administrative burden to you.

Minimizing Healthcare Costs

A few strategies that will help you save money without compromising the quality of the medical care received by your employees. Keep these guidelines in mind:

FOR EXAMPLE

Benefit vs. Cost

When a large clothing retailer added a less expensive HMO option to its existing PPO healthcare benefits, many employees jumped at the chance to save some money in their paychecks. Other employees, many of whom had doctors who did not participate in the HMO plan, decided to stick with the more expensive PPO, simply for the sake of convenience and security.

▲ **Affiliate with the largest group possible:** The larger the group of companies with which you affiliate, the more competitive the rates you're likely to pay. Most regional business associations and local chambers of commerce, for example, offer group plans for member companies.

▲ **Raise the deductible:** Increasing the deductible amount for which employees are responsible for covering on a typical indemnity plan can save you anywhere from ten percent to fifty percent on premiums, depending on the size of the deductible. However, in some states the deductible can't exceed $1,000.

▲ **Consider consumer-directed health plans (CDHPs).** CDHPs are a relatively new experiment in finding ways for companies to reduce healthcare costs. CDHPs usually consist of a high-deductible medical insurance plan coupled with **Health Savings Accounts (HSAs)**. HSAs were created by the Medicare bill signed by President Bush in 2003 and are designed to help individuals save for future qualified medical and retiree health expenses on a tax-free basis.

▲ **Manage drug benefits:** Many companies have eliminated copay arrangements for prescription drugs, opting instead for plans that require coinsurance and/or deductibles on a cost-sharing basis. One cost-cutting aspect is to provide preferred coverage for generic drugs. Some plans offer reduced costs to participants who elect home delivery by mail for long-term prescription needs.

▲ **Consider working with a benefits consultant:** Bringing in an outside benefits expert to analyze your company's healthcare needs and recommend the best approach to health insurance may cost you money in the short run. But the recommendations can more than offset the initial expense.

9.3.2 Examining Employee Welfare Benefits

Benefits other than health insurance are a common part of an organization's indirect compensation. However, because these benefits are so common, businesses seeking to use them as recruiting and retention tools must find some way to differentiate their plans from those of their competitors. To increase the attractiveness of their benefit packages, companies may want to reduce or eliminate the employee contribution toward premiums for themselves or for their families.

Dental Insurance

Dental insurance has become an increasingly popular employee benefit in recent years. According to the California Dental Association, more than forty-eight percent of all Americans—113 million people—currently have dental insurance.

That's nearly ten times as many as had it in 1970. Companies sometimes offer dental care as part of a health-insurance package and sometimes as a separate policy or an add-on. Costs and deductibles vary widely by region and by extent of coverage.

Vision Care

Most benefit plans usually restrict vision coverage to routine eye exams, and most plans impose a ceiling on how much is covered toward the purchase of eyeglasses. These plans, moreover, don't cover serious eye diseases and other conditions that, in most cases, the employee's regular health-insurance policy covers.

Prescription Coverage

Even though most medical plans include some form of coverage for prescription drugs, these plans are also offered separately. The cost of the plans is managed by controlling the amount of the required copayment and requiring the use of generic drugs instead of named brands.

Insurance Programs

▲ **Life insurance:** Many insurance companies bundle basic life insurance with medical or dental insurance for a very low rate and offer supplemental insurance for employees willing to pay an additional premium for coverage.

▲ **Accidental Death and Dismemberment Insurance (AD&D) insurance:** AD&D insurance can provide insurance for employees and their dependents in the event of an accident (not an illness) that results in the death of the covered person or the loss of a bodily function.

▲ **Short- and long-term disability insurance:** Disability insurance protects employees from income loss due to disability caused by illness or accident. Disability protection generally begins with sick leave provided by employers. When employees exhaust their sick leave, they may become eligible for short-term disability insurance, which can be in effect for anywhere between three and six months. Employees who are still disabled when short-term disability ends become eligible for long-term disability coverage, which can last for anywhere from two years until age sixty-five.

▲ **Flexible Spending Accounts (FSAs):** FSAs allow employees to set aside pretax funds for medical expenses they plan to incur during the calendar year. Employees should be conservative when projecting the amounts they plan to spend during the year because any funds left in the FSA will be forfeited. A downside for employers is that employees may be reimbursed for expenses before the funds have been withdrawn from their paychecks;

in fact, if they leave the company before the funds have been withheld, they are not required to reimburse the company for those expenses. A similar **dependent care account** can be used by employees to set aside a maximum of $5,000 to be used to care for dependent children or elders.

SELF-CHECK

1. Define *gatekeeper*.
2. A Preferred Provider Organization typically costs less for employees than an HMO. True or false?
3. A health savings account allows individuals to set aside money to pay for medical expenses on a tax-free basis. True or false?

9.4 Administering Other Benefits

In addition to health insurance, organizations frequently offer a number of other benefits to employees. Here's a rundown of the most common benefits and what you should know about them.

9.4.1 Planning for Retirement

Next to health insurance, perhaps the most important voluntary benefits are related to employee retirement. Deferred compensation refers to tax-deferred retirement plans, such as individual retirement accounts (IRAs), 401(k) programs, or traditional employer pension plans. While there are no federal laws requiring employers to provide any of them, there are some federal laws that regulate the pensions or benefits included in a total rewards package (see "Retirement Regulation"). The more common of the voluntary retirement benefits are discussed in the following sections.

Defined Benefit Plans

A **defined benefit plan** is an employer-sponsored pension or retirement plan that promises to pay a specified amount (based on a predetermined formula) to each person who retires after a set number of years of service.

Pension: A sum of money paid regularly as a retirement benefit.

With a defined benefit plan, investment risk and portfolio management are entirely under the control of the company. There are also restrictions on when and how an employee can withdraw these funds without penalties.

A defined benefit plan is based on a formula that looks at two factors: salary and length of service with the company. In most traditional defined benefit plans, the retirement benefit is based on the salary earned during the last five to ten years of earnings, but it may also be based on career average earnings, a flat dollar amount for each year of service, or a unit benefit plan in which the benefit payment is based on a percentage of earnings multiplied by the years of service. In these plans, the company is committed to pay a specified benefit amount when an employee retires.

Defined Contribution Plans

A **defined contribution plan** is a retirement plan wherein a certain amount or percentage of money is set aside each year for the benefit of the employee. There are restrictions as to when and how you can withdraw these funds without penalties. In these plans, the amount of the contribution is fixed, but the amount of the benefit available upon retirement can vary based on the type of investments that are made and the returns earned on them. There are several types of defined contribution plans:

▲ **Profit sharing plans:** Profit-sharing plans allow employers to contribute deferred compensation based on a percentage of company earnings each year. The percentage of the contribution may vary from year to year, and the company may elect to make no contributions in some years. Because the contributions may vary from year to year, profit sharing plans work well for companies with erratic profit levels.

▲ **Money purchase plans:** A money purchase plan uses a fixed percentage of employee earnings to defer compensation. This type of plan works well for organizations with relatively stable earnings because the percentage is fixed and, once established, contributions must be made every year.

▲ **Target benefit plans:** Generally speaking, a target benefit plan is a cross between a money purchase plan and a defined benefit plan. Like a defined benefit plan, contributions are based on projected retirement benefits. However, the benefits provided to participants at retirement are based on the performance of the investments, and are therefore not guaranteed.

▲ **401(k) plans:** A common type of deferred compensation is the 401(k) plan, established by the Revenue Act of 1978. A 401(k) plan allows for contributions from both employees and employers. Employees may defer a part of their pay before taxes up to certain limits; employers may make contributions as well. Plans similar to the 401(k) are available for nonprofit workers (403(b) plans) and for public employees (457 plans). Employees are ultimately responsible for ensuring that the funds are properly managed until they are ready to retire.

RETIREMENT REGULATION

The Employee Retirement Income Security Act of 1974 (ERISA) is the law that protects the retirement assets of Americans, by implementing rules that qualified plans must follow to ensure that plan managers do not misuse plan assets. ERISA was amended in 1986 by the Consolidated Omnibus Budget Reconciliation Act (COBRA) and the Health Insurance Portability and Accountability Act (HIPAA) in 1996.

9.4.2 Providing Family Assistance

The much documented increase in the number of two-income families, single working mothers, **domestic partner** arrangements, and employees who care for both children and their aging parents has led to an accelerating demand for childcare and eldercare assistance from employers. And you can expect the need to intensify in the years ahead. The following list describes some ways in which companies are providing this benefit:

▲ **On-site care:** On-site child care is a great convenience to the working parent. But only a handful of companies provide a day-care facility at the work location itself. The big problem is cost—liability insurance, in particular.

▲ **Contracted day-care for children and elders:** This option is much more feasible for many employers but is still considered progressive. The company contracts with one or more outside providers to provide services for both the children and parents of employees. However, by selecting a particular provider, your company is vouching for that provider's quality of care and services.

▲ **Vouchers:** Vouchers are simply subsidies that you pay to employees to cover all or part of the cost of outside child care. Voucher systems are the simplest form of child-care assistance to administer.

▲ **Dependent Care Reimbursement Accounts:** These accounts enable an employee to use pretax dollars to pay for dependent care.

IMPLEMENTING FAMILY-FRIENDLY POLICIES

What follows is a partial list of progressive benefit categories that are generally classified as family-friendly:

▲ Adoption assistance.
▲ After-school and holiday care.

▲ Child-care centers and family day care (on- or off-site).

▲ Domestic partner coverage.

▲ Eldercare.

▲ Flexible benefit plans (includes dependent-care assistance plans).

▲ Flexible scheduling options (compressed work week, part-time, job-sharing).

▲ Housing/relocation assistance.

▲ Lactation programs.

▲ Leave (parental, personal, family).

▲ Long-term care.

▲ Paid time of f (sick leave, paid leave banks, leave donation programs).

▲ Sick-child care.

▲ Telecommuting.

9.4.3 Managing Time Off

Although many employees take the practice for granted, paying employees for days they don't work—whether for holidays, vacation, sick days, or personal days—is an important benefit. Each company has its own philosophy, but the following list offers general observations about paid days off:

▲ Most companies provide employees with a fixed number of paid holidays a year, such as New Year's Day, Independence Day, Thanksgiving Day, Christmas Day, and so on.

▲ According to a 2005 study of international vacation policies conducted by the Economic Policy Institute, the typical American employee is awarded 8.9 days of vacation time after one year on the job. This figure rises throughout the employee's tenure: eleven days are granted after three years of service, 13.6 after five, and up to 19.2 after twenty-five years with a single company.

▲ Vacation accrual policies differ widely from one company to the next. Some companies enable their employees to bank vacation time, and others require employees to take all vacation during the year in which they earn it.

▲ Some companies combine sick time, personal time, and vacation time into a single paid time-off program. Figure 9-1 shows a memorandum outlining a company's holiday schedule.

Figure 9-1

MEMORANDUM

TO: All U.S. Staff

FROM: Mike Williams

DATE: October 5, 2007

SUBJECT: ***2008 HOLIDAY SCHEDULE***

We are pleased to announce the holiday schedule for 2008. During 2008, the Company will observe the eleven holidays listed below. In addition, we will have two floating holidays to provide you with some flexibility to meet your diverse individual preferences. The Company-observed holidays are:

New Year's Eve	*Monday, December 31*
New Year's Day	*Tuesday, January 1*
Martin Luther King, Jr. Day	*Monday, January 21*
President's Day	*Monday, February 18*
Memorial Day	*Monday, May 26*
Independence Day	*Friday, July 4*
Labor Day	*Monday, September 1*
Thanksgiving Day	*Thursday, November 27*
Friday after Thanksgiving	*Friday, November 28*
Christmas Eve	*Wednesday, December 24*
Christmas Day	*Thursday, December 25*

FLOATING HOLIDAYS:

If you are employed with Company XYZ prior to January 1, 2007, you are eligible for two floating holidays during 2007. You must schedule these in advance with your supervisor. If you are hired during 2007, you become eligible for floating holidays after completing your New Employee Orientation Period. Thereafter, you become eligible for floating holidays in accordance with this schedule:

DATE OF EMPLOYMENT	*FLOATING HOLIDAY ELIGIBILITY (DAYS)*
January 1 - March 31	*2*
April 1 - September 30	*1*
October 1 - December 31	*0*

You may use these days to observe holidays that are not observed by the Company, to extend your vacation, as additional personal time or for other reasons acceptable to your supervisor.

You must schedule this time off with, and receive advance approval from your supervisor.

If you work part-time, you are eligible for Company-observed holidays only if you are scheduled for work on the day the holiday is observed, and only for the number of hours you would have worked. Employees who are scheduled to work 35 hours or more bi-weekly are eligible for floating holidays.

A sample holiday schedule.

Sick Days

Formal sick-leave policies generally limit how many sick days the company is willing to pay for (anywhere from six to twelve days a year). In addition, companies usually impose a limit on the number of sick days that employees can take in succession (after which employees may be entitled to nonpaid leave of absences). Most companies have short-term and long-term disability plans to supplement sick days (see Section 9.3.2).

Sometimes companies offer a reward for employees who don't use their allotment of sick-days—for example, a cash payment for a percentage (usually half) of an employee's unused sick leave at year-end or if he leaves the company.

Leaves of Absence

A **leave of absence** is an arrangement whereby employees take an extended period of time off (usually without pay) but still maintain their employment status. In other words, they resume their normal duties when the leave is over. Employees either request or are granted leaves of absence for a variety of reasons: maternity, illness, education, travel, military obligations, and so on.

With certain key exceptions (military obligations and situations covered by the Family and Medical Leave Act, for example), the specific policies you adopt regarding leaves of absence aren't subject to federal and local law. (See Section 9.2.3 for more on the Family Medical Leave Act.)

Various states also have additional pregnancy leave requirements. Under FMLA regulations, you must maintain the employee's health coverage under any group health plan for the duration of the unpaid leave, and you must restore the employee to the same or equivalent job when she returns. The law also requires you to post notices advising workers of their rights under the law.

GUIDELINES FOR DOMESTIC PARTNERS

Extending benefits to domestic partners (either opposite-sex or same-sex nonmarried partners) has become a rapidly accepted practice at thousands of companies across the United States. This new benefit speaks powerfully to the ways corporations have become aware of the changing lifestyle arrangements of many of their employees. Though no official, nationally recognized set of requirements determine eligibility for this benefit, here are a few to keep in mind should you decide to offer it:

▲ Both partners occupy common residence, as proven by lease or title deed, for at least six consecutive months.

▲ Both partners are at least eighteen years of age and not related by blood.

▲ Joint bank account, joint credit cards, or other evidence of shared financial responsibility exists.

▲ They're registered as partners in a state or locality that permits registration of domestic partner relationships.

9.4.4 Setting Up an Employee Assistance Program

Employee Assistance Programs (EAPs) originated in the early 1970s as a mechanism for helping employees deal with certain types of personal problems (alcohol abuse, for example) that had on-the-job implications. EAPs addressed employee well-being in a variety of areas that previously hadn't been covered by benefit programs. Today, EAPs are usually presented as a benefit rather than included in work environment programs. The following are some areas in which EAP providers can assist employees:

▲ Stress management and conflict resolution.

▲ Social, psychological, and family counseling.

▲ Pre-retirement planning.

▲ Termination and career transition services (sometimes called *outplacement*).

▲ Alcohol and substance abuse.

▲ Mental-health evaluation and referral.

▲ Gambling addiction and other compulsive behaviors.

▲ Marriage counseling.

▲ Financial issues and credit counseling.

Many large companies operate their own in-house EAPs, staffed with psychologists, social workers, counselors, and support staff. Smaller companies that have EAPs generally rely on outside sources, such as EAP providers. These providers range from fully staffed organizations to small groups of individuals who have arrangements with outside firms. You can obtain a list of EAP providers in your region from the Employee Assistance Professionals Association (www .eapassn.org).

FOR EXAMPLE

Assistance Pays Off

Although organizations facing tight budgets may be tempted to cut employee assistance programs, there's growing evidence that these programs play an important role in preventing workplace turmoil, including violence and injury. A U.S. Department of Justice study found that, as a result of workplace violence, more than 500,000 employees miss 1,800,000 days of work annually, resulting in more than $55,000,000 in lost wages, not including days covered by sick and annual leave.

If you offer an EAP, remember that confidentiality is essential for legal and practical reasons. Employees must have confidence that they can talk privately to a counselor without repercussions (information reported back to a supervisor, for example).

SELF-CHECK

1. Define *pension*.
2. List three types of family-friendly employee benefits.
3. An Employee Assistance Program enables an employee to use pretax dollars to pay for dependent care. True or false?

SUMMARY

In today's competitive market, an organization's benefits package should be used to attract and retain valuable employees. More and more employees are demanding benefits that address certain family challenges and lifestyle goals. Making decisions about the benefits package that is most appropriate for a particular organization's workforce requires consideration of many factors: demographics, industry standards, local area practices, the financial situation of the company, and the organizational culture among them. Employers are required by law to include benefits such as unemployment insurance, Medicare, Social Security, and workers compensation. In addition to those benefits that are mandated by law, employers can offer many other voluntary benefits as part of an attractive total compensation package: flextime, telecommuting, 401(k) plans, onsite child care, and paid sick days among them. Health insurance, certainly an organization's most costly offering, is also highly sought after by employees; without such coverage, many Americans face serious financial hardship. The next most valued voluntary benefits are in the area of retirement planning; with traditional pensions going by the wayside, other retirement options such as profit sharing plans and 401(k)s should be considered. Finding the right mix—healthcare, retirement, and otherwise—can significantly affect an organization's ability to attract and retain employees. In fact, many large companies now offer cafeteria benefits, which give employees a number of choices; the downside of this, of course, is that employees have more to manage with each additional choice offered. Effective communication, with a system for employee feedback, is a critical part of HR's role in benefits administration.

KEY TERMS

Base Plan	Health insurance that covers certain services, usually in connection with hospitalization.
Benefit	Any form of indirect compensation that isn't part of an employee's basic pay or directly connected to job performance.
Cafeteria benefits	Flexible benefits that give employees a menu of choices.
Defined benefit plan	An employer-sponsored retirement plan that promises to pay a specified amount to each person who retires after a set number of years of service.
Defined contribution plan	A retirement plan wherein a certain amount or percentage of money is set aside each year for the benefit of the employee.
Dependent care account	Employees can set aside a maximum of $5,000 to be used to care for dependent children or elders.
Domestic partners	Opposite-sex or same-sex nonmarried partners.
Employee Assistance Programs (EAPs)	A mechanism for helping employees deal with certain personal problems (such as alcohol abuse).
Family Medical Leave Act	Created to help employees balance the needs of their families with the demands of their jobs.
Flexible Spending Accounts (FSAs)	Accounts that allow employees to set aside pretax funds for medical expenses they plan to incur during the calendar year.
Gatekeeper	A primary physician who decides whether a member needs to seek specialty services within the network or services outside the network.
Health Maintenance Organizations (HMOs)	Healthcare option that offers a wide range of medical services but limit choices to those specialists or organizations that are part of the network (also known as HMOs).
Health Savings Accounts (HSAs)	Designed to help individuals save for future qualified medical and retiree health expenses on a tax-free basis.
Indemnity plans	Insurance programs (also known as fee-for-service plans) that reimburse members for defined benefits.

Leave of absence   An arrangement giving employees extended time off (usually without pay); employee still maintains employment status.

Lifestyle benefits   Relatively inexpensive rewards or services that make life a little easier for employees.

Major Medical   Healthcare option that covers such services as routine doctors' visits and certain tests.

Medicare   A federal health insurance program for people sixty-five and over.

Pension   A sum of money paid regularly as a retirement benefit.

Preferred Provider Organizations (PPOs)   Healthcare that gives employees a range of choices about doctors (also known as PPOs).

Social Security   A system to provide basic retirement income for workers who have contributed to the plan.

Unemployment insurance   Provides basic income for workers who become unemployed through no fault of their own.

Workers' compensation   Insurance that provides protection for workers who suffer injuries or become ill on the job.

ASSESS YOUR UNDERSTANDING

Go to www.wiley.com/college/messmer to assess your knowledge of benefits design and administration.
Measure your learning by comparing pre-test and post-test results.

Summary Questions

1. Social Security is an involuntary employee benefit. True or false?
2. Perks or services that appeal to individual employees are called
   (a) indemnity plans.
   (b) cafeteria benefits.
   (c) voluntary benefits.
   (d) lifestyle benefits.
3. The federal government mandates medical insurance for all full-time employees. True or false?
4. How are Social Security and Medicare funded?
   (a) employees
   (b) employers
   (c) both employees and employers
   (d) federal subsidies
5. Which of the following benefits is not federally mandated?
   (a) life insurance
   (b) health care continuation
   (c) unemployment insurance
   (d) worker's compensation
6. A worker's compensation benefit is contingent upon a judgment of employer negligence. True or false?
7. Under which type of health insurance plan are employees responsible for paying for and submitting bills to a carrier?
   (a) Health Maintenance Organization
   (b) Preferred Provider Organization
   (c) Indemnity Plan
   (d) Major Medical
8. Explain one way that employees can save money on prescription costs.
9. Which type of insurance covers an employee's income loss between the period covered by sick leave and the period covered by long-term disability?

10. Which retirement plan is a combination of two other types of retirement planning?

    (a) profit sharing plan

    (b) money purchase plan

    (c) target benefit plan

    (d) pension plan

11. With a 401(k) plan, an employer is responsible for the risk management of retirement funds. True or false?

12. Which benefit is designed to help employees with family counseling and conflict resolution?

    (a) Leave of absence

    (b) Employee Assistance Program

    (c) Onboarding

    (d) Target benefit plans

Applying This Chapter

1. If you were designing a benefits plan for an alternative health care clinic, and you only had financial support for ten programs (both mandated and voluntary), which would you choose?

2. One of your restaurant employees has just announced that she's having a baby in six months. Briefly explain how the Family Medical Leave Act would apply to her and her husband, who is also an employee of the restaurant.

3. As the owner of a day care facility, you are faced with the choice of cutting staff or making cost-saving changes to your health benefits. Come up with three ways of cutting costs without having to lay off employees.

4. Although your company has only been in business for two years, in order to compete with other website design firms for the area's top talent, you need to add some sort of retirement benefit to your compensation package. Which type of plan would you choose and why?

YOU TRY IT

Grading the System

Evaluate the benefits in place in your company, organization, or school, then conduct a small survey of employee satisfaction about the benefits.

- Is the organization meeting all of its legal requirements in relation to employee benefits?
- On a scale of 1 to 10, how do the benefits rate according to the employees?
- Which, if any, area would be the top priority for change?

Side by Side

Compare the benefits plans of two companies in the same industry or two similar schools.

- In what ways are the plans similar?
- In what ways are the plans different?
- From the standpoint of a potential employee, which plan is most appealing and why?

Progressive Planning

Using the Internet or other resources research a company that is known for its work/life benefits; that is, a company that utilizes a progressive and flexible approach to voluntary employee benefits. At what point in the company's history did this changeover begin and why?

10

DEVELOPING EMPLOYEE RELATIONS
Promoting High Performance and Job Satisfaction

Starting Point

Go to www.wiley.com/college/messmer to assess your knowledge of the basics of employee relations.
Determine where you need to concentrate your effort.

What You'll Learn in This Chapter

▲ Ways in which employee relations factor into an organizational strategic plan
▲ Characteristics of employee-friendly workplaces
▲ Types of alternative work arrangements
▲ The role of human resources in encouraging employee performance
▲ The importance of employee feedback

After Studying This Chapter, You Will Be Able To

▲ Distinguish between methods of top-down and bottom-up communication
▲ Analyze a company's commitment to employee satisfaction
▲ Evaluate the effectiveness of alternative work arrangements for given situations
▲ Propose ways in which employee recognition programs would benefit an organization
▲ Choose the most effective technique for eliciting employee feedback

INTRODUCTION

When people think about human resources, what usually comes to mind are activities related to employee relations: the work environment and employee involvement, among others. In today's workplace, in order to have success, employee relations must be a part of an organization's strategic plan. It is more important than ever that this strategy is focused on creating a people-oriented workplace, with such features as alternative work arrangements. This chapter explores the role played by HRM in creating an environment that encourages a high level of performance and increases job satisfaction—a winning situation for both employee and employer.

10.1 Building Employee Relations into a Strategic Plan

Employee relations can be defined as the policies and practices concerned with the management and regulation of relationships between an organization, individual staff members, and groups of staff within a working environment.

Let's look at the connection between employee relations programs and the achievement of organizational goals. From an employer's point of view, employees are hired to produce the goods or services that are needed to satisfy customers and achieve business goals. To the extent that the work environment furthers this goal, employee relations programs are beneficial to organizations because the way an employer treats its employees can directly affect whether or not they are as productive as possible. Although it can be difficult to tie individual employee relations activities to specific organization goals, these activities are an essential element of an HRM program. From a strategic point of view, a company should consider several aspects as it develops an employee relations program.

▲ **Organizational culture:** An **organizational culture** establishes standards of behavior, many of which are unwritten, for all employees. The tone for the culture begins with senior organization leaders, heavily influenced by the CEO and other members of the executive team. How the organization's leaders treat employees—with dignity and respect, as cogs in a production wheel, or somewhere between—is generally emulated by managers at lower levels in the organization and, in turn, affects the way individual employees do their jobs.

▲ **Management style and philosophy:** Senior managers also influence an organization's culture through their leadership and management styles. Some managers lead by building consensus among employees, encouraging them to take risks and be creative in doing their jobs. Other managers use a more directive approach and expect employees to do what they are told without questioning the reasons.

▲ **Employee involvement:** The level of employee involvement in an organization is often related to the management style and philosophy of its

---

FOR EXAMPLE

Trickle Down Culture

The CEOs of many companies are workaholics who spend sixteen hours every day at their jobs (think Robert Nardelli, the former CEO of Home Depot). Typically, the executives who report to them will do the same in order to impress their bosses. Managers who want to impress those executives will also put in sixteen-hour days, and, as this work ethic trickles down through the organization, front-line employees will do so as well. To be successful in this culture, employees at all levels spend at least as much time at work as their managers do. On the other hand, CEOs who maintain a balance between their work lives and outside activities create an atmosphere that encourages other employees to do the same.

---

leaders. When organizations encourage a high level of employee involvement, employees have a sense of control over their daily activities. The more involved employees are in decisions that affect them, the greater is the level of "buy-in" they have for implementing those decisions, and this involvement usually results in a higher level of productivity.

10.1.1 Building a Communication Plan

It almost goes without saying that communicating with employees is an integral part of all human resource management functions, and it is one of the key elements of an effective employee relations program. Just as communicating with customers, owners, and suppliers is crucial, keeping employees informed about business needs and developments is equally important for organizational success.

An employee communication program can do the following:

▲ Motivate employees and build their enthusiasm for their work.
▲ Allow employees to give input to leaders developing operating plans.
▲ Provide a means for clearing up misinformation.

One of the most important considerations in developing a communication process is to allow opportunities for two-way communication, so that information flows both from the top down and from the bottom up. All organizations allow information to be disseminated from the top (management) down (employees). It is equally important to provide a means for information to flow from employees to management, or from the bottom up. This two-way flow of information is important to ensure that organization leaders are fully aware of activity within the organization; it's also important to ensure that employees have an avenue to report problems that occur, such as sexual harassment or other breaches of company policy.

▲ **Top-down communication:** The channel of communication in which information flows from the organization to employees. Examples include all-hands (town hall) meetings, team briefings, newsletters, emails, bulletin boards, and intranets.

▲ **Bottom-up communication:** The communication channel in which information flows from employees up through the organization; examples such as employee surveys and exit interviews are discussed in Section 10.5.

▲ **Lateral communication:** Communication that takes place between employees in different departments within the organization. Encouraging employees to share information with each other can reduce duplicated efforts and build camaraderie. One way to develop lateral communication is through the formation of cross-functional project teams.

SEEING A SHIFT

Historically, organizational communication has moved from top to bottom, originating with the president or CEO and ending with those on the front lines. Today, power is becoming more decentralized as the structure of organizations has changed; in the process, organizations are creating teams and enabling more lateral and bottom-up communication in the workplace.

Information sharing takes many forms, from frequent email and website updates to planned departmental meetings to impromptu discussions and, as appropriate, printed literature, DVDs, and special events that involve the entire company. And good communication addresses the widest possible set of corporate topics. Short-term objectives, long-term strategies, data on new products and services, research on competitors, updates on employee benefits—all are fair game.

The best way to maintain a steady flow of information is to impress upon managers the importance of creating an overall atmosphere that encourages employees to become involved and to openly communicate their concerns. As the best companies demonstrate, communication is a two-way street.

SELF-CHECK

1. Explain the role of employee relations programs.
2. Define *organizational culture.*
3. Employee involvement is critical to the success of an employee relations program. True or false?
4. List the three types of organizational communication.

10.2 Creating a People-Oriented Workplace

The cornerstone of a great place to work is trust built on open, engaged relationships between management and employees. Only from that foundation can employees feel the profound sense of engagement that marks a great company. The following sections provide more information on how that spirit plays out.

10.2.1 Promoting Job Satisfaction

Job satisfaction, or how content an individual is with his or her job, is an important consideration in an employee relations program. Job satisfaction implies doing a job one enjoys, doing it well, and being rewarded for one's efforts. The factors that affect job satisfaction vary from one worker to another and from day to day, but include the following:

▲ The nature of the work (the tasks involved, and the interest and challenge the job generates).
▲ The level of compensation.
▲ The perceived fairness of the promotion system within a company.
▲ The quality of the working conditions.
▲ Management style.
▲ Social relationships in the workplace.

Along with contributing to a general sense of personal wellbeing, job satisfaction is perceived to be linked to a positive work attitude and increased productivity.

10.2.2 Treating Employees as Assets

Companies known for their "people-friendly" HR policies have adopted the notion that employees are a cherished asset—and need to be treated accordingly. The steps that organizations actually take to integrate this value into their day-to-day business practices vary from one company to the next. Of course, the existence of this value doesn't mean that human concerns always take precedence over fundamental principles. It simply means that the welfare of employees is routinely taken into consideration when companies are making bottom-line decisions.

At minimum, a business must follow operational and physical standards if it expects employees to be productive, loyal, and satisfied. The Occupational Safety and Health Administration (OSHA) establishes protective workplace standards and enforces those standards; Chapter 13 covers OSHA in more detail.

10.2.3 Committing to Job Security

Though even the most employee-friendly businesses in today's marketplace can't guarantee lifetime employment, companies that place a high value on the personal well-being of their people tend to view massive layoffs as a last resort, not a reflex response to a business downturn. Layoffs may end up being inevitable, but the takeaway message from you to senior managers should be as follows: Staffing is a long-term process, so make sure that a short-term crisis doesn't derail your bigger objective of building a successful company. As part of this emphasis on job security, employers should create an atmosphere where employees feel comfortable sharing their ideas, thoughts, and feelings without fear of retribution (see Section 10.4.1).

10.2.4 Providing People-Friendly Facilities

Virtually all businesses today are obligated by state and federal law to provide a safe working environment. Employee-friendly companies, though, go above and beyond, creating facilities and introducing policies that far exceed legal requirements. A 2005 article in Workforce Management magazine praises Abbott Laboratories' headquarters and its $10 million state-of-the-art childcare center that more than 400 preschool children attend daily. According to The Wall Street Journal, a major reason why Analytical Graphics, a Pennsylvania-based software company, topped the "Best Small and Medium Companies to Work For" list in 2005 was its on-site laundry, car maintenance, and haircut services.

Other more modest but progressive investments have included private lactation areas for breast-feeding mothers; on-site automatic teller machines; fitness centers; and employee cafeterias with healthy menus, ultra-low prices, and after-hours take-out service. Every step your company takes to make life easier for its employees, no matter how large or small, sends a big message to employees: You care.

FOR EXAMPLE

Friendliest Company: Google

What do you have to do as a company to become known in today's highly competitive market as employee-friendly? That's the basic question asked by the Great Place To Work Institute, a research and management firm that each year identifies the "100 Best Companies To Work For," a study published in Fortune magazine. Google, ranked #1 in 2007, sets some high and innovative standards. As employees strive to achieve the company's mission "to organize the world's information and make it universally accessible and useful," they have access to free meals, a climbing wall and swimming pool, and free doctors onsite. No wonder Google receives 1,300 résumés a day.

10.2.5 Being Sensitive to Work-Life Balance Issues

A company's ability to attract and retain employees with the expertise it requires relates increasingly to the "human" side of the day-to-day working experience—the general atmosphere that prevails in the workplace. This includes, in particular, the extent to which company practices help people balance the pressures they face at work with the pressures they have to deal with at home.

Benefits packages in employee-friendly companies often feature policies to help staff better balance work and personal priorities. These policies may include anything from allowances for childcare and eldercare to a sensitivity to simpler, occasional needs (see Chapter 9). Workers in employee-friendly companies can count on the support of their employers whenever a medical emergency occurs, for example, or, on a happier note, some special event takes place at their child's school.

HEALTH BENEFITS OF EMPLOYEE RELATIONS

Conducting seminars, distributing literature, and offering information on topics such as stress, nutrition, sleep, and other health-related subjects can go a long way toward encouraging employees to stay healthy—and, in turn, decreasing healthcare costs. Some companies go further, building on-site facilities that offer exercise equipment or offering discounts on memberships at local health clubs. HR can nurture a corporate culture where employees are urged to take good care of themselves, for example, by being on the lookout for employees who work themselves to the brink of exhaustion and end up getting sick.

10.2.6 Offering Employee Autonomy

The one thing you almost never find these days in companies known for their employee-friendly policies is the traditional "command-and-control" management style, with its highly structured hierarchy and military-like "chain of command." **Employee empowerment** in employee-friendly companies is more than simply a catch phrase; it's one of the key values that drives day-to-day company operations (see Section 10.4.1). The rationale behind true employee empowerment is that most people work harder and do a better job when they're accountable for their own decisions and actions, as opposed to simply "following orders."

BY THE NUMBERS: WORK-LIFE BALANCE

Here's a look at some of the statistics driving the need for programs that support employees' efforts to balance work and personal priorities:

▲ Percentage of couples where both members are in the workforce: seventy-eight percent (2002), up from sixty-six percent in 1977.

▲ Percentage of American children living in single-parent households in 2004, according to The Annie E. Casey Foundation: thirty-one.

▲ Percentage of large U.S. employers (1,000 or more employees) that provide on- or near-site childcare, according to Families and Work Institute: seventeen.

▲ Percentage of women with children under eighteen who currently work, according to the U.S. Department of Labor (2004): 70.7.

▲ Percentage of Americans under the age of sixty who expect to be responsible for the care of a relative within ten years, according to a 2004 study conducted by the National Partnership for Women and Families: more than sixty percent.

SELF-CHECK

1. Give three examples of employee-friendly policies.
2. On-site childcare centers increase employee satisfaction and loyalty. True or false?
3. Employee autonomy is a result of a chain of command management style. True or false?

10.3 Adopting Alternate Work Arrangements

One of the most popular management concepts of recent years has been the scheduling concept known as **alternate work arrangements**. Broadly speaking, an alternate work arrangement is any scheduling pattern that deviates from the traditional Monday-through-Friday, 9-to-5 workweek.

Alternate work arrangements, flexible scheduling in particular, are an approach employees care about very much. Flexibility is the basic idea behind alternate work arrangements. You give employees some measure of control over their work schedules, thereby making it easier for them to manage nonjob-related responsibilities. The business rationale behind the concept is that by making it easier for employees to deal with pressures at home, they'll be more productive when they're at work—and less likely to leave if a competitor offers them a bit more money.

10.3.1 Options for Alternate Work Arrangements

Alternate work arrangements are generally grouped into the following categories:

▲ **Flextime:** Flextime refers to any arrangement that gives employees options on structuring their work day or work week. Typically, employees working under flextime arrangements are expected to be on the job during certain core hours of the workday. They're given the opportunity to choose (within certain parameters) their own starting and quitting times—as long as they work the required number of hours each day.

▲ **Compressed work week:** Under this arrangement, employees work the normal number of hours but complete those hours in fewer than five days. The most common variation of the compressed work week is the so-called 4/10, in which employees work four 10-hour days instead of five 8-hour days.

▲ **Job-sharing:** As the term implies, job-sharing means that two part-time employees share the same full-time job. Salary and benefits may be prorated on the basis of what proportion of the job each worker shares. Apart from the obvious consideration (both people need to be qualified for the job), a successful job-sharing arrangement assumes that the employees sharing the job can work together harmoniously to make the arrangement work.

▲ **Telecommuting:** Telecommuting refers to any work arrangement in which employees—on a regular, predetermined basis—spend all or a portion of their work week working from home or from another non-company site. Section 10.3.3 provides more details about this option.

▲ **Permanent part-time arrangements:** The hours in these arrangements usually vary from twenty to twenty-nine hours per week, with employees sometimes given the right to decide which days they work and how long they work on those days. The key attraction of this arrangement is that the employees may be entitled to company benefits, albeit on a prorated basis.

▲ **Phased retirement options:** A phased retirement allows tenured employees to gradually ease their way out of the organization by reducing the number of hours they spend on the job. This option gives your company the ability to retain valuable institutional knowledge and provides a better means of transitioning job responsibilities.

AVOIDING BURNOUT

The Japanese have a word for it: karoshi. The term means, literally, "death from overwork." **Burnout** may not be a major cause of death in the United States, but almost everywhere you look—even in companies known for employee-friendly policies—you sometimes hear complaints and concerns raised about employee burnout. Often it relates to the psychological, social, and physical problems that result when workers literally "wear down" from stress and become unable to cope with workday demands. The prime cause of employee burnout is overwork, or, to be more precise, sustained periods of overwork. Employee burnout can manifest itself any number of ways. If you can become sensitive to the warning signs of burnout, you can frequently avert a crisis. Among the most obvious signs are the following:

▲ Noticeable increase in staff absenteeism or tardiness.

▲ Any obvious change for the worse in the general mood of the workplace.

▲ Uncharacteristic emotional outbursts from normally calm employees.

▲ Increased customer complaints about the quality of goods and services.

Burnout doesn't happen overnight; it's a gradual process. At some point even the most dedicated employees will reach their physical, emotional, and mental limits. When they reach this point, you have two options: hire additional full-time employees or hire supplemental workers to ease the burden.

10.3.2 Making Alternate Arrangements Work

Many studies show that alternative work arrangement policies improve morale and job satisfaction, reduce absenteeism, cut down on turnover, and minimize burnout—and with no measurable decline in productivity. However, these arrangements don't work for every company at every level, and so the practices may have to be carefully and consistently implemented with some legally sound ground rules.

▲ **Establish guidelines:** Flexible work arrangement policies don't have to be set in stone. At the very least, though, you need a set of guidelines that serve as the basis of the program. Some specifics:

- Make sure that the flexible work arrangement policies your company develops are logically keyed to the nature and the demands of your business.

- Be consistent. Decisions regarding who should be offered the option of flexible scheduling should be based on the nature of the job as opposed to the needs of the individual.

- Make sure that managers and supervisors have some say in policies.

▲ **Pay attention to legal implications:** With certain groups of employees (hourly employees or unionized workers, in particular), flexible arrangements can easily run counter to existing agreements. Check to see whether

> ## FOR EXAMPLE
>
> ### Delivering Success
>
> FedEx Kinko's, a company that prides itself on round-the-clock service, invariably must have its stores managed by people who know how to cope with a variety of flexible schedules. Accordingly, aspiring local managers are put through a nine-month training program. The program includes courses taught by the company's chief executive officer, chief technology officer, and chief financial officer. The involvement of these senior managers drives home the message that the company really cares about how it conducts its business.

flexible scheduling violates state or local laws, and, in particular, how certain arrangements may affect overtime obligations.

▲ **Get managerial buy-in:** Regardless of how thrilled your employees may be with a flexible work arrangement, the policy itself will face rough sledding if it doesn't have the enthusiastic support and involvement of both senior management and line supervisors.

10.3.3 Telecommuting Takes Hold

Telecommuting is one of the fastest-growing alternate work arrangements in corporate America. Strictly speaking, **telecommuting** is when employees of a company regularly work out of their homes or other locations all or part of the work week. The key word in the previous definition is regularly. The structured aspect of the arrangement is what differentiates telecommuters as a group from those employees who routinely take work home from the office.

Telecommuting arrangements vary. Typically, a company's telecommuters spend part of the week—one or two days, usually—working out of their homes and the rest of the week in the office. Candidates for a successful telecommuting arrangement can include, but should not be limited to, those who:

▲ Perform a function that doesn't require extensive interaction with other employees or the use of equipment found only on company premises.

▲ Have a compelling personal reason (a long commute, for example, or family responsibilities) for working part of the time from home.

▲ Have the temperament and the discipline to work alone.

▲ Can be absent from the office without creating an inconvenience for others.

These factors are just a few to consider when selecting telecommuting candidates. Beyond these managerial issues, you should also take into account a number of sticky legal and operational aspects:

▲ **Worker safety and health:** Although OSHA enforces safety and health standards in all industries, such matters are tricky to create and monitor when employees work from home-based offices. Check with your legal counsel or insurance carrier to see what additional coverage, if any, you may need.

▲ **Security:** In an era when the internet is an integral part of many people's job, technology-driven security measures are a real concern with telecommuters. At the very least, you should have a written agreement that spells out the company's confidentiality policies and sets down specific guidelines.

▲ **Local zoning issues:** Many communities have zoning restrictions against conducting certain business activities in residential areas. While these rules generally are loosely enforced, the restrictions can create legal problems.

SETTING UP A TELECOMMUTING AGREEMENT

Consider preparing a formal agreement with any employee who is going to be telecommuting. The agreement, at the very least, should spell out the following:

▲ The specific scheduling terms—that is, how much time is to be spent at home or at the office.

▲ The specific equipment the company is willing to provide, and how the equipment is to be installed and maintained.

▲ Reporting requirements: How often should the telecommuter send email updates? Should he be part of a weekly departmental conference call? What kind of voice mail setup will the employee have?

▲ How proprietary information is to be controlled and handled.

SELF-CHECK

1. Define *flextime.*
2. Explain the difference between flextime and a compressed work week.
3. Discuss the implications of OSHA on telecommuters.
4. Give three typical symptoms of burnout.

10.4 Encouraging Performance

The human resources professional is probably the one person in an organization who is ideally positioned to help the broadest range of employees understand and maximize the opportunities created by today's progressive management model. Because you work with all levels and departments, you're best qualified to spearhead management practices that foster extraordinary employee performance. Creating a workplace environment that taps full employee potential is a monumental challenge, but, if you're successful, you can significantly impact productivity and profitability.

10.4.1 Making the Case for Employee Empowerment

Employee empowerment is an all-purpose term whose cornerstone notion is that employees ought to have as much control and autonomy as is reasonably possible in the performance of their day-to-day tasks. In an empowered environment, in other words, the authority to make decisions doesn't originate at the top and work its way down on a diminishing scale, as was the case decades ago. Individual judgment replaces "rules" and "procedures" as the decision-making mechanism in day-to-day situations. The need for supervision and micromanaging declines. Employees become increasingly accountable for their own actions.

In theory, employee empowerment is a terrific concept. It's clear that productivity as well as most measures of job satisfaction—low turnover, high morale, strong team spirit—are considerably higher in companies that encourage employee initiative and participation than they are in companies that operate under the traditional "command-and-control" structure. The problem is that, in far too many cases, companies fail to provide the support or make the changes that employees needed in order to exercise the "power" they've been granted. When that doesn't happen—when, for example, a supervisor repeatedly shoots down his team's ideas or shows up late for meetings that his subordinates have called—employees feel less motivated. And motivation is really what's at the heart of empowerment.

As you consider this concept for your organization, keep in mind that effective motivation is a trial-and-error process, one that requires constant experimentation and vigilant study—not just of your company dynamics, but also that of others. Here's a look at the principles of an environment in which employees are motivated—and where employee empowerment is not a buzzword but a way of life.

▲ **Create a safe-to-fail environment:** Successful companies encourage employees at all levels to develop and experiment with new ideas. But effective managers don't abandon employees who suggest ideas that don't pan out. Instead, they reflect collectively, talking candidly and supportively with their team. What worked? What needs to be improved? And, most importantly, how can this problem or project be better tackled in the future?

▲ **Providing training and support:** Empowerment initiatives invariably create the need for new skills at all levels of the organization. Front-line workers who are being called upon to make on-the-spot decisions frequently need training in problem solving, decision-making, and time management.

▲ **Rewarding initiative:** Employees in empowered environments are more motivated by the desire to be creative, resourceful, and responsive to customer needs than they are by the fear of making mistakes. The most progressive companies allow staff to do whatever they consider necessary to please the customer, with no "rule book" to determine what is or isn't permitted.

10.4.2 Putting Team Power to Work

Teamwork is not an abstract or trendy concept. By now, organizational experts who've studied high-performance work teams report that when the concept of team play is successfully implemented, it produces dramatic results in productivity, employee morale, and customer satisfaction.

The better you understand the challenges of making teamwork a reality, the more you'll be able to keep things in perspective. Moreover, if you're called upon to spearhead a teamwork initiative in your company, you'll move ahead with a realistic understanding of the issues. The following sections describe the fundamental factors that characterize effective teams.

▲ **Task appropriateness:** Not every function or challenge in a company lends itself to a team approach. So the first question that needs to be asked is whether the work that needs to be done will benefit from a team approach.

▲ **Shared vision:** Teams that succeed are unified by a clear sense of mission. Members of the team understand why the team was formed, what its goals are, and what steps are needed to achieve its goals. To create a shared vision:
  • Take time to formulate a clear statement of purpose.
  • Ensure that the team mission is embraced by all team members.
  • Make sure that the mission is consistent with the overall mission and strategic vision of the company.

▲ **Strategic focus:** The specific tasks that teams perform need to be driven by the strategic goals of the organization. To develop these goals:
  • Set priorities. Make sure that team members are focused at all times on the issues that are directly keyed to strategic considerations.

- Ensure that goals are realistic and are accompanied by specific action plans that have their own measures of success.
- Make sure that teams can measure their progress.

▲ **Role clarity:** Team members must understand—and accept—the role that they play within the team and must also be aware of the responsibilities of their team members. For example, if the team chooses a leader, the group should agree on and clearly define his or her responsibilities. It may be necessary to establish protocols for intervening when people aren't living up to their responsibilities.

▲ **Individual motivation:** Team members should be given the opportunity to develop new skills at the same time that they're contributing to the success of the team's mission. To help develop those skills:

- When assigning tasks, pair team members who have expertise in a particular area with other team members who can benefit from that expertise.
- Set aside time for group learning, giving individual team members the opportunity to share their knowledge and experience.
- Create reward mechanisms for team members who share information.

▲ **Conflict resolution:** Good teams anticipate disagreement and diversity and have developed means for resolving differences. To effectively resolve conflict when it occurs, establish ground rules and encourage team members to voice concerns about the performance of others early on in the process.

▲ **Appropriate reward mechanisms:** Because appraisal and merit systems have traditionally been based on individual performance, creating reward mechanisms that support team initiatives has emerged as one of the prime challenges facing companies that want to move to a team-oriented system.

PROBLEMS AND PITFALLS IN TEAM SITUATIONS

Even under the best of circumstances, the road to successful teamwork is filled with minefields. Here's a look at some pitfalls you need to be aware of:

- ▲ Dissension and disagreement among team members.
- ▲ Abuse of authority by team leaders.
- ▲ Management interference, especially when an individual manager is not committed to team concepts.
- ▲ Conflict between team mission and company policies.
- ▲ Resentment by workers not included in teams, which can cause morale and productivity problems.

▲ Team practices that conflict with existing union contracts and EEO and civil rights laws.

▲ Legal problems. (Team activities that involve both exempt and non-exempt employees may create payment/scheduling situations in conflict with the Fair Labor Standards Act and other similar laws.)

10.4.3 Developing Employee Recognition Programs

Employee recognition programs have been a staple in the human resource professional's tool kit for decades, and it's easy to see why. When recognition programs are planned intelligently and implemented with care, they're a proven method of enhancing performance, increasing morale, and building employee loyalty. And recognition programs don't necessarily have to be costly. The idea and the spirit behind the programs—the mere fact that a company is singling out and showing gratitude toward employees who are doing a great job—can be as motivational as the material rewards that may be given.

As you may expect, HR professionals should play a key role in any recognition initiative. For example, the rationale behind any reward needs to correlate to your company's overall business goals and objectives. The traditional recognition programs, such as length of service awards, attendance, and safety, still have a place in most companies. But in today's performance-driven business environment, the trend is toward recognition that is productivity-based, which can have a more direct impact on both the company's bottom line and the employee's commitment. Figure 10-1 shows a sample employee recoginition program.

The decisions involving the actual mechanics of the employee recognition programs—budget, in particular—should be well-coordinated and equitable. Otherwise, you run the risk of creating discord between those teams or departments in your company that have recognition programs and those that do not. Consider the following guidelines for developing effective recognition programs:

▲ **Think it through carefully:** Think through every aspect of a recognition program, particularly the criteria you intend to use as the basis for the rewards. Ideally, the performance targets you set up for each program ought to be challenging enough to instill an extra measure of motivation, but not so challenging that they're considered out of reach. On the other hand, if too many people meet the criteria for special recognition, you'll dilute its impact.

Figure 10-1

Employee Recognition Program

In keeping with our commitment to recruit, retain, and develop exceptional employees, XYZ Company's five-tier employee recognition program enables us to recognize and reward our employees for their commitment and contributions, both to us and our clients. Nominations for all of our five awards can be made by any employee of XYZ Company, and awards will be announced on a quarterly basis.

1. The CEO Award. Monetary awards and CEO recognition for employees who provide outstanding client service and/or project management.

2. The Most Valuable Performer (MVP) Club. Recognition for exceptional performance in one or more of the following:

- Health and Safety
- Technical Competence, Professional Knowledge and Self-development
- Commitment, Initiative and Productivity
- Teamwork, Cooperation and Building Relationships

3. Marketing Director Award. Monetary reward for top-performing office in each division, given quarterly, to advocate the importance of teamwork in achieving goals.

4. Achievement Certificates. Formal acknowledgement for employees who go above and beyond for clients and coworkers.

5. Service Anniversary Awards. CEO acknowledgement and gift selection for employees at milestone service anniversaries.

An example of an employee recognition program.

Make sure that all employees eligible for formal rewards are made aware of how these decisions will be measured. Finally, consider the possibility that the same person or group of people may win the rewards repeatedly.

▲ **Make sure that the recognition means something:** Regardless of what form they take—a certificate, an acknowledgment in the company newsletter, or an all-expenses-paid trip to Tahiti—the fundamental purpose of a recognition program is to motivate exemplary performance. As a result, rewards should have real value to recipients, regardless of how much money is spent. A paperweight or elegant plaque, for example, can be meaningful and motivational because they're visible to all coworkers.

▲ **Share the wealth:** Formal reward programs ought to be as all-inclusive as possible. If you've set up a program for one group of employees—sales reps, for example—give thought to instituting a reward program for nonsales/back office personnel as well. The nature and amount of the rewards don't necessarily have to be the same for every group, but everyone has the potential to contribute and should therefore be eligible for formal recognition.

▲ **Communicate the criteria:** One of the downsides to recognition programs is that occasionally employees will feel that the "winners" are not deserving. To help prevent this, make sure, early on, that the criteria for rewards are not only well-defined, but communicated clearly to all employees. Another suggestion: Get as much employee input as possible when you're setting up the program.

▲ **Spread the news:** To get the most mileage out of a recognition program, you need to do a good job of publicizing it—in a newsletter, color brochure, company-wide memo, bulletin board, or notices on your company's intranet.

BUDGET-CONSCIOUS REWARD PROGRAMS

The success of a recognition program isn't determined solely by the monetary value of its prizes. With a little imagination and employee input, you should be able to develop dozens of rewards that are easy and inexpensive to administer. Here are some ideas to get started:

▲ Time off or extra vacation days.

▲ A note or letter of appreciation from the company president.

▲ Dinner (for two) at a local restaurant or a group lunch for an outstanding department.

▲ A designated employee-of-the-month parking spot.

▲ Lunch or dinner with the company CEO (provided that the CEO enjoys these functions; otherwise, it can make for an awkward session).

▲ A photo and brief article in the company newsletter.

▲ A press release to the local newspaper.

▲ Inexpensive plaques or paperweights.

▲ Special gear (T-shirt, tote bag, and so on) with the company logo.

▲ Movie tickets.

SELF-CHECK

1. Define *employee empowerment.*

2. A team approach can be used to meet any strategic goals. True or false?

3. Explain how an employee recognition program can benefit an organization.

4. An employee reward must be expensive to be meaningful. True or false?

10.5 Utilizing Employee Feedback

A key component of effective employee relations programs is staying in touch with how well your employee relations programs are meeting the needs of employees. To do so, employers need to utilize a bottom-up communication process (see Section 10.1.1). The following sections outline some commonly used methods for eliciting employee feedback.

10.5.1 Surveys: Keeping Tabs on Company Morale

Employers interested in developing a high-performance workforce know that they must find out what motivates and satisfies their employees. Employees are typically thrilled when management solicits their opinions. But what's the best way to go about it? The most powerful vehicle to accomplish this goal is an anonymous employee opinion survey.

Filling out an employee opinion survey is easy for most individuals. The majority of survey formats include simple instructions and use a 1-to-5 response system that consists of a range from strongly agreeing to strongly disagreeing with a given statement. Although the wealth of information uncovered by an employee opinion survey can at times be astounding, it also can serve as the employer's motivation to fix what's been apparent all along. Any company thinking about tapping the benefits of employee brain power should pay close attention to the before and after phases of the process. Here are some tips:

▲ Before writing the survey, spend time thinking about what the survey should specifically emphasize. This might require a focus group or special meetings in which issues are identified and isolated.

▲ Watch your timing. Don't conduct surveys when many employees may be taking days off. And avoid exceptionally heavy workload periods.

FOR EXAMPLE

Feedback Pays Off

At the Atlanta-based Holder Construction Co. employees participate regularly on committees that help make company decisions. As a result, the company has implemented a number of employee suggestions. For example, employees proposed that the company close at 3:30 P.M. on Fridays so they could beat Atlanta's horrific rush hour traffic. The company agreed to try it. What happened, says Chairman and CEO Tommy Holder, is that people finished their work early, so the new schedule worked well for everyone. At Holder, employees aren't hesitant to make requests because they know the company will consider them, make a decision, and explain the reasons for that decision.

▲ Think carefully about your objectives before crafting your survey questions. What do you want to find out? What do you intend to do with the information?

▲ Share survey objectives with employees, but do so in language that's relevant to them. In other words, instead of using HR terms such as "We want to assess employee attitudes," tell them that "We want to hear your thoughts since we merged with Company X."

▲ Before you unveil your survey to the entire company, test it out on a small group of employees to see what may need refining.

▲ A key step: Assure employees that their comments are confidential.

▲ Communicate to employees the results of the survey on a timely basis and take action, as appropriate, when employees make recommendations. Employee morale tends to deteriorate if no action is taken after they have participated in a survey in which their opinions were supposed to count Let employees know how their input has affected company policy.

10.5.2 Open-Door Policies

An **open-door policy** is a strategy that is often used in organizations to encourage employees to come forward with questions and concerns about issues that are affecting them at work. Whether the issues have to do with work processes, barriers to getting work done, new ideas to improve workflow, or personal issues that are affecting an employee's ability to achieve results, open-door policies can be very effective—but only if management is willing to follow through on it.

Successful open-door policies often include requirements that employees first approach their direct supervisor with questions or complaints before moving to the next level; however, employees should never be punished for bringing problems to their supervisors.

10.5.3 Management By Walking Around (MBWA)

Management By Walking Around (MBWA) was developed at Hewlett-Packard in the 1940s. The idea behind MBWA is that managers who get out of their offices and onto the production floor can see the results of their decisions in action and get a feel for how well those decisions are working for the organization. MBWA is a simple and cost-effective way for managers to talk to employees about working conditions and processes, and having the general manager or CEO come to the production floor to talk to them makes employees feel important and valued by the organization. Although MBWA provides opportunities for bottom-up communication, it is time-consuming for executives with a lot on their plate, and some employees may find it intimidating to see the "big boss" on their turf. Employees who do have questions might find that the boss doesn't have an answer immediately available, so it's crucial that a way of providing the information promptly is found when that occurs.

10.5.4 Employee Involvement Committees

One way to get employees involved in solving problems is to create an employee involvement committee that includes them on a task force or committee designed to solve a particular problem. Participating on a committee gives employees an opportunity to be heard, gives them a sense of control over their work, and increases their level of buy-in to the results. As with committee work in any organization, there are some drawbacks:

▲ Left to their own imaginations, employees can make some pretty unrealistic proposals.

▲ There's no guarantee that what the committee proposes reflects what all employees want.

▲ Committee recommendations can be time-consuming and delay implementation of needed changes.

10.5.5 Brown-Bag Lunches

A **brown-bag lunch** is an informal way for senior executives to meet with small groups of employees and talk with them about what is happening in the company. It presents an opportunity for employees who would not otherwise have a chance to talk to organization leaders to do so and to ask questions in a less-intimidating situation than an all-hands meeting.

ONE CUP OF SATISFACTION

Although the results of employee relations programs can be difficult to measure, there are two indicators of employee satisfaction that can be measured: absenteeism and turnover. Excessive unplanned absences can be an indication of employee stress, dissatisfaction with job requirements, supervisory conflicts, and feeling undervalued by the employer. Measuring absence and turnover rates over time can provide feedback on the success of employee relations programs, as well as provide indicators of supervisory issues that may be resolved through coaching or training.

10.5.6 Suggestion Programs

Suggestion programs are effective when they are taken seriously by the organization. In many companies, employees find the "suggestion box" to be a source of humor because nothing ever happens based on suggestions that are made. The first rule about a suggestion program, then, is that employers must read and respond to the suggestions. Whether or not the suggestions are viable, it is important for employees to understand why they are not implemented. When appropriate suggestions are implemented, it's important to follow up and let employees know that the change occurred as a result of a suggestion. Allowing employees to make suggestions anonymously may increase their willingness to take risks and make suggestions that go against the status quo and result in significant savings.

ANALYZING AND REPORTING FEEDBACK RESULTS

When an organization undertakes a feedback initiative, the results must be reported back to both management and employees. The human resources professional should carefully review the data to ensure that it is accurate. If the results are quantified, they should be viewed critically to make sure they make sense and accurately reflect what is truly happening in the organization.

10.5.7 Exit Interviews

Some of the most candid employees are often those who are leaving your company. To gain valuable ideas about improving your working conditions and making the workplace more inviting, consider conducting exit interviews with employees who have resigned or are otherwise voluntarily leaving your company. (People you've had to fire, while potentially the most candid of all, are not good subjects for two reasons: They're unlikely to cooperate and, if they do, their input will probably be overly negative rather than constructive.) Consider the following ideas:

▲ Use third parties to conduct exit interviews, keeping the results anonymous.

▲ Conduct exit interviews six months after employees leave. Former employees are often more open about their experiences once they have had a chance to gain some perspective.

STRAIGHT FROM THE GRAPEVINE

To some degree, although it is not an official form of feedback, the office "grapevine" can provide employers with some useful information about employee satisfaction. Of course, this approach has to be managed carefully.

SELF-CHECK

1. Explain the value of employee feedback in employee relations programs.
2. List three examples of techniques for eliciting employee feedback.
3. Define *open-door policy*.
4. Which of the following feedback methods was developed in the 1940s?

    a. All-Hands Meetings

    b. Employee Involvement Committees

    c. Management By Walking Around

    d. Employee Surveys

SUMMARY

Effective management of employee relations is a critical element of a successful business. Employees who are treated with respect and given the tools they need to succeed reward employers with increased production and loyalty. Part of the success of an employee relations program lies in how the plan is communicated to employees; it is equally important for employees to have a means of communicating their concerns and questions to management. Other aspects of an employee relations program should take into consideration the various elements that affect job satisfaction—working conditions and management style among them. For today's workforce, alternative work arrangements that address work-life balance issues are a particularly appealing aspect of an employee relations program. As flexibility becomes increasingly valuable to employees, more companies are choosing to offer such options as flextime, job-sharing, and telecommuting. Programs should also consider employee recognition programs and other means of encouraging quality performance. Keep in mind that recognition can come in many different forms, from vacation packages to parking spots and gift certificates. Finally, to be totally effective, an employee relations programs must make a concerted effort to solicit and carefully consider employee feedback, making changes and adjustments when called for; options for soliciting feedback include surveys, committees, brown bag lunches, and even suggestion boxes.

KEY TERMS

Alternate work arrangements	Any scheduling pattern that deviates from the traditional workweek.
Bottom-up communication	Information that flows from employees up through an organization.
Brown-bag lunch	An informal way for senior executives to meet with and talk to small groups of employees.
Burnout	When workers wear down from stress and become unable to cope with work-day demands.
Compressed work week	Employees work the normal number of hours but complete those hours in fewer than five days.
Employee empowerment	Philosophy that employees ought to have as much control and autonomy as is reasonably possible in the performance of their day-to-day tasks.
Employee relations	The policies and practices that are concerned with the management and regulation of relationships in an organization.
Flextime	Any arrangement that gives employees options on structuring their work day or work week.
Job satisfaction	How content an individual is with his or her job.
Job-sharing	Two part-time employees share the same full-time job.

Lateral communication	Communication that takes place between employees in different departments within the organization.
Management By Walking Around (MBWA)	A way for managers to talk to employees about working conditions and processes.
Open-door policy	Strategy to encourage employees to come forward with questions and concerns about work issues.
Organizational culture	Establishes standards of behavior, many of which are unwritten, for all employees.
Phased retirement options	Program that allows tenured employees to gradually ease their way out of the organization by reducing the number of hours they work.
Telecommuting	Any work arrangement in which employees regularly work out of their homes or other locations all or part of the work week.
Top-down communication	Information that flows from the organization to employees.

ASSESS YOUR UNDERSTANDING

Go to www.wiley.com/college/messmer to assess your knowledge of employee relations.

Measure your learning by comparing pre-test and post-test results.

Summary Questions

1. Organizational culture is most influenced by employee feedback. True or false?

2. Which of the following is an example of top-down communication?

    (a) exit interview

    (b) brown-bag lunch

    (c) management by walking around

    (d) all-hands meeting

3. Explain the value of bottom-up communication to a company's success.

4. Which benefit addresses an employee's work-life balance issues?

    (a) dental insurance

    (b) eldercare

    (c) 401(k)

    (d) pension

5. Employee empowerment makes it easier for workers to follow the orders of management. True or false?

6. Alternative work arrangement policies increase employee

    (a) burnout

    (b) turnover

    (c) absenteeism

    (d) job satisfaction

7. A telecommuter is an employee who occasionally works out of his or her home. True or false?

8. A phased retirement requires employees to work from home all or part of the work week. True or false?

9. With job sharing, employees work the normal number of hours but from different locations. True or false?

10. Explain the necessity of creating guidelines for alternative work arrangements.

11. Employee empowerment initiatives fail for which reasons?

    (a) poor ideas

    (b) lack of employer support

    (c) budget restrictions

    (d) corporate regulations

12. Give three examples of employee recognition awards.

13. The current trend in employee recognition programs is to reward

    (a) length of service

    (b) safety

    (c) attendance

    (d) productivity

14. Employee feedback utilizes which methods of organizational communication?

    (a) top-down

    (b) bottom-up

    (c) lateral

    (d) voluntary

15. Open-door policies fail because employees don't follow through on ideas. True or false?

16. The anonymity of suggestion boxes enables employees to be more honest in their feedback. True or false?

Applying This Chapter

1. A former member of the military has signed on to run a security systems manufacturing company. Though he spends time "patrolling" the work environment, employee morale is suffering. Suggest ways in which the organizational culture could be changed to improve employee relations.

2. In an effort to improve employee motivation, the manager of an eldercare home started offering bagels to workers on Fridays and bought a ping-pong table for the break room. But employee burnout is at an all-time high. Propose other more substantial motivational techniques that could be more effective in decreasing absences and turnover.

3. A mortgage company has a six-person customer service department, and the phones are answered from 8 A.M. to 7 P.M. The peak period—when the most calls come in—is between noon and 3 P.M. As the owner, set up a flextime arrangement that obliges all six representatives to be in their offices from noon to 3 P.M. but also gives employees the latitude

to work together to set up their own eight-hour days so that the department is never left unstaffed.

4. You've been chosen to create an employee recognition program for your hotel. It should reward an employee for productivity. What type of criteria should you have and what should be the reward?

5. To be effective, managers must become great listeners. Which of the employee feedback methods would be most useful for the owner of a large chain of car dealers?

Communicating at Work

Examine the communications methods in place at a large company like Starbucks. Identify both the top-down and bottom-up communication channels in use. How do they differ from your own organization or one in your neighborhood? Compare those communication channels with those of a small business. How do they compare?

Taking on Telecommuting

Research shows that telecommuting leads to higher productivity, less pollution, and reduced stress. Research a company that allows telecommuting and consider the following:

- The percentage of employees in the program.
- The positions they're in.
- How the policy came about and any restrictions.
- How other employees feel about the program.
- Any problems with the program.

Surveying the Field

The twenty-five employees of a small insurance company have gone without retirement benefits since the company was started seven years ago. Although the owners of the company treat the employees very well, they have resisted the financial commitment of retirement planning. To begin the process, management decides to survey employees for their opinions. Write a ten-question survey that would give the company a clear understanding of how to best satisfy the needs of the company and the employees.

11

MANAGING DISCIPLINE AND EMPLOYEE RIGHTS

Dealing with Difficult Workplace Situations

Starting Point

Go to www.wiley.com/college/messmer to assess your knowledge of discipline management.
Determine where you need to concentrate your effort.

What You'll Learn in This Chapter

▲ Ways to avoid legal issues in matters of employee discipline
▲ The steps of a disciplinary procedure
▲ Guidelines for implementing a grievance procedure
▲ Criteria for a fair and effective termination approach
▲ Common reasons for employee layoffs

After Studying This Chapter, You Will Be Able To

▲ Analyze the effectiveness of an organization's disciplinary procedures
▲ Assess the ability of a disciplinary process to withstand the scrutiny of the legal system
▲ Choose the appropriate method of dispute resolution
▲ Evaluate how a termination approach respects an employee's rights
▲ Assess possible alternatives to employee layoffs

INTRODUCTION

Regardless of how well you've organized the human resources function in your company, and regardless of how diligently you handle your day-to-day responsibilities, your organization is going to face some personnel-related challenges. Even your best employees are going to make mistakes and get into occasional squabbles. And as unpleasant as the prospect may seem, you or the managers will be obliged at some point to take some sort of corrective action—including termination—against an employee whose job performance or conduct falls short of company expectations. And most important perhaps, you (more than likely) have to make sure that your company's disciplinary and termination policies minimize your company's exposure to wrongful discharge lawsuits.

11.1 Playing by the Rules

As the person responsible for HR in your company, you have a crucial role to play in making sure that job performance and workplace conduct issues are handled promptly, intelligently, and fairly. The best overall way to reduce the number of difficult situations you have to deal with is to prevent them from happening in the first place. You can never hope to avert all employee improprieties, poor judgments, and disputes, of course, but establishing a culture based on ethical behavior can go a long way in diminishing these situations in your organization.

▲ Become a company that emphasizes the importance of employees' ethical behavior in all interactions. Including integrity and consideration of others as one of your core values prevents many unpleasant situations from occurring.

▲ Have a formal code of conduct that is not buried on a shelf, but actively reinforced by all of your managers (see Section 1.3.1). When employees hear one set of values but see another enforced by managers, the inconsistent messages cause them to question your commitment to your basic principles.

11.1.1 Getting the Meaning of At-Will Employment

Employers in the United States have long operated under a doctrine generally known as employment-at-will.

▲ **Employment-at-will** (also referred to as **termination-at-will**) means that in the absence of any contractual agreement that guarantees employees certain job protections, you (as an employer in the private sector) have the right to fire any of your employees at any time and for any (or no) reason.

In other words, you may terminate an employee with or without cause and with or without notice. At the same time, your employees have the right to leave at any time, for any (or no) reason, even without giving notice.

You should note that the concept of at-will employment is specific to the United States. Other countries have their own sets of requirements concerning termination. At-will employment is, however, subject to a number of limitations. If your company is unionized, for example, your employees' jobs are likely subject to contractual constraints.

Court decisions involving wrongful termination cases, particularly in recent years, recognize employment-at-will so long as the employer's actions do not violate certain public policies. For example, you can't terminate an employee for refusing to forge reports to the government or to violate antitrust laws. Your company still has the right to set behavioral standards, take corrective action when those standards aren't met, and fire employees who don't perform their job duties. However, you must be sure that in the process, you're not impinging on public policies.

BE WARY OF WRONGFUL TERMINATION

Wrongful termination occurs when an employer terminates an employee for a reason that is prohibited by statute or breaches a contract. For example, an employee may not be terminated because he or she is a member of a protected class. If an employer gives a different reason for the termination, but the employee can prove that the real reason was based on a discriminatory act, the termination would be wrongful. Similarly, an employee may not be terminated as retaliation for whistle-blowing activity or for filing a worker's compensation claim.

FOR EXAMPLE

At Will in Alabama

The University of Alabama states on its website its position regarding employment agreements: The State of Alabama is an employment at will state. Although it is desirable for employees of the University to form long-standing employment relationships with the University, either the employee or the University may terminate the relationship at any time, for any reason, with or without notice. Neither the University's policies or practices nor its employee handbooks are intended to alter an employee's at will relationship.

11.1.2 Staying Out of Court

According to the Bureau of National Affairs, the number of wrongful discharge suits working their way through the courts more than doubled during the 1980s, and the trend continues today. Even more sobering is the fact that plaintiffs win most wrongful discharge suits that reach trial largely because juries tend to favor employees over employers. How does a company protect itself? In short, protection comes from preventive action. Here are seven key principles to bear in mind:

▲ Review all company recruiting and orientation literature to ensure that no statements, implicitly or explicitly, "guarantee" employment. Be especially careful about the use of the word "permanent" in any employee literature or in conversations that occur before an employee is hired. Courts have held this term creates an implied contract of employment. If you need to differentiate between classes of employees, "regular" or full-time are better terms.

▲ Establish and document specific, easy-to-understand performance standards for every position in your company and make sure that every employee is aware of those standards.

▲ Train managers to maintain careful, detailed records of all performance problems and the disciplinary actions that have been taken in response to those problems. Keep in mind that the verdict in many wrongful discharge suits hinges on whether the discharged employee was given "fair warning." Juries do not like it when they think an employee was surprised when terminated.

▲ Make sure that all disciplinary and dismissal procedures are handled in a manner consistent with your company's stated policy.

▲ Make sure that all the managers and supervisors in your company are well-versed in your company's disciplinary and termination procedures. Confer with them on a regular basis to ensure that they're following procedures. If you discover they're not, let them know that failure to follow proper disciplinary and termination procedures is unacceptable and can prove extremely costly.

▲ Seek legal advice whenever you are uncertain about any aspects of your company's disciplinary or legal policy.

▲ Be sensitive to the possibility that an employee who leaves your company voluntarily as a result of a change in assignment or work practices may be able to convince a jury that the change in assignment or work practices represented a deliberate attempt on your company's part to force the employee to quit.

11.1.3 Respecting Employee Rights

Employee rights provide only limited protection for getting fired from a job. That's mostly because of the concept of employment at will (see Section 11.1.1).

As such, in the absence of employment agreements or contracts that indicate otherwise, employment relationships are presumed to be voluntary and indefinite. Although employers generally may fire employees for any, no or even unfair reasons, employees do maintain some rights:

▲ Employers cannot illegally fire employees. But, just because getting fired from a job seemed unfair, doesn't mean that it was illegal. For information about firings that might be illegal, read "Be Wary of Wrongful Termination" in Section 11.1.1.

▲ Even if an employee is "legally" fired from a job, that employee still might be entitled to collect state unemployment insurance benefits.

▲ Employees might also be entitled to continue employer-provided health insurance benefits at group rates, under COBRA (see Sections 2.2 and 9.2.5).

▲ Employees have the right to final paychecks immediately or within thirty days after being fired. Exactly when your employer must issue a final paycheck depends on state laws.

SELF-CHECK

1. A formal code of conduct can help prevent discipline problems in a company. True or false?

2. Define *employment-at-will*.

3. Give an example of *wrongful termination*.

4. An employee who is fired is never eligible for unemployment insurance. True or false?

11.2 Taking Disciplinary Action

It would be great if all employees came to work on time every day with no other goal than to do a great job. Unfortunately, this is not always the case, and sometimes organizations must take actions to correct substandard or inappropriate behavior.

When it is necessary, many organizations utilize disciplinary policies that begin with an attempt to correct behavior or performance problems and to provide documentation of steps taken to improve performance prior to terminating an employee. Disciplinary policies help to ensure that employees throughout the organization are treated fairly and consistently.

Each organization determines how to implement a disciplinary process; some organizations may have three steps; others may have four. The goal is to ensure that employees are not surprised by a performance-related termination. Disciplinary processes provide organizations with the documentation necessary to demonstrate that a terminated employee was treated fairly, given an opportunity to correct behavior or improve performance, and warned in writing that the possible consequences of not improving could result in termination.

11.2.1 Developing Disciplinary Procedures

Some companies like a formalized disciplinary process, one that reasonably and systematically warns employees when performance falls short of expectations.

A formal disciplinary procedure works best in companies that are highly centralized, where personnel decisions for the entire company are made within one department (most likely HR), which makes sure that each step of the disciplinary process is implemented properly. The advantage is that the rules and regulations of job performance are consistently communicated to everyone. The disadvantage, however, is that if your company doesn't abide by these self-imposed rules, not even a lawyer can help you.

On the other hand, some companies don't like such a process. Using a formalized disciplinary process doesn't work as well for organizations that are decentralized, where personnel decisions are made within each office or department on a case-by-case basis in accordance with a company's general expectations. In these situations, ensuring that each office or department follows the same disciplinary procedure is difficult.

The specifics of a formal disciplinary process can take a variety of forms, but most practices are structured along similar lines. To one degree or another, they all mirror the following phases:

1. **Initial notification:** The first step in a typical disciplinary process is informing the employee that his or her job performance or workplace conduct isn't measuring up to the company's expectations and standards. The employee's manager typically delivers this initial communication verbally in a one-on-one meeting. Details from this and all later conversations should also be documented. The report needn't be lengthy; a few bullet points highlighting the main topics are perfectly acceptable.

2. **Second warning:** This phase applies if the performance or conduct problems raised in the initial phase worsen or fail to improve. The recommended practice is for the manager to hold yet another one-on-one meeting with the employee and accompany this oral warning with a memo that spells out job performance areas that need improvement. At this stage in the process, the manager needs to make the employee aware of what the consequences are for failing to improve or correct the problem. The

manager needs to work with the employee to come up with a written plan of action that gives the employee concrete, quantifiable goals and a timeline for achieving them.

3. **Last-chance warning:** The "last-chance" phase of discipline usually takes the form of a written notice from a senior manager or, in smaller companies, from the company president. The notice informs the employee that if the problems continue, the employee will be subject to termination.

4. **Corrective action:** Corrective action is some form of discipline administered by the company prior to termination. In union contracts, for example, this action may take the form of a suspension, mandatory leave, or possibly a demotion. In small companies, disciplinary actions become a little trickier to implement—so much so, that corrective action can become termination itself.

5. **Termination:** Termination is the last step in the process—the step taken when all other corrective or disciplinary actions have failed to solve the problem.

11.2.2 Meeting Plan Criteria

These progressive disciplinary steps serve as general guidelines and aren't intended as a substitute for legal counsel. However you decide to structure your disciplinary plan, the process itself—apart from being fair—should meet the following criteria:

▲ **Clearly defined expectations and consequences:** Every employee in your company should be aware of the expectations and standards that apply to her particular job. Your company needs to communicate standards and expectations early on in the employee's tenure. The same principle applies to workplace rules. Courts have repeatedly held that employers can't fire employees for violating rules of which they were unaware.

▲ **Early intervention:** This nip-the-problem-in-the-bud principle is that an employer steps in as early as possible when an employee's job performance or workplace conduct isn't satisfactory. Failing to provide pointed performance feedback early on can hurt you in two ways:

- Employees can interpret the lack of any intervention as an implicit sign that they're doing just fine.

- If you take action against another employee who is having similar problems, you leave yourself open to charges of favoritism or discrimination.

▲ **Consistency:** You need to apply your company's policies and practices consistently—no favoritism or bending of the rules allowed. Solid, legitimate, nondiscriminatory reasons are the only justification for deviation.

▲ **Rigorous documentation:** Supervisors and managers must get into the habit of recording all infractions and problems, along with the steps taken to remedy those problems. When deciding whether to terminate an employee, review evaluations, warning notices (if any), personnel policies or work rules, witness statements, witness evaluation notes, and other relevant documents, such as customer complaints, production reports, and time cards. If the documentation is not deemed sufficient, ask the manager for more information and hold off on taking action until you've determined you have sufficient documentation.

11.2.3 Workplace Behavior Issues

Employees are human beings whose behavior at work is influenced by many factors. Regardless of the source, these factors influence the way employees behave while they are at work. Employee behavior and management's response (or in some cases, lack of response) affects the productivity and morale of the entire workgroup.

▲ **Absenteeism:** Employees call in sick for many different reasons—sometimes they themselves are ill or perhaps a child or parent needs care. Some employees call in sick to go surfing, go shopping, or have a "mental health" day. Regardless of the reasons given, more often than not the absence causes problems for the work group. When one employee has an excessive number of absences, an absentee policy provides the basis for disciplinary action. An effective policy should clearly state the following:
  • How much sick leave is provided.
  • If the absences are counted on a fiscal, calendar, or rolling year basis.
  • When a doctor's note is required before sick leave may be used.

▲ **Dress code:** Dress code policies let employees know what clothes need to be worn in the workplace. Some types of clothing may not be appropriate for safety reasons (such as to prevent a piece of clothing from getting caught in a machine) or to ensure a professional appearance. A policy should describe what type of clothing is appropriate for different jobs, give examples to clarify, and let employees know the consequences for inappropriate attire.

▲ **Insubordination:** Insubordinate behavior can be as blatant as employees refusing to perform a legitimate task when requested by their managers. It can also be more subtle, such as employees who roll their eyes whenever a manager gives them direction. Few organizations have specific policies for insubordination, but a code of conduct that describes the organization's expectations for treating all employees with dignity and respect provides managers with the tools they need to correct unacceptable behavior.

11.2.4 Conducting Workplace Investigations

A workplace investigation is conducted when allegations or suspicions of misconduct come to the attention of the organization. These investigations occur when claims of sexual harassment are made, after an accident occurs in the workplace, or when management suspects that other misconduct has occurred.

Conducting an effective workplace investigation for the first time can be intimidating and overwhelming, so it is helpful to establish a standard plan of action before an investigation is needed. When developing this plan, be sure to include the following activities:

▲ Create a checklist for conducting investigations so you are sure to cover all the bases if the need arises.

▲ Select an investigator who is seen by all parties as neutral in the investigation.

▲ If possible, have the accuser make a written statement about the incident(s) and sign it; if this is not possible, take careful notes and have the accuser read, date, and sign it. Get the names of any witnesses so that they can be interviewed.

▲ Interview the accused to get the other side of the story, and get the names of any additional witnesses.

▲ Interview the witnesses and get their statements.

▲ Make a determination based on the facts that were gathered.

▲ Make a written report of the facts and findings for the record.

▲ Take appropriate action based on the results.

In cases where employee actions create a dangerous situation for the employer, as in theft of company property or violence in the workplace, the employer should move immediately to the termination phase of the disciplinary process. When this occurs, the best course of action is to suspend the employee pending an investigation, conduct the investigation in a fair and expeditious manner, and, should the results of the investigation support termination, terminate the employee.

SEXUAL HARASSMENT INVESTIGATIONS

When an employee comes to HR alleging that workplace harassment or other misconduct has occurred, it is essential that HR conduct an investigation into the allegation. Workplace investigations must be conducted in a timely manner (two or three days at the most), particularly if the allegation concerns sexual harassment. Letting a situation involving sexual harassment continue without an immediate investigation could result in additional liability for the employer if the allegations are found to be justified.

Establishing an effective program to prevent harassment from occurring in the first place and to deal with allegations quickly and fairly protects both employees and their employers (see Section 2.6).

11.2.5 Grounds for Dismissal

Certain employee infractions and misdeeds are so blatant that you may be able to terminate the employee without going through the normal disciplinary channels. Your orientation literature should spell out the offenses that lead to immediate dismissal. Here's a list to get you started:

▲ Stealing from the company or from other employees.

▲ Possession or use of drugs.

▲ Distribution or selling of illegal drugs.

▲ Blatant negligence that results in the damage to or loss of company machinery or equipment.

▲ Falsifying company records.

▲ Violation of confidentiality agreements.

▲ Misappropriation of company assets.

▲ Making threatening remarks to other employees or managers.

▲ Engaging in activities that represent a clear case of conflict of interest.

▲ Lying about credentials.

FOR EXAMPLE

No Excuses

The contract for a county's service maintenance workers is comprehensive when it comes to absences, listing fifteen valid reasons for missing work. When an employee has one unexcused day of absence, his supervisor must informally advise the employee that he could be at risk for corrective action should he have further unexcused absences. This is not considered to be corrective action and no documentation is maintained. Following that, however, the next unexcused absence results in a formal written notification and is included in the employee's personnel file. After the third unexcused absence, the employee faces corrective action, including weekly supervisory meetings, a three-day suspension, and, finally, termination.

SELF-CHECK

1. Identify the steps of a disciplinary process.
2. Explain the benefit of careful documentation in disciplinary matters.
3. Give an example of a work behavior that is cause for disciplinary action.
4. Sexual harassment is an offense that is cause for immediate dismissal. True or false?

11.3 Settling Grievances and Disputes

An effective, well-balanced disciplinary process does more than provide a means for dealing with the problem behavior of employees. It also gives employees an opportunity to be heard when they're not happy with the way things are going in the workplace. This disciplinary process is known as a **grievance procedure**. In unionized companies, the grievance procedure is a multistep and often cumbersome process that begins with an employee airing the complaint to the union steward (see Chapter 13 for more on union relations).

Chances are, your company doesn't need a highly structured series of steps to resolve complaints, but you do need to provide employees with the opportunity to voice their complaints without fear of repercussion. Here are suggestions on how to implement such a process.

▲ **Offer complaint-reporting options:** As a general rule, instruct employees to bring their complaints to the attention of their immediate supervisors. If the complaint involves the supervisor, however, employees should have the right to break the chain of command. In certain circumstances, directing complaints through a different channel, such as a trained and designated member of the human resources department, may be appropriate.

▲ **Stress the importance of prompt response:** Everyone in the company who's responsible for receiving employee complaints should make it a point to address the complaint as promptly as possible. Ideally, an employee should know within twenty-four hours that you've received his complaint and you're handling it. Whenever the complaint involves an alleged serious workplace safety or health violation, sexual harassment, discrimination, or criminal activity, alert senior managers immediately. Ignoring any complaint that deals with serious issues greatly increases your company's exposure.

▲ **Investigate with an open mind:** Until you have reason to believe otherwise, consider all information important. Never assume that simply because your company has never experienced a particular problem before that the problem doesn't exist.

▲ **Report back to the employee:** Whether the complaint is substantiated or not, you need to keep the employee who registered it informed of what you're doing to deal with the situation. If you ultimately find that the complaint isn't substantiated explain why you feel more action isn't warranted.

If the complaint is justified, indicate that corrective action is being taken. Depending on the circumstances, such as workplace safety, you may even want to communicate the nature of the action to the complainant. On the other hand, given privacy considerations, don't communicate to the complainant the nature of the disciplinary action taken against another employee.

▲ **Protect the employee from reprisals:** Ensure employees that if they follow the company's recommended procedure for filing complaints, they will not be penalized in any way—regardless of the nature of the complaint, if it is offered in good faith. When handling a complaint, remind all parties involved of your company's antiretaliation policy. And if you need to resolve a dispute between an employee and a supervisor, caution supervisors about taking any actions that may be perceived as retaliatory, such as unfavorable work assignments, an inappropriate transfer, or a demotion, while an investigation is underway or shortly after its completion.

11.3.1 Settling Disputes

One of the functions of an HR department is to assist in the dispute resolution process: working with managers and employees or with coworkers who have disagreements—about issues such as problem behaviors, time off, back pay, or reinstatement to a position. Line managers are responsible for managing their direct reports, so the role of the human resource function is to facilitate communication or coach managers through the process, providing assistance as needed. Many times, line managers will approach HR practitioners and ask them to take care of uncomfortable situations (such as an employee's lack of hygiene) or increasing absenteeism. To be truly supportive, practitioners should work with managers to provide the tools necessary for them to feel comfortable addressing these issues with employees directly.

Similarly, when employees come to HR to complain about their managers or about coworkers with whom they are having difficulty, the role of HR is really to provide employees with the necessary tools to handle the situation on their own. Often, employees just need someone who is willing to listen to them and make suggestions for ways to address the problem themselves.

Methods of Dispute Resolution

Workplace conflicts sometimes escalate past the point where the parties involved can resolve them without assistance. The worst-case scenario for dispute resolution is costly litigation, so many organizations try to solve problems by using some form of **Alternative Dispute Resolution (ADR)**. The first level of ADR might be an internally-facilitated, problem-solving meeting between the parties to the disagreement. In employee relations disputes, these meetings are often facilitated by an HR practitioner. If resolution is not achieved at this level, organizations may utilize other forms of ADR, such as the three described as follows.

- ▲ **Peer review panel:** A **peer review panel** is an internal method used to resolve disputes. These panels are made up of management and non-management personnel who receive training on company policies, procedures, and work rules. Panel members listen to the parties to the disputes and then make decisions. These panels can be very effective in resolving problems.

- ▲ **Ombudsman:** Some companies establish an **ombudsman** or ombuds, an impartial person not involved in the dispute who speaks with both parties and suggests alternative solutions. An ombudsman can be someone within the company or an outsider.

- ▲ **Mediation:** Similar to the ombudsman approach, the objective of **mediation** is to resolve a dispute by bringing in a third party who, presumably, has no ax to grind and whose job is to help the two parties come up with a solution that is acceptable to both parties. The key qualities of an effective mediator are patience, listening skills, and the ability to find common ground between differing viewpoints. To verify if indeed the mediator has these skills, it's best to ask for references. The advantage of mediation is that the process generally (though not always) leaves both parties at least reasonably satisfied. The downside of mediation: This time-consuming process doesn't always guarantee a resolution.

- ▲ **Arbitration:** Arbitration is a form of alternative dispute resolution used by management and employees to effectively resolve disputes that normally arise during the course of employment. As with mediation, **arbitration** requires the participation of a disinterested third party who listens to both sides of the story. But unlike a mediator, an arbitrator has the power to impose a financial settlement. The key precursor to any arbitration arrangement is the willingness of both parties to accept the judgment of the arbitrator as final.

The dispute resolution procedures in this section are designed only for the usual personality conflicts that arise in the workplace. They generally do not address or resolve complaints of illegal conduct, such as discrimination or sexual harassment.

FOR EXAMPLE

Mediation Saves the Day

All Kentucky state employees in the executive branch are eligible to participate in the Kentucky Employee Mediation Program (KEMP). KEMP was established as a way for employees to solve problems with another employee or with a supervisor. With KEMP, a trained neutral mediator meets with the people in a conflict and helps them reach their own solution. Mediation is available at no cost and can be used to resolve personality conflicts, issues with supervisors, discrimination problems, as well as with topics such as flex time, ADA, suspensions, and workplace environment. The company's goal is to resolve problems before they escalate into much bigger problems, avoiding formal grievances and lawsuits. The company credits KEMP with a sixty-three percent increase in settlement of appeals with an average cost savings of $6,500 for every case settled.

Whenever possible, settle disagreements or disputes at the local level. Encourage employees who are in conflict with one another to come to an agreement themselves with help from their manager or a fellow team member trained in dispute resolution procedures.

SELF-CHECK

1. Explain the purpose of a *grievance procedure*.
2. A quick response is important in cases of employee complaints. True or false?
3. Define *arbitration*.
4. List three methods of *alternative dispute resolution*.

11.4 Contending with Terminations

Even when you have ample cause for doing so, firing employees is always emotional—not only for the employees losing their jobs and the supervisors making the decision, but the coworkers as well.

You can do only so much to ease the disruption that terminations create. You can do a great deal, however, to help ensure that your company's approach to firing meets two criteria:

▲ It protects the dignity and the rights of the employee being terminated.

▲ It protects your company from retaliatory action or wrongful dismissal claims by a disgruntled former employee.

11.4.1 Pre-Termination Preparation

Before a termination can be approved, the employee's personnel file must be reviewed to ensure that it includes the proper documentation to support the action. As part of this process, evaluate the possibility that the termination will produce a wrongful discharge lawsuit or a discrimination claim. Use the following checklist to evaluate a termination proposal:

▲ Were statements ever made, contrary to the usual employment-at-will doctrine, that implied a contract for a specific term?

▲ Is there sufficient documentation in the personnel file to support the termination?

▲ Did the employee recently file a claim—workers' compensation, sexual harassment, or discrimination—against the company? If so, the employee may claim that the discharge is in retaliation of his claim.

▲ Is the employee a member of a class protected against discrimination by employment laws: racial and ethnic minorities, people over forty, or pregnant or disabled employees?

▲ Has the employee made claims about any illegal activity within the company?

▲ Has the company used the reason for termination to discharge other employees in the past?

When there is sufficient proof that termination is necessary, HR should meet with the supervisor to coach him or her on how to appropriately conduct the meeting. By this stage in the process, the employee should not be surprised by the termination, since it should have been referred to as a consequence if improvement did not occur. Regardless of why an employee is leaving your company, keep the termination meeting as conclusive as possible, which means you need to prepare prior to the meeting. The following list covers some issues to consider.

▲ **Final payment:** Ideally, any employee being dismissed should walk out of the termination meeting with a check that covers everything he or she is entitled to, including severance. (Some states, such as California, impose penalties for failing to pay all wages due at the time of termination.) Depending on your company's policy—and on the circumstances that led to the employee's departure—the amount of the final check probably includes money from some or all of the following:

- Salary obligation (pro-rated to the day of dismissal).

- **Severance pay** (money in addition to wages and any other money that employers owe employees when their employment ends) if applicable.

- Any outstanding expense reimbursements due to the employee.

- Money due from accrued vacation, sick days, or personal days.

▲ **Security issues:** Think about company security, including keys, access cards, and company credit cards. If the employee has been using a password to access company files, ask your IT department or consultant (or whoever sets up your computers) to change it on the system. Do the same with credit card privileges.

▲ **Company-owned equipment:** The employee should return any company-owned equipment immediately. If the equipment is off-site (a computer in the employee's home, for example), arrange for its pickup.

▲ **Extended benefits information:** If your company is subject to COBRA regulations (see Sections 2.2 and 9.2.5), you're generally obligated to extend the employee's medical coverage—with no changes—for eighteen months. Who pays for the benefits—your company or the employee—is your call, though you're under no legal obligation to pick up the tab. Make sure, though, that you have all the information the employee needs to keep the coverage going. Also resolve all questions regarding an employee's 401(k), pension or stock plan during the meeting, providing up-to-date information on what options, if any, the employee has regarding those benefits.

▲ **Notification of outplacement or other support mechanisms:** If your company has set up outplacement arrangements (or any other services designed to help terminated employees find another job), provide all the relevant information. In some companies, the outplacement counselor is already on the premises and is the first person the terminated employee talks to following the meeting.

A WAIVER OF RIGHTS

Some companies ask a discharged employee to sign a statement that addresses confidential agreements and also releases the company from legal liabilities. Often called a **severance agreement**, firms require employees to sign this document and return it by a specified date before they receive a severance payout. Note that this payout is separate from any compensation regulated by state or federal law, such as accrued benefits or regular compensation. Such a document should be closely reviewed by an employer's legal counsel, and the employee should also be encouraged to consult legal counsel. In fact, it is a good practice to discourage employees from signing the document during the exit interview. This is because an argument may be made later that the employee signed the document while under duress.

11.4.2 Holding the Termination Meeting

The standard practice in most companies is for the immediate supervisor to deliver the termination notice. Other guidelines can help make the process go smoother:

▲ The message should be delivered in person and in a private location.

▲ The timing of the "best" day and time is a subject of disagreement. Taking steps to ensure that the termination occurs with as little embarrassment for the employee as possible should be the guiding factor in making this decision.

▲ Depending on the circumstances, include a third person, such as another supervisor or member of the human resources department, at the meeting. Do not involve coworkers. (*Note:* Some union contracts require the presence of a third person, such as a union official.)

▲ Deliver the news as soon as the termination meeting starts. Even if you've had a previous discussion about problems and infractions, employees being discharged have the right to be told why the decision was made. Keep the conversation short and to the point and don't try to fill in awkward silences.

▲ If the company has confidentiality agreements, remind employees—in writing—of their legal obligations.

In all cases, remind managers that whatever they say during the termination interview (for example, "It wasn't my idea. Management is simply trying to cut back.") can come back to haunt your company in a wrongful discharge lawsuit (see Section 11.1.1).

11.4.3 Following Post-Termination Protocol

Once completed, and, of course, depending on corporate policy and the circumstances surrounding the termination, the employee should be escorted from the building. Company policies differ on this part of the process: some companies have a security officer escort the employee from the building; others allow the employee to

FOR EXAMPLE

Termination News

An in-house physician for a New York company was fired for refusing to breach the confidentiality of employee medical records. She pursued a wrongful discharge suit and was successful because as a doctor her obligation to her employer was to "do nothing to prevent her from practicing medicine in compliance with the ethical standards of the medical profession." The court held that the doctor's complaint sufficiently alleged that she was engaged in the practice of medicine in her employment and that the company could not require the doctor to perform an act that was in violation of the ethical standards of the medical profession, such as revealing confidential information about employees to whom she provided treatment.

pack up personal items from the desk with a supervisor or security officer present. While the supervisor is conducting the termination meeting, facilities and IT personnel are often simultaneously taking steps to prevent the employee from accessing the company network or facilities once the termination has been completed.

SELF-CHECK

1. Define *severance pay.*
2. A final termination meeting should cover the employee's health continuation rights. True or false?
3. Give an example of *wrongful termination.*
4. Explain the purpose of a *severance agreement.*

11.5 Coping with Layoffs

Layoffs differ from firings in a variety of ways, but one critical aspect comes to mind: The people being let go haven't done anything to warrant losing their jobs. Layoffs occur for a number of reasons, which can include:

▲ Seasonal shifts in the demand for a company's products or services.

▲ An unexpected business downturn that requires the company to make drastic cost reductions.

▲ A plant/company closure.

▲ An initiative that restructures work practices, leaving fewer jobs.

▲ A merger or acquisition that produces redundancy in certain positions.

Generally, when someone is laid off, there is no expectation that she will be returning to work. Some companies use the term in a different sense, however.

When business is slow and they don't need the entire current workforce, some firms (particularly those operating in a unionized environment) notify workers that they will be placed on **furlough** for a period of time and will be offered the opportunity to return to work on a certain date or in stages.

Some companies (especially seasonal businesses and those for which losing a major project creates a significant worker surplus) call this arrangement a "layoff" even though they plan to bring people back to work if and when conditions allow.

Whatever the reason for a layoff, the pressure on the HR function is the same. You need to help your company navigate this difficult turn of events with as few long-term repercussions as possible. The following sections guide you through the process.

11.5.1 Viewing Layoffs as a Last Resort

You should always view layoffs as the last resort in responding to any change in the business environment. When you or your management are weighing the possibility of layoffs, make sure that the management team is considering more than the bottom-line implications and thinking about the impact on customers and remaining staff members. Layoffs may turn out to be inevitable, but management should be aware that the short-term cost-cutting benefits of layoffs may well be offset by the following factors:

▲ Severance and outplacement costs for the laid-off employees (including accrued vacation and sick pay).

▲ The impact on your company's future unemployment compensation obligation.

▲ The effect on morale and productivity.

▲ The impact on future recruiting efforts.

11.5.2 Knowing the Law

If the number of full-time employees in your company exceeds one hundred (fewer in certain states), your layoff strategy needs to consider the Worker Adjustment and Retraining Notification Act (WARN). WARN obligates companies with one hundred or more full-time employees to give sixty days' notice of a mass layoff or reduction in hours. A **mass layoff** at a single site is generally defined as one that affects 500 or more workers or fifty or more workers if they comprise at least thirty-three percent of the active, full-time workforce. A reduction in hours is a fifty percent cut in hours worked each month for six months or more.

Employers covered by WARN don't have to comply in the case of smaller layoffs. Beware, though, that multiple layoffs in a short period of time—for example, fifty days—may trigger WARN obligations. And also note that a number of states have their own WARN-like laws. These matters can be tricky, so consult your legal counsel. You need to be careful, too, that you're not laying off a disproportionately high number of employees who are in any group protected by Equal Employment Opportunity Commission (EEOC) legislation. (For more details on EEOC and WARN, see Chapter 2.)

11.5.3 Easing the Burden

Moral considerations notwithstanding, it is in your best long-term interests to do whatever is reasonably possible and fiscally responsible to ease both the financial and psychological pain that layoffs invariably create. Of course, be as generous as you can with severance packages. But you can take additional steps that will help employees get back on their feet again.

▲ **Outplacement specialists** help dismissed employees (usually middle managers and above) regroup and find new jobs. In a typical outplacement program, managers who've been let go get an opportunity to attend seminars or one-on-one sessions in such areas as career counseling and in job-hunting basics. Typically, too, the job seekers are given office space, access to a phone, and administrative help for a predetermined period of time.

▲ **Staffing companies** can help workers get back into the workforce with opportunities for project-based and full-time positions. These firms maintain existing networks with many employers and may even specialize in particular industries, such as high-tech, legal, or finance. The big advantage is that they don't charge your company or the worker. When the employee is placed by the staffing firm, his or her new employer pays the staffing firm's placement fees.

11.5.4 Finding Alternatives to Layoffs

If the purpose of the layoff is to cut down on costs (as opposed to reduce redundancy), you may want to explore options that, at the very least, can reduce the number of people who need to be terminated:

▲ **Temporary pay cuts:** Reducing salary costs is probably the simplest and most direct way to cut staffing costs without cutting staff. The key to this

FOR EXAMPLE

Early Retirement in the News

In 2007 *The Boston Globe* announced that twenty-four journalists had accepted buyout offers from the newspaper. The move was made in an effort to avoid layoffs "in the face of some of the harshest conditions for newspapers and other mass media in years." The paper had intended to cut nineteen jobs with the early retirement offer, but many more people applied. Because online and other competitors are cutting into newspaper circulation and advertising revenue, other newspapers have been forced into making similar moves: *The Philadelphia Inquirer* laid off about seventy editorial employees and *The Minneapolis Star Tribune* cut twenty-four jobs through buyouts.

strategy is to ensure that everyone—including senior managers—shares the pain. *The downside:* No matter how justified the cuts, some workers will resent losing pay—and the decision to cut back on pay may induce your best and most mobile workers to quit. Though there is no legal limit on the duration of a temporary pay cut, the sooner you can communicate when wages will be restored, the more positive the impact on morale.

▲ **Work w4eek reductions:** This option is worth exploring for companies that have large numbers of hourly workers. You maintain the same hourly rates, but employees work fewer hours. As an inducement to accept the lower take-home pay, most companies pledge to maintain benefits at full-time levels. *The downside:* Reduction of hours has no effect on salaried employees and managers who are not paid by the hour.

▲ **Early retirement:** An often-used method of reducing payroll costs is to encourage early retirement, when retirement is elected before the normal retirement age, generally through financial incentives. Because senior employees are usually the most highly paid, trimming their ranks can result in significant savings. *The downside:* Senior employees are often your most valued, and losing too many of them at one time can significantly weaken the leadership of your firm. Remember, too, that under the Age Discrimination in Employment Act, it is illegal, with rare exceptions, to force anyone to retire.

SELF-CHECK

1. Explain the difference between firing and laying off an employee.
2. Define *furlough.*
3. What is the role of the Worker Adjustment and Retraining Notification Act?
4. Give two alternatives to layoffs.

SUMMARY

As HR managers face the challenge of dealing with employee discipline it is critical that they have a clear understanding of laws regulating disciplinary proceedings and employee rights. The disciplinary policies developed and enforced by a company help to ensure that employees throughout the organization are treated fairly and consistently. With wrongful discharge lawsuits on the rise, employers must be more cautious than ever about how disciplinary matters are handled, consulting lawyers when in doubt. Although disciplinary processes will vary between organizations, their goal is to ensure that employees are kept informed of any issues that develop. At the same time, an organization's disciplinary process should provide an organization with sufficient documentation required to prove that a disciplinary matter was handled properly. An effective disciplinary process will also provide employees with a grievance procedure or an opportunity to voice workplace concerns. In some cases, workplace conflicts will need to be settled using various methods of dispute resolution such as mediation and arbitration. When terminations are necessary, they are often incredibly difficult situations. HR professionals need to be able to provide support for managers who must take this action. Of particular importance is any pre-termination preparation that is required—assembling documentation and reviewing records, for example. Finally, employers should have a grasp on the nuances of layoff procedures, including ways of avoiding such measures.

KEY TERMS

Alternative Dispute Resolution (ADR)	An alternative to battles in court; involves mediation or arbitration.
Arbitration	A neutral third party listens to both sides of the dispute; unlike a mediator, an arbitrator has the power to impose a financial settlement.

Early retirement	When retirement is elected before the normal retirement age; a method of reducing payroll costs.
Employment-at-will	Employee or employer can terminate a relationship with no liability if there was no express contract for a definite term governing the employment.
Furlough	Generally used in unionized environments to temporarily lay off employees; employees often return to work on a certain date or in stages.
Grievance procedure	A disciplinary process that provides a means for dealing with problem behavior among employees.
Layoffs	Termination of employees, but in cases when the people being let go haven't done anything to warrant losing their jobs.
Mass layoff	A layoff that affects 500 or more workers or 50 or more workers if they comprise at least 33 percent of the active, full-time workforce.
Mediation	Process in which a neutral third party is brought in to help two parties come up with a solution that is acceptable to both parties.
Ombudsman	An impartial person not involved in a dispute who speaks with both parties and suggests alternative solutions.
Outplacement specialists	Companies that help dismissed employees, usually middle managers and above, regroup and find new jobs.
Peer review panel	Dispute-resolution method in which management and non-management personnel listen to disputing parties and make decisions.
Severance agreement	A statement that addresses confidential agreements and releases a company from legal liabilities.
Severance pay	Money in addition to wages and any other money that employers owe employees at termination.
Staffing companies	Companies that can help workers get back into the workforce; sometimes specializing in particular industries.
Termination-at-will	Also known as employment-at-will.
Wrongful termination	When an employer terminates someone for a reason prohibited by statute or breaches a contract.

ASSESS YOUR UNDERSTANDING

Go to www.wiley.com/college/messmer to assess your knowledge of discipline management.
Measure your learning by comparing pre-test and post-test results.

Summary Questions

1. Employment at will allows
   (a) employees to apply for a job.
   (b) employers to fire employees.
   (c) employees to quit a job.
   (d) both b and c.

2. Juries favor employers over employees in cases of wrongful dismissal. True or false?

3. The employment-at-will doctrine only applies to 45 of the 50 states. True or false?

4. Which step of the disciplinary process typically involves the first written communication to the involved employee?
   (a) initial notification
   (b) second warning
   (c) final warning
   (d) termination

5. Wrongful dismissal suits have increased in the past twenty years. True or false?

6. In investigations of workplace misconduct, the accused is the subject of all questioning. True or false?

7. What type of policy protects an employee who has filed a complaint against reprisal?

8. Methods of alternative dispute resolution are used to settle disputes in court. True or false?

9. Which ADR method can result in financial settlements?
   (a) peer review
   (b) grievance procedure
   (c) mediation
   (d) arbitration

10. A termination meeting should be held on a Friday at 4:30. True or false?

11. Which of the following should be included in a termination meeting?
    (a) supervisor
    (b) coworker
    (c) relative
    (d) CEO
12. Outplacement arrangements assist an employee by
    (a) mediating a termination meeting.
    (b) providing employment assistance.
    (c) setting up a peer review panel.
    (d) arranging COBRA benefits.
13. If a company has more than 100 employees it must adhere to the guidelines of which legislation when considering layoffs?
    (a) COBRA
    (b) FLSA
    (c) ADA
    (d) WARN
14. Name two ways in which employers can assist employees that are laid off in pursuing future employment.
15. Explain how a work-week reduction program can help avoid employee layoffs.

Applying This Chapter

1. You've been asked to draft a memo from the HR department of a sporting goods manufacturer to department managers regarding disciplinary procedures. In it, list three things that managers should consider when dealing with employee discipline problems.
2. A member of your telemarketing team has consistently failed to meet her sales goals. Describe what steps you would take before having to fire her.
3. A female employee complained to human resources that a supervisor was touching her and making sexually inappropriate comments. A week later she was fired for allegedly using language that threatened violence against the company. Without assuming that the employee would be successful, what two legal complaints could she file against the company?
4. Imagine that you are the supervisor of an employee with a serious and unresolvable insubordination issue. John, who has been with your

company for five years, is a talented employee, but he has suffered from attitude problems since being passed over for a promotion six months ago. He has been officially warned about his disrespectful behaviors (eye-rolling and sarcasm), but you have seen no improvement. Draft what you will say in his termination meeting.

5. With twenty employees at your local home renovation company, the people who work for you almost seem like family. A steep decline in the market has forced you to consider letting five employees go. Develop an alternative plan that might save those five jobs.

YOU TRY IT

Policy Maker

Using research from the Internet or other sources, create an employment-at-will policy for a music recording label. Ensure that it does not imply a contract of employment that could be used against the company in a lawsuit.

Problem Behaviors

Investigate the disciplinary procedures in place in your organization.

- Is information on the process available to employees?
- How many steps are in the process? How does it differ from the example cited in this chapter?
- Has the organization been involved in any wrongful discharge suits?

Firing Line

Interview friends and coworkers who've been discharged or laid off from jobs in the past. In what ways could the experiences have been improved for those employees?

12

MANAGING WORKPLACE HEALTH AND SAFETY
Complying With OSHA Regulations

Starting Point

Go to www.wiley.com/college/messmer to assess your knowledge of the basics of workplace health and safety.
Determine where you need to concentrate your effort.

What You'll Learn in This Chapter

▲ The three employer requirements of the Occupational Safety and Health Act
▲ Three types of environmental hazards identified by OSHA and NIOSH
▲ Common safety standards developed by OSHA
▲ Aspects of an employer-sponsored safety and health plan

After Studying This Chapter, You Will Be Able To

▲ Categorize workplace hazards according to OSHA priorities
▲ Propose ways of securing assistance with health and safety issues
▲ Evaluate a workplace for potential environmental health hazards
▲ Assess an organization's OSHA compliance efforts

INTRODUCTION

Employers must obviously provide a place for employees to work, and human resource professionals should be familiar with what is required to make the workplace a healthful, safe, and secure environment. The key piece of federal legislation affecting virtually every business in the United States is the Occupational Safety and Health Act (OSH Act). This chapter describes the legal requirements of OSHA, discusses the various occupational health hazards, and covers some of the issues employers face in providing a hazard-free workplace.

12.1 Understanding the Occupational Safety and Health Act

For more than a hundred years, sporadic legislation was enacted by different states and the federal government to address specific workplace safety concerns, usually in regard to mine safety or factory conditions, but there was no comprehensive legislation requiring employers to protect workers from injury or illness. That changed with the **Occupational Safety and Health Act of 1970** (the OSH Act), a comprehensive piece of federal legislation that continues to impact employers in virtually every company in America.

The intent of Congress, as stated in the preamble to the OSH Act, is to ensure safe and healthful working conditions for American workers. To accomplish this purpose, the act establishes three simple duties:

1. Employers must provide every employee a place to work that is "free from recognized hazards that are causing or are likely to cause death or serious physical harm."
2. Employers must comply with all safety and health standards disseminated in accordance with the act.
3. Employees are required to comply with occupational safety and health standards, rules, and regulations that impact their individual actions and behavior.

12.1.1 Setting Safety Standards: OSHA

A key component of the Occupational Safety and Health Act of 1970 was the creation of the **Occupational Safety and Health Administration (OSHA)**, which now sets safety standards for virtually every business in the United States. OSHA enforces those standards with the use of fines, and in the case of criminal actions, can call on the Department of Justice to file charges against offenders.

In creating OSHA, the OSH Act gave the agency the authority to develop and enforce mandatory standards applicable to all businesses engaged in interstate commerce. The definition of interstate commerce is sufficiently broad to cover most businesses, with the exception of the following:

▲ Sole proprietors without employees.

▲ Family farms employing only family members.

▲ Mining operations, which are covered by the Mine Safety and Health Act.

The act encouraged OSHA to work with industry and build on standards already developed by specific industries, and it authorized enforcement action to ensure that employers comply with the standards. OSHA was charged with developing reporting procedures to track trends in workplace safety and health so that the development of preventive measures would be an ongoing process that changed with the development of new processes and technologies.

WHAT ABOUT ERGONOMICS?

Changes in technology and industry have resulted in evolving worker safety concerns. Consider the current emphasis on ergonomics, the study of workplace design and the physical and psychological impact it has on workers. For occupations ranging from poultry processing to data entry, for example, carpal tunnel syndrome is a concern. OSHA's website features specialized information on the topic of ergonomics, with guidelines and assistance for both employees and employers (www.osha.gov/SLTC/ergonomics/). (See Section 12.2.1 for more on physical hazards such as ergonomic injuries.)

FOR EXAMPLE

Cost of Noncompliance

Congress intended the OSH Act to reduce the occurrences of injuries, illnesses, and deaths affecting Americans in their places of work. Though it can be difficult to measure how much money individual employers save when safety and health standards are implemented, in 2003, OSHA levied fines totaling more than $82,000,000 against employers who did not comply with established standards. Despite the fact that businesses did not develop concern for the health, safety, and security of their employees of their own accord, employers realize a number of benefits from providing safe work environments. Cost savings are also realized when fewer claims for workers' compensation insurance premiums are filed. Fewer injuries and illnesses also mean improved productivity and employee morale.

Evaluating Occupational Hazards: NIOSH

The OSH Act also created the **National Institute of Occupational Safety and Health (NIOSH)** as part of the Department of Health and Human Services. NIOSH is charged with researching and evaluating workplace hazards and recommending ways to reduce the effect of those hazards on workers. NIOSH also supports education and training in the field of occupational safety and health by developing and providing educational materials and training aids and sponsoring conferences on workplace safety and health issues. The NIOSH website (www.cdc.gov/niosh/homepage.html) provides a wealth of information for human resources professionals.

Giving States the Lead

The OSH Act encourages states to take the lead in developing and enforcing safety and health programs for businesses within their jurisdictions by providing grants to help identify specific issues and to develop enforcement and prevention programs.

12.1.2 OSHA Enforcement

OSHA's success is the result of strong enforcement of the standards it has developed. As demonstrated in the nineteenth and twentieth centuries, without the threat of financial penalty, some business owners would choose to ignore injury and illness prevention requirements. That being the case, OSHA established fines and penalties that can be assessed against businesses when violations occur. Table 12-1 describes the violation levels and associated penalties for noncompliance.

OSHA Inspections

OSHA is empowered by the OSH Act to inspect workplaces. Most inspections are conducted without notice by a **Compliance Safety and Health Officer (CSHO)** who has been trained on OSHA standards and how to recognize safety and health hazards in the workplace. OSHA has established a hierarchy of situations to give priority to inspection of the most dangerous workplace environments.

During fiscal year 2004, OSHA conducted 39,167 inspections. Table 12-2 provides a breakdown of the numbers of inspections, as well as the costs of violations identified during the inspections.

Table 12-3 describes the priorities OSHA uses in allocating time for inspections. In most cases, an OSHA inspection occurs as the result of a serious work-related injury or death, or of a complaint from an employee about dangerous working conditions. Inspections are conducted by a Compliance Safety and Health Officer and follow a distinct procedure. In advance of the inspection, the CSHO prepares by reviewing records related to any previous incidents or inspections or employee complaints. The inspector also determines what, if any, special testing equipment will be necessary for the inspection. Upon arrival at the worksite, the

Table 12-1: Categories of OSHA Violations

Violation	Description	Fine
Willful	Assessed when there is evidence of an intentional violation of the OSH Act or "plain indifference" to its requirements.	$5,000 to $70,000 per violation
Serious	Assessed when there is substantial probability of death or serious physical harm as a result of the hazard.	Up to $7,000
Other-than-Serious	The hazard could have a direct and immediate effect on the safety and health of employees.	Up to $7,000
Repeat	OSHA has previously issued citations for substantially similar conditions.	Up to $70,000 per violation
Failure to Abate	The employer failed to abate a prior violation.	Up to $7,000 per day past the abatement date
de-minimus	Assessed for violations with no direct or immediate relationship to safety or health.	$0

Source: OSHA Facts, www.osha.gov/as/opa/oshafacts.html

Table 12-2: Violations and Penalties from 2004 Inspections

Violations	Percent	Type	Current Penalties
462	0.5%	Willful	$14,553,171
61,666	71.1%	Serious	$54,526,440
2,360	2.7%	Repeat	$9,755,960
301	0.3%	Failure to Abate	$1,611,943
21,705	25%	Other	$1,960,084
214	0.2%	Unclassified	$2,785,342
86,708	TOTAL		$85,192,940

Source: OSHA Facts, www.osha.gov/as/opa/oshafacts.html

Table 12-3: OSHA Inspection Priorities

Priority	Hazard	Description
First	Imminent Danger	A reasonable certainty that immediate death or serious injury from existing workplace hazards will occur before normal enforcement procedures can take place.
Second	Catastrophes and Fatal Accidents	Employers must report fatal accidents or serious injuries resulting in the hospitalization of 3 or more employees within 8 hours. OSHA will inspect to determine if any safety violations contributed to the accident.
Third	Employee Complaints	Employees may request inspections when they feel violations exist that threaten physical harm.
Fourth	Programmed High-Hazard Inspections	Based on statistical analysis, OSHA conducts planned inspections of industries or jobs that have high incident rates for death, injury, and illness.
Fifth	Follow-up Inspections	CSHOs follow up on previously issued citations to ensure that the employer has taken action to correct the violation.

Source: OSHA Facts, www.osha.gov/as/opa/oshafacts.html

inspection commences with an opening conference, proceeds to a workplace tour, and ends with a closing conference; see explanations that follow:

▲ **Presentation of CSHO credentials:** At the beginning of an inspection, CSHOs present their official credentials and ask to speak with the employer's representative.

▲ **Opening conference:** During the opening conference, the CSHO informs the employer of the reason for the inspection and explains the inspection process.

▲ **Facility tour:** Activities that can occur during an inspection include the following:
  • Review of the **safety and health program**.
  • Examination of records, including OSHA logs, records of employee exposure to toxic substances, and medical records.

- Ensuring that the OSHA workplace poster is prominently displayed.
- Evaluation of compliance with OSHA standards specific to the worksite.
- Pointing out unsafe working conditions to the employer and suggesting possible remedial actions.

▲ **Closing conference:** The closing conference usually includes both the employer and employee representatives and it is during this time that the employer representative has an opportunity to provide records and documents to demonstrate compliance activities that have been occurred. The CSHO discusses any possible citations or penalties that may be issued. Should a citation be issued, the employer must post it at or near the worksite involved, where it must remain for three working days or until the violation has been abated, whichever is longer.

WORKING WITH OSHA

Like it or not, OSHA is a fact of life for most businesses in the United States. Although some business owners may find the safety standards costly and inefficient, OSHA does make an effort to work with them to reduce those costs:

▲ **OSHA assistance:** OSHA provides many sources for employers and employees to obtain information about workplace health and safety issues. Its extensive website (www.osha.gov) provides access to the laws, regulations, and standards enforced by OSHA as well as general information on prevention. In addition, OSHA publishes pamphlets, brochures, and training materials that are available to employers.

▲ **OSHA consultants:** The agency provides consultation services to work with individual businesses to solve safety and health problems without going through an OSHA inspection. The benefit of the consultation process is that it provides a means for the employer to find out whether or not its operations are in compliance with standards without the risk of incurring fines and penalties. The result of a consultation is a list of workplace hazards that must be corrected. The OSHA consultant works with the employer to establish a time frame for abating the hazards and follows up from time to time to ensure that the changes are being implemented. An employer who requests a consultation must be willing to make the changes identified during the process; if not, the consultation findings are referred to an enforcement officer for appropriate action and could result in the assessment of fines.

Safety and Health Plans

OSHA requires employers to develop plans describing how safety, health, or emergency situations will be handled if they should occur. There are some common elements to all these plans, including a clear policy statement and the commitment of senior management to its implementation, a description of the ways in which employees are able to participate in creating the plan, and an identification of the employees responsible for specific tasks outlined in the plan. The plans must also define the process for employees to use when reporting workplace hazards and outline the training program that will be used to inform employees about safety and health requirements. Section 12.3.2 has more on how these plans are administered.

SELF-CHECK

1. Explain the intended purpose of the Occupational Safety and Health Act of 1970.
2. How does a safe, healthful, and secure workplace benefit an employer?
3. What is the difference between OSHA and NIOSH?
4. Which type of hazard is the first priority of OSHA?
   a. imminent
   b. fatal accident
   c. high-hazard inspection
   d. follow-up inspection

12.2 Identifying Occupational Hazards

The connection between illness and the work environment became known as long ago as the ancient Greek and Roman civilizations when the effects of lead and mercury poisoning on mine workers was first identified. For many centuries, mines were the chief source of workplace illness. When the Industrial Age began in the eighteenth century, mines were no longer the only source of occupational illnesses, and side effects from other industrial processes began to affect the health of workers (cancer, for example). As industrialization increased during the nineteenth century, other illnesses were identified and connected to manufacturing processes.

Table 12-4: Examples of Environmental Health Hazards

Chemical	Physical	Biological
Asbestos	Ergonomic design	Bacteria
Battery acid	Stress	Contaminated water
Corrosives	Extreme temperatures	Dusts
Gas fumes	Light, noise	Fungi
Pesticides	Electrical currents	Molds
Polyurethane foam	Radiation	Plants
Solvents	Vibrations	Viruses

12.2.1 Recognizing Environmental Health Hazards

As discussed in Section 12.1, the Occupational Safety and Health Act of 1970 created two federal agencies to identify hazards, develop standards for preventing illness and injury, and enforce the use of these standards in American workplaces. Working in collaboration, and as illustrated in Table 12-4, OSHA and the National Institute for Occupational Safety and Health (NIOSH) have identified three categories of **environmental health hazards**—chemical, physical, and biological—and established standards designed to protect workers from them. The following sections describe how these issues affect the health of employees.

Chemical Hazards

Although they are most often found in manufacturing processes, **chemical hazards** that pose a physical or health hazard to workers can also affect workers in other environments as well. Over the years, a number of hazardous chemicals have been identified, and OSHA has developed standards designed to eliminate or reduce their harmful effects. These standards protect workers who are exposed to asbestos, corrosives, pesticides, gas fumes, or solvents during the course of their work by requiring the use of appropriate preventative measures.

For the most part, when people think of hazardous chemical exposures, they think of manufacturing and industrial work areas. Chemical risks, however, can occur in other work environments, such as office buildings. As an example, the carbonless copy paper often used for multi-part forms has been linked to irritations of the skin, eyes, and upper respiratory tract. These symptoms can be prevented or reduced with simple measures such as washing hands after handling

---

FOR EXAMPLE

Toxic Exposure

Exposure to chemical substances can result in a wide variety of health effects. Those effects resulting from the collapse and subsequent fires at the World Trade Center on September 11, 2001, have been the subject of much study and concern. The towers' collapse pulverized cement, glass windows, insulation (asbestos and fiber glass), and other building elements. Smoke from this fire contained the toxins from computers, wiring, carpet, furniture, fuels, and more. Because the long-term effects on rescue and recovery workers are unknown, medical monitoring programs will help to determine the health effects of 9/11-related exposure. The World Trade Center Medical Monitoring Program provides free medical exams to workers and volunteers who responded to 9/11 attacks in New York City. The goal of the exams is to provide workers with information about health; the information gained will also be valuable in understanding how to protect worker health in future emergencies.

---

the paper; limiting contact between hands, eyes, and mouths; and ensuring that the workplace has adequate ventilation, humidity, and temperature controls.

To aid employers in identifying possible chemical hazards in their workplaces, OSHA requires chemical manufacturers to provide a material safety data sheet (MSDS) for each chemical product they produce. The MSDS is to be included with the product when it is delivered to the end user to aid in identifying preventative measures. Employers are required to maintain copies of the MSDS sheets in areas where the chemicals are present, and in the event of an inspection by an OSHA investigator, must be able to produce the documents if requested. Even products as common as toner cartridges for copy machines include an MSDS that should be maintained in or around the office copy machine.

Physical Hazards

Electrical currents, excessive noise, too much or too little light, radiation, and vibrations are all examples of **physical hazards**. When exposure to any of these elements exceeds established standards, the results can, at a minimum, have long-lasting negative (even fatal) effects on worker health and productivity.

With the increased use of computers in the workplace, ergonomic injuries have become more prevalent in workers whose work requires them to spend the bulk of their time typing. An **ergonomic injury** is one that is related to the way the physical environment is designed; for example, the placement of the keyboard relative to the height of the employee's chair can affect the occurrence of a musculoskeletal disorder (MSD), such as carpal tunnel syndrome. (See "What About Ergonomics?" earlier in this chapter.)

Biological Hazards

Bacteria, molds, contaminated water, and dust are **biological hazards** known to cause illness to workers. Many of the illnesses resulting from these hazards have long-lasting effects and may even be fatal to workers. These illnesses, which are most often the result of mining and industrial operations, include byssinosis, silicosis, and pneumoconiosis. Byssinosis, also known as brown lung disease, affects textile workers who breathe the dust created during the processing of cotton, flax, and hemp. Silicosis is found in workers who are exposed to silica dust as a result of their work in mines or metal casting operations; it results in symptoms that include chronic coughing, shortness of breath, weight loss, and fever. Pneumoconiosis, which is better known as black lung disease, is found in coal miners and produces shortness of breath and a chronic cough.

The occurrence of these diseases has been reduced with the use of preventative measures that include the use of facemasks by workers and steps taken by employers to reduce dust levels in the workplace.

12.2.2 Understanding Safety Standards

The OSH Act of 1970 established OSHA to work with unions, employers, and industry associations to develop standards for safe work environments. Subsequent to the establishment of OSHA, many state legislatures created similar agencies to address workplace safety issues specific to the businesses and environmental conditions in their states. Employers must be aware of and comply with safety standards established by either federal or state agencies; when the agencies have conflicting requirements, business owners must comply with the regulation that has the strictest requirement.

Many of the safety standards developed by OSHA deal with situations specific to a single industry or production process, whereas other safety standards have broad application across industries and businesses. The following are some of the more common standards that HR practitioners may encounter.

- ▲ **General Duty Standard:** The **general duty standard** applies to all businesses and requires business owners to provide a safe work environment for their employees. Employees also have a responsibility under this standard to conduct themselves in a way that complies with all OSHA standards and rules pertaining to the jobs they perform for the company.

- ▲ **Hazard Communication Standard (HCS):** The **hazard communication standard** requires employers to inform employees of the dangers of chemicals used in the workplace. This is the standard that requires chemical manufacturers to provide MSDS sheets, as discussed in "Chemical Hazards," in Section 12.2.1.

- ▲ **Occupational Noise Exposure Standard:** The **occupational noise exposure standard** sets allowable levels of workplace noise and identifies procedures for measuring noise and audiometric testing for employees who must work in noisy environments.

▲ **Personal Protective Equipment (PPE) Standard: Personal protective equipment standards** require employers to provide appropriate garments and equipment for dealing with different types of hazards, such as compressed gas, radiation, explosive substances, and ammonia. The standard also requires employers to train workers in the proper use and maintenance of the equipment.

▲ **Lockout/Tagout Standard:** The **lockout/tagout standard** is designed to reduce injuries and deaths by preventing machinery or equipment from starting unexpectedly during repairs and maintenance.

▲ **Blood-Borne Pathogens:** A blood-borne pathogen is a microorganism in human blood that can cause disease. Although health care workers are most at risk of contracting illnesses transmitted by blood and other body fluids (such as Human Immunodeficiency Virus [HIV]), workers in other industries can be exposed to them as well. The **blood-borne pathogen standard** requires employers to develop a written exposure control plan that advises employees of the steps they can take to prevent or reduce the effects of exposures.

SEEKING OUTSIDE ASSISTANCE

Employers can often partner with their workers' compensation insurance carriers, who have a vested interest in ensuring safe work environments, to establish workplace safety programs that comply with federal and state requirements. These insurance carriers often employ workplace safety specialists who provide assistance for employers through onsite visits designed to assist employers in complying with OSHA regulations, and thus reduce workers' compensation costs. These specialists might offer suggestions with regard to noise issues, air quality, lifting, forklift handling, and other safety issues. Employers whose business processes involve the use of industrial chemicals will find assistance with the vendors who manufacture these substances, including onsite training.

SELF-CHECK

1. List the three types of environmental hazards.
2. The purpose of an MSDS is to inform workers of the dangers of chemicals used in the workplace. True or false?
3. Give two examples of biological hazards in the workplace.

12.3 Overseeing Health and Safety Programs

American employers are legally obligated to provide a workplace in which neither the environment nor the work practices subject employees to any unreasonable risk in safety or health. However, the safety- and health-related regulations vary considerably, within an industry and according to state or federal regulations. Consequently, no one single standard or list of safety- and health-related regulations apply across the board to every company.

The regulations that apply depend on your particular company and industry. In addition, although the Occupational Safety and Health Act is applicable throughout the United States, it permits states to implement their own plans with requirements above and beyond the federal regulations. More than twenty states have adopted their own plan, so it's important that you familiarize yourself with both federal and state laws regarding safety and health. When in doubt, consult an attorney.

HEALTH AND SAFETY: THE BOTTOM LINE

Although most people agree that a healthful, safe, and secure work environment benefits employees, some business owners question how this environment contributes to the achievement of corporate goals. They argue that the cost of improving health and safety adds no value to the bottom line; instead, it has the opposite effect of making it more difficult to compete in world markets by increasing product costs. The answer to this argument is that occupational health and safety programs make significant contributions to the achievement of corporate goals by reducing costs, building good will in the community, protecting assets, and improving productivity.

12.3.1 Employer Responsibilities and Rights

As discussed in Section 12.1 of this chapter, the OSH Act has three requirements, two of which pertain to employers. Not only must employers provide a workplace that is safe and healthful for employees, they must also comply with established standards. OSHA has established other requirements for employers as required by the law:

▲ Employers are expected to take steps to minimize or reduce hazards and ensure that employees have and use safe tools, equipment, and personal protective equipment (PPE) and ensure that they are properly maintained.

▲ Employers are responsible to inform all employees about OSHA, posting the OSHA poster in a prominent location and making them aware of the standards that apply in the worksite.

▲ Appropriate warning signs that conform to the OSHA standards must be posted where needed to make employees aware of potential hazards.

▲ Compliance with OSHA standards also means that employers must educate employees and train them to follow safe operating procedures.

▲ Businesses with 11 or more employees must maintain records of all workplace injuries and illnesses and post them from February 1 through April 30 each year.

▲ Within eight hours of a fatal accident, or one resulting in hospitalization for three or more employees, a report must be filed with the nearest OSHA office.

▲ An accident report log must be made available to employees, former employees, or employee representatives when reasonably requested.

▲ Businesses with more than 11 employees must adhere to OSHA record-keeping requirements. (See Handling Administrative Responsibilities in Section 12.3.2.)

▲ When employees report unsafe conditions to OSHA, the employer may not retaliate or discriminate against them.

Employers have some rights as well, including the right to seek advice and consultation from OSHA and to be active in industry activities involved in health and safety issues. Employers may also participate in the OSHA Standard Advisory Committee process in writing or by giving testimony at hearings. Finally, employers may contact the National Institute of Occupational Safety and Health (NIOSH) for information about substances used to determine whether or not they are toxic.

At times, employers may be unable to comply with OSHA standards due to the nature of specific operations. When this happens, they may apply to OSHA for temporary or permanent waivers to the standards along with proof that the employer has developed protections that meet or exceed those of the OSHA standard.

EMPLOYEE RESPONSIBILITIES AND RIGHTS

When the OSH Act was passed in 1970, employees were granted the basic right to a workplace with safe and healthful working conditions. The act intended to encourage employers and employees to collaborate in reducing workplace hazards. Employees have the responsibility to comply with all OSHA standards and with the safety and health procedures implemented by their employers. The act gave employees the following specific rights to:

▲ Seek safety and health on the job without fear of punishment.

▲ Know what hazards exist on the job by reviewing the OSHA standards, rules, and regulations that the employer has available at the workplace.

▲ Be provided with the hazard communication plan containing information about hazards in the workplace and preventive measures employees should take to avoid illness or injury, and to be trained in the measures.

▲ Access the exposure and medical records employers are required to keep relative to safety and health issues.

▲ Request an OSHA inspection, speak privately with the inspector, accompany the inspector during the inspection, and respond to the inspector's questions during the inspection.

▲ Observe steps taken by the employer to monitor and measure hazardous materials in the workplace, and access records resulting from those steps.

▲ Request information from NIOSH regarding the potential toxic effects of substances used in the workplace.

▲ File a complaint about workplace safety or health hazards with OSHA and remain anonymous to the employer.

12.3.2 Administering a Health and Safety Plan

As mentioned in Section 12.1.2, OSHA requires employers to develop plans describing how safety or health situations will be handled if they should occur. A health and safety plan (sometimes referred to as an injury and illness prevention program) should be tailored specifically to a workplace situation and the tasks involved. Such plans should include a clear policy statement and the commitment of senior management to its implementation, a description of the ways in which employees are able to participate in creating the plan, and an identification of the employees responsible for specific tasks outlined in the plan. The plans must also do the following:

▲ Establish a process for communication between employees and employer.

▲ Identify and assess hazards that are known to exist in the organization, and describe the steps that have been taken to correct those hazards.

▲ Include a process that ensures an ongoing review of the work environment so that new hazards can be identified and corrected.

▲ Include a description of proper procedures that are to be used for maintenance of machinery and equipment.

▲ Define the procedures to be followed to report and investigate any workplace accidents that do occur.

SAFETY AND LOSS PREVENTION

In some organizations, a health and safety program covers issues in the arena of workplace security, ranging from protecting physical assets from damage to preventing theft of intellectual property and financial assets. Programs of this scope may begin with a risk assessment, which looks at external and internal threats to an organization. A resulting security plan may call for the implementation of protective measures such as fire alarms, door locks, and security guards.

Taking the Safety Lead: The Safety Manager

Depending on the size and nature of the organization, responsibility for health, safety, and security functions can be assigned to individuals along with other unrelated duties, assigned to a single individual who focuses on the safety manager function, or (in very large organizations) have entire departments devoted to health and safety.

In the event that you've been given the responsibility for safety, probably in addition to your regular duties, three steps will help get you started:

1. *Understanding Your Responsibilities*

Meet with the person who appointed you to obtain a clear understanding of your role and responsibilities as well the expectations of managers and supervisors. This stage will help you identify how much time is needed, what you need to know, and how much support is available. Here are key questions to ask senior management:

▲ What are my responsibilities?
▲ Will I have any authority to enforce safety polices?
▲ What are the safety expectations of managers and supervisors?
▲ How will senior management support the program?
▲ What type of training will I receive?

What does a safety person do? The purpose of most safety managers is to oversee the overall safety program and OSHA compliance, and help prevent workplace injuries. A safety manager will usually be involved in tasks ranging from program development to setting up compliance systems. The following list offers an idea of some typical tasks of a person responsible for safety:

▲ Develop and update safety policies.
▲ Set up safety training programs for supervisors, employees, and new hires.

▲ Review employee accident reports and help investigate accidents.

▲ Maintain OSHA-required documentation.

▲ Serve as the safety committee facilitator.

▲ Provide recommendations to management to reduce workplace injury rates.

▲ Conduct safety inspections and audits with supervisors.

▲ Assist in managing the workers' compensation and return-to-work programs.

In many companies, the safety person manages the overall program, and the supervisors are responsible for implementing and enforcing safety policies in their departments. Accident investigation, conducting job specific safety training, and correcting hazards are usually the supervisors' responsibility.

Whatever the arrangement, make a point to meet with managers and supervisors before developing the program. To help reduce resistance to change and to create buy-in, ask senior management to meet with supervisors to ask for their ideas and explain the benefits of the safety program. This critical step sets the tone for your entire program and ensures that safety will be a shared responsibility.

SAFETY SMARTS

Assess and build safety knowledge: Because your role carries legal responsibilities and involves the safety of others, it's important to assess your safety knowledge. Are you familiar with workplace hazards such as machine guarding, respiratory protection, and chemical safety? If you lack knowledge in a particular area, seek technical assistance from OSHA or other safety organizations. The American Society of Safety Engineers (ASSE) offers a wide variety of technical books and resources: www.asse.org.

---

2. *Learning the Safety Requirements for Your Organization*

OSHA requirements can vary from state to state. For example, monthly safety inspections are required in some states, but in others you can choose the frequency. Standards vary because some states have their own state OSHA. States that don't must follow federal OSHA standards. Here are a few OSHA tips:

▲ To find out if your company falls under a state OSHA or federal OSHA plan, visit the federal OSHA website map at: www.osha.gov or contact your local OSHA Consultation office. Many OSHA websites also have safety program and training information to help you get started.

▲ Safety standards are constantly changing; therefore, you will need to have up-to-date information. Consider a regulatory update subscription service to keep track of new requirements or check the OSHA website.

▲ When federal OSHA changes or adopts new safety standards, state OSHAs have a certain timeframe to adopt similar or more stringent standards. You may need to change or update your program when this occurs. To make sure your policies stay current, plan to review them at least annually.

MODELS OF SAFETY

The OSHA website is an invaluable resource for anyone involved in the development of a health and safety plan. Every organization will be different, but the agency offers some plan models that may be prove helpful. For instance, model plans and programs for the OSHA Blood-borne Pathogens and Hazard Communications Standards can be found at www.osha.gov/Publications/osha3186.html.

---

3. Setting Up a Safety Committee

It is important to set-up key processes—record-keeping, accident reporting, training and workplace inspections—to ensure programs are effectively implemented. The most common system you will probably set up is a safety committee.

Even though safety committees are not required in every state, it's an effective way to ensure two-way communication between management and labor, and involve employees in the process. Before you schedule a committee meeting, take some time to design the overall structure and define the purpose and mission of the team. Ask yourself "What's the purpose of the team?" "Who should be on the team?" "What do we want to accomplish?"

Handling Administrative Responsibilities

There are several administrative tasks that are part of an occupational health and safety program. The most important of these is the OSHA recordkeeping requirement that applies to businesses with eleven or more employees. There are three forms that are required by this process, described as follows.

▲ **OSHA Form 300, Log of Work-Related Injuries and Illnesses:** Employers use this form to keep track of all work-related injuries and illnesses that occur during the year.

▲ **OSHA Form 300A, Summary of Work-Related Injuries and Illnesses:** Each year between February 1 and April 30, employers are required to post a summary of the injuries and illnesses that occurred during the previous year. This form allows information to be posted without listing names of employees.

▲ **OSHA Form 301, Injury and Illness Incident Report:** This form must be completed within seven days after the employer is notified that a work-related injury or illness has occurred. It includes information about the employee and the circumstances surrounding the incident, and is used to complete Form 300.

OSHA requires that these forms be maintained for five years after the year in which the incidents were reported. Detailed guidance about completing the forms is available at www.osha.gov/recordkeeping/detailedfaq.html#1904.0.

WHICH EMPLOYERS ARE EXEMPT?

Some employers are exempt from OSHA's recordkeeping requirements. In addition to employers with fewer than eleven employees, OSHA identifies industries with historically low incidents of workplace injury and illness and exempts them from maintaining records. This list includes businesses that operate in the retail, service, finance, insurance, and real estate industries. Businesses in one of these industries must complete the OSHA reports only if they are notified in writing by either the federal Bureau of Labor Statistics or by OSHA to do so.

Measuring Results

As with all other aspects of human resources, managers should be able to demonstrate with meaningful measurements that health and safety programs are adding value to the organization. Occupational health and safety is one area of HRM that lends itself to the collection and maintenance of statistics. For example, a warehousing operation might require employees to lift heavy boxes and items on a frequent basis. If employees are not lifting in the correct way or are otherwise not following established safety procedures, the result could be an increase in the number of back injuries. When HRM becomes aware of this problem, either from an increase in the absentee rate or claims for workers' compensation, or when completing the annual OSHA Form 300A, it is possible to establish a baseline measure that reflects the current number of back injuries and implement training programs to retrain employees in proper lifting techniques. A statistic that is very useful for this purpose is OSHA's recordable case rate formula. Figure 12-1 demonstrates how this formula is used.

Figure 12-1

$$\text{Back Injury Rate (BIR)} = \frac{\text{Number of back injuries} \times 200{,}000}{\text{Total hours worked by all employees during the period}}$$

Total number of employees: 350 FTE
Number of back injuries = 53

$$\text{BIR} = \frac{53 \times 200{,}000}{350 \times 2{,}000} = \frac{10{,}600{,}000}{700{,}000} = 15.15\%$$

Total number of employees: 375 FTE
Number of back injuries = 35

$$\text{BIR} = \frac{35 \times 200{,}000}{375 \times 2{,}000} = \frac{7{,}000{,}000}{750{,}000} = 9.3\%$$

OSHA's Recordable Case Rate Formula.

This formula establishes a baseline for how much time is normally worked by 100 employees during one year. Assuming that they work an average of forty hours per week and fifty weeks per year, 100 employees would work a total of 200,000 hours per year if no injuries occur. To calculate the back injury rate (BIR), the formula also assumes that employees in the organization work forty hours per week and fifty weeks per year.

FOR EXAMPLE

Safety in Numbers

Some manufacturing organizations communicate the success of their safety programs by keeping track of the number of days worked without an accident. These organizations issue press releases or post the statistic on large billboards at the front of the factory as a reminder to employees as they come to work each day. This measurement can become a source of pride for employees, and can be used as part of a friendly competition between work teams. It also has the benefit of being easy to calculate—whenever an accident occurs, the count starts over at one and continues until another accident occurs. A major poultry processor, for example, may announce that it has surpassed two million manhours of work and four years without a lost-time accident. Or a coal mine might measure success by announcing that it completed a year of mining without a lost-time accident—and at the same time set a company coal production and sales record of nearly thirty million tons.

SELF-CHECK

1. A company should be solely concerned with the requirements of the federal OSH Act. True or false?

2. Companies with fewer than twenty employees are exempt from OSHA regulations. True or false?

3. Which OSHA form must be posted between February 1 and April 30 of each year?

SUMMARY

Human resources professionals are largely responsible for managing an organization's employee relations program, and protecting worker health and safety should be a high priority. It was not until the Occupational Safety and Health Act of 1970 was passed that employers were required to protect workers from injury or illness. Today's HR professionals should be familiar with the Act as well as the Occupational Safety and Health Administration, the agency charged with enforcing OSHA's safety standards. As part of a successful health and safety program, an organization must make every effort to identify all workplace hazards. OSHA has set standards to protect workers from environmental health hazards, categorized as chemical, physical, and biological. Employers are required by OSHA to minimize hazards and supply employees with any necessary tools and personal protective equipment. Employers must also post OSHA information posters and warning signs, educate employees about safety procedures, and comply with OSHA recordkeeping requirements. An effective health and safety plan will be administered by a safety manager who has the complete support of senior management; the plan should follow OSHA regulations and be a cooperative, organizational effort.

KEY TERMS

Biological hazards	Bacteria, molds, contaminated water, and dust that are known to cause illness in workers; most often the result of mining and industrial operations.
Blood-borne pathogen standard	Requires employers to develop an exposure control plan of how to prevent or reduce the effects of exposure to pathogens.

Chemical hazards	Hazards such as asbestos, corrosives, pesticides, gas fumes, or solvents that pose a physical or health risk to workers.
Compliance Safety and Health Officer (CSHO)	An individual trained on OSHA standards who conducts workplace inspections.
Environmental health hazards	Chemical, physical, and biological dangers in the workplace.
Ergonomic injury	An injury that is related to the way the physical environment is designed.
General duty standard	Applies to all businesses and requires business owners to provide a safe work environment for their employees.
Hazard communication standard	Requires employers to inform employees of the dangers of chemicals used in the workplace.
Lockout/tagout standard	Designed to reduce injuries and deaths by preventing machinery or equipment from starting unexpectedly during repairs and maintenance.
National Institute of Occupational Safety and Health (NIOSH)	Agency charged with researching and evaluating workplace hazards; suggests ways of eliminating risks.
Occupational noise exposure standard	Sets allowable levels of workplace noise and identifies procedures for measuring noise.
Occupational Safety and Health Act of 1970	Federal legislation requiring employers to protect workers from injury or illness.
Occupational Safety and Health Administration (OSHA)	Agency that sets and enforces safety standards for virtually every business in the United States.
Personal protective equipment standards	Requirement that employers provide appropriate garments and equipment for dealing with different types of hazards; also requires employers to train workers in the proper use and maintenance of the equipment.
Physical hazards	Elements such as electrical currents, excessive noise, too much or too little light, radiation, and vibrations that can have negative effects on worker health.
Safety and health plan	Strategy that identifies and assesses workplace hazards, and describes the steps taken to correct those hazards (also known as an injury and illness prevention program).

ASSESS YOUR UNDERSTANDING

Go to www.wiley.com/college/messmer to assess your knowledge of workplace health and safety.

Measure your learning by comparing pre-test and post-test results.

Summary Questions

1. List the six categories of OSHA violations.
2. Which business would be exempt from mandatory OSHA standards?
   (a) railway transportation company
   (b) family-operated daycare center
   (c) tax preparation company
   (d) family-run dairy farm
3. The role of NIOSH is to provide consultation services to businesses facing OSHA violations. True or false?
4. Which of the following is a physical hazard?
   (a) solvents
   (b) radiation
   (c) asbestos
   (d) dust
5. Contaminated water is an example of a chemical hazard. True or false?
6. An ergonomic injury is the result of which type of hazard?
   (a) chemical
   (b) repetitious
   (c) physical
   (d) biological
7. MSDS sheets are required for chemicals because of which safety standard?
   (a) lockout/tagout
   (b) personal protective equipment
   (c) general duty
   (d) hazard communication
8. An employee who reports unsafe handling of chemicals at work is protected by the OSH Act from retaliation and discrimination. True or false?
9. How long are OSHA forms required to be maintained after an incident is reported?
   (a) five months
   (b) two years

(c) five years

(d) eleven years

10. A safety manager is appointed by OSHA to enforce health and safety regulations. True or false?

11. OSHA Form 301 is used to

   (a) report an injury or accident.

   (b) report employee sick days.

   (c) summarize a year's worth of injuries and illnesses.

   (d) track injuries for employers with less than eleven employees.

Applying This Chapter

1. In the past two years, three legal assistants at a law firm have been treated for carpal tunnel syndrome. Which category of environmental hazard does this injury fall under? What resources might be available to help the employer prevent future injury?

2. The Occupational Safety and Health Act gives employees the right to file complaints about workplace safety and health hazards. Assume you are an employee of an auto body painting shop. Although you've asked for better respirators for your crew, the company has not responded. What is your recourse?

3. A Compliance Safety and Health Officer has arrived for an unannounced inspection of a perfume manufacturer. What types of hazards might the inspector be looking for? Compare those hazards to those found in an insurance office.

4. As the safety manager of an ice cream distributor, what would be your responsibilities as far as complying with the OSH Act? What technique would you use to measure the success of your safety program?

YOU TRY IT

Employer Solutions

Nearly thirty percent of the 11.6 million employees of restaurants and other eating and drinking businesses in the United States are under twenty years of age. Many teens' first work experience is in the restaurant industry. Using the OSHA website's "e-tools" section, research teen restaurant worker safety issues.

- Select one common hazard that should be of concern to a restaurant owner.
- Prepare a statement that addresses the most effective employer solution to the hazard.
- Determine what, if any, employee responsibilities are involved in coping with this hazard.

A Safe Desk Job?

Although the health and safety risks associated with mining, manufacturing, and other hazardous industries are widely publicized, the average office worker faces his or her own occupational hazards. Using the NIOSH website, review the subject of worker safety and health in an office environment. List five to ten common office hazards that a safety manager would need to address, and include possible solutions on how to prevent them.

Inspection Time

Take a look at your own organization's health and safety issues. First, assemble a list of any workplace hazards you can find. Then, compare your concerns with your organization's health and safety plans, if they exist. How do they differ? And are there any hazards that you believe are being overlooked? Is there a designated health and safety manager? Propose changes or additions to the plans; if no plan exists summarize the need for one.

13

WORKING WITH ORGANIZED LABOR
Bringing Labor Relations into Employee Relations

Starting Point

Go to www.wiley.com/college/messmer to assess your knowledge of the basics of labor relations.
Determine where you need to concentrate your effort.

What You'll Learn in This Chapter

▲ How the history of unionization affects labor relations today
▲ The major union-related laws and regulations
▲ The steps of the union-organization process
▲ Examples of unfair labor practices
▲ The role of a collective bargaining agreement
▲ Common types of union actions

After Studying This Chapter, You Will Be Able To

▲ Examine the relationship between employee rights and unions
▲ Discuss the relevance of historical labor laws today
▲ Assess the extent to which union organization is taking place in a company
▲ Differentiate between union and employer unfair labor practices
▲ Examine the clauses contained in a collective bargaining agreement
▲ Differentiate between lawful and unlawful strikes

INTRODUCTION

Although the labor union movement is not as active today as it was during its peak in the 1950s, HR professionals should be prepared to work with unions as part of an employee relations plan. To build a foundation of cooperation, those in human resources should be familiar with the laws passed throughout the labor movement. Today, labor unions are active in collective bargaining about issues such as wages, benefits, and working conditions for their membership. Union actions—strikes, lockouts, picketing—may also come into play in a union-employer relationship.

13.1 The Role of Unions in Employee Relations

The extent to which you need to concern yourself with labor relations in your company depends mainly on two things: the number of people in your company and whether the company is unionized. A **union** is an organized association of workers who have united to represent their collective views for wages, hours, grievance procedures, and working conditions.

If your company is unionized, chances are that you may spend a considerable amount of your time negotiating and administering labor agreements. What's more, you're likely to be the person that union representatives approach whenever they have grievances.

Organizations that create work environments in which employees are valued and treated with dignity and respect typically have employees who, in the long run, will be more productive. Some organizations don't see the value in creating this type of supportive environment, choosing instead to focus on cost-saving tactics that may have a negative impact on workers. Employees in such organizations may come to believe that to be treated fairly they need to form a union to represent their interests. Unions are usually happy to oblige employees who want to unionize their workplaces, promising better compensation and improved working conditions or job security. **Labor relations** refer to the relationship between employers and employees who are represented by unions.

Many changes occur to the employment relationship when a union is involved. The focus moves from employee relations to labor relations, and it now involves a third party, the union, in the relationship. Unions bargain with the employer to develop a contract, known as a **Collective Bargaining Agreement (CBA)**. Each time the CBA is negotiated, the union and the employer agree on how different issues will be handled while the CBA is in effect. The goal of the union is to ensure job security for their members, so it becomes more difficult for employers to terminate workers who do not perform as well as they should. Salary increases, benefits, and working conditions are also negotiated with the union and become part of the CBA. In this environment, management loses some of its authority with workers. Most employers prefer to avoid unions by establishing fair and consistent policies designed to treat employees with dignity and respect, compensate them fairly, and establish methods for resolving workplace disputes.

WORKING WITH UNION LEADERSHIP

An organization will have much of its union contact through the **union steward** (aka shop steward), the person union members elect to represent them to management with grievances and other requests. He or she is the first person a member will look to for guidance and interpretation of their collective agreement, and for informed representation when there is a dispute with the organization.

13.1.1 Following the History of Unions

The history of American labor relations goes back to the late 1700s, when a group of shoemakers joined as a united front in Philadelphia. Other groups followed suit as years passed, and in 1869, in what is credited as a major event in labor relations history, the Knights of Labor was formed. This organization was an advocate of the 8-hour work day when twelve or fourteen hours per day was the norm. Labor unions grew in importance for the next century. By the end of the nineteenth century, unions became powerful enough to threaten business profitability and federal anti-trust laws were used to hinder their growth. In reaction, Congress enacted labor legislation that supported union growth. At their peak in 1953, unions represented 35.7 percent of the private sector workforce. Numbers released by the Bureau of Labor Statistics in January 2006 revealed that unions represented only 7.8 percent of the private sector workforce in 2005. However, unions are far more prevalent in today's public sector: 36.5 percent of public sector employers are unionized. As unions struggle to maintain membership levels, they have had to re-examine their strategies for attracting new members.

Most labor unions in the United States today are members of one of two larger umbrella organizations: the American Federation of Labor-Congress of Industrial Organizations (AFL-CIO) or the Change to Win Federation, an organization that split from the AFL-CIO in 2005. Both organizations advocate policies and legislation favorable to workers in the United States and Canada.

13.1.2 Recognizing Employee Union Rights

One of the significant union-related laws in the United States, the National Labor Relations Act (NLRA), grants employees the right to organize, join unions, bargain collectively, and engage in other "concerted activities" for mutual aid or protection, as well as the right to refrain from doing so (see Section 13.2 for more on union laws and regulations). The NLRA also protects the right of employees to strike and identifies lawful versus unlawful strikes:

▲ **Lawful strikes:** One type of lawful strike is an economic strike in which the union stops working in an effort to obtain better pay, hours, or working conditions from the employer. In an economic strike, employers may hire permanent replacements for striking employees and are not required to rehire the strikers if doing so means the replacement workers would be fired. If employees make an unconditional request to return to work, they may be recalled at a later time when openings occur. The other type of lawful strike is one that occurs when the employer has committed an unfair labor practice (see Section 13.6) and employees strike in protest. In this case, strikers may not be discharged or permanently replaced.

▲ **Unlawful strikes:** Strikes can be characterized as unlawful for several reasons, such as:

- Strikes in support of union unfair labor practices.
- Strikes in violation of a no-strike clause in the contract.
- Lawful strikes can become unlawful if strikers engage in serious misconduct.

FOR EXAMPLE

Labor Relations in the Air

Some strikes garner more attention than others. Garbage strikes, thanks to their inconvenient nature, are often the subject of media and public attention. In August 2006, Local 813 of the International Brotherhood of Teamsters ended a nearly four-month strike by 115 drivers, maintenance workers and helpers who collected trash from 10,000 businesses in New York City and Westchester County. Waste Management, a private garbage-hauling company, announced that it had reached an agreement with the union; the approved contract made changes to the workers' health plan and addressed overtime issues. The strike was the first against a private garbage hauler in the New York City in more than fifteen years.

SELF-CHECK

1. Define *labor relations*.
2. Explain the role of a *shop steward*.
3. Name the two major union organizations in the United States.
4. Explain the purpose of the *National Labor Relations Act*.

13.2 Knowing the Labor Laws

Current federal law regulating labor-management relations is largely a product of the New Deal era of the 1930s. Although no major new labor laws have been passed over the past several decades, the following sections highlight the laws that are still relevant today.

Sherman Anti-Trust Act

The first piece of legislation to impact the labor movement was the Sherman Anti-Trust Act, passed in 1890. This legislation was originally intended to control business monopolies that conspired to restrain trade in the United States. The act allowed **injunctions**, court orders that either require or forbid an action by one party against another, to be issued against any person or group that conspired to restrain trade. It was first used to obtain an injunction against the American Railway Union in 1894 to end its strike against the Pullman Palace Car Company.

Railway Labor Act

In 1926, Congress enacted the Railway Labor Act, the intention of which was to avoid interruptions due to strikes, protect the rights of employees to join a union, and allow for a cooling off period of up to 90 days if the president deemed a strike to be a national emergency. Originally intended to cover the railroad companies, today this act applies to airlines as well.

Norris-La Guardia Act

The Norris-La Guardia Act was passed in 1932 and protected the rights of workers to organize and strike without the interference of federal injunctions. It also outlawed **yellow dog contracts**, which employers had used to prevent employees from joining unions by requiring them to sign an agreement that the employee was not a member of a union, would not become one in the future, and that joining a union would be sufficient grounds for dismissal.

National Labor Relations Act (NLRA), or Wagner Act

In 1935, the National Labor Relations Act (NLRA), or Wagner Act, was passed as part of President Franklin Roosevelt's New Deal. At the time, it was referred to as "labor's bill of rights" and represented a marked change in government attitudes toward unions. The NLRA allowed employees to organize, bargain collectively, and engage in "concerted activities for the purpose of collective bargaining or other mutual aid or protection." The right to engage in concerted activities applies not only to union employees, but to nonunion employees as well.

The NLRA went on to identify five employer unfair labor practices and created the **National Labor Relations Board (NLRB)**, which is charged with conducting elections and preventing and remedying unfair labor practices. The NLRB does not instigate actions on its own; it only responds to charges of unfair labor practices or petitions for representation elections filed in one of its offices.

Taft-Hartley Act, or Labor-Management Relations Act (LMRA)

In 1947, when a Republican majority was elected to Congress, the Taft-Hartley Act, or Labor-Management Relations Act (LMRA) was passed in response to employer complaints about union abuse. The LMRA established the Federal Mediation and Conciliation Service to "prevent or minimize interruptions of the free flow of commerce growing out of labor disputes." An important feature of Taft-Hartley is the power granted to the president to obtain an injunction ending a strike or lockout for an 80-day "cooling off" period if, in the president's estimation, the continuation of the strike could "imperil the national health or safety." This power is rarely invoked since its record of leading to successful long-term agreements is mixed.

The Labor-Management Reporting and Disclosure Act (LMRDA)

The Labor-Management Reporting and Disclosure Act (LMRDA) of 1959, also known as the Landrum-Griffith Act, placed controls on internal union operations. Congress felt this was necessary due to "a number of instances of breach of trust, corruption, disregard of the rights of individual employees, and other failures to observe high standards of responsibility and ethical conduct" on the part of union leadership. Landrum-Griffith gave employees the right to sue the union and provided safeguards against retaliatory disciplinary actions by the union. The act also prohibited "extortionate picketing" by unions and required that union leadership elections be conducted no less often than every three years for local unions and every five years for national or international officers.

> ### FOR EXAMPLE
>
> #### Union Watchdog
>
> Although the National Legal and Policy Center (NLPC) was founded in 1991 to promote government ethics, in 1997, NLPC launched the Organized Labor Accountability Project, becoming the nation's only clearing house on union corruption. Since then the NLPC has investigated and exposed union corruption, publishing the newsletter, *Union Corruption Update* (www.nlpc .org/ucu.asp). The newsletter has been referenced in publications such as *The New York Times* and the *Chicago Tribune*.

SELF-CHECK

1. Name the first major piece of U.S. labor legislation.
2. Define *injunction.*
3. Explain the difference between the NLRA and the LMRA.
4. Which piece of legislation was passed to deal with union corruption?
   a. The Sherman Anti-Trust Act
   b. The National Labor Relations Act
   c. The Labor-Management Reporting and Disclosure Act
   d. The Norris-La Guardia Act

13.3 Keeping Up with Union Organization

By the time management notices signs of union activity, the organizing process may already be well underway. One early indication that an organizing campaign has begun is a noticeable change in employee behavior. For example, employees may begin to challenge management decisions using union terminology related to benefits or employee rights.

13.3.1 What Can an Employer Do?

To begin with, employers can make truthful statements about the consequences of unionization in response to union claims—as long as they do not threaten, interrogate, promise, or spy on employees (referred to as TIPS; see Section 13.4.1 for more). Just as union organizers work to convince employees to join the union, management may communicate their reasons for opposing unionization. During any organizing campaign, an experienced labor attorney should review management statements about the union before they are disseminated. All members of the management team should be coached on ULPs and how to avoid them, particularly first line supervisors since they interact most frequently with rank-and-file employees. First line supervisors also have more influence with their direct reports than any other member of management, and employers should make use of this relationship by providing them with the information they will need to effectively represent the management view to employees.

Finally, unions understand that the enthusiasm and support for the union peaks at a certain point and then support begins to dwindle. For that reason, unions like to schedule elections to coincide with the peak of interest, and they gear their organizing activities to that goal. If an employer can delay the election, the chances of prevailing against the union are improved.

13.3.2 Union Organizing Process

There are seven basic elements in the recognition process, but not all of them occur in every situation. The process consists of authorization cards, a demand for recognition, a petition to the NLRB, an NLRB conference, a pre-election hearing, a campaign, and finally, the election.

▲ **Authorization Cards:** The goal of the union during the organizing process is to obtain signed authorization cards from employees. An **authorization card** is the means by which the NLRB determines that there is sufficient support for a union to hold an election. The NLRB will hold an election if thirty percent of the eligible employees in the anticipated bargaining unit sign the authorization cards. In practice, the union would like to have far more signed cards before submitting a petition for an election—generally they would like to have signed cards from at least fifty percent of the eligible employees.

▲ **Demand for Recognition:** When the union has a sufficient number of signed authorization cards, they are ready to approach the employer with a demand for recognition. This usually comes in the form of a letter to the employer in which the union claims to represent a majority of workers and demands to be recognized by the employer as the exclusive bargaining agent for employees. An employer may choose to recognize a union voluntarily under some circumstances, but this should only be done after conferring with legal counsel.

▲ **Petitioning the NLRB:** If management refuses to grant voluntary recognition, the union files a petition for an election with the NLRB, along with evidence of employee interest in union representation. The NLRB reviews the petition to determine that it represents an appropriate level of interest in union representation and those signatures on the petition or authorization cards are valid.

▲ **NLRB Conference/Pre-election Hearing Issues:** When the NLRB is satisfied with the legitimacy of the petition, it schedules a conference with the employer and employee representatives. During the conference, an NLRB representative reviews any jurisdictional issues, the makeup of the bargaining unit, eligibility of voters in the proposed unit, and the time and place of the election. If either party disputes issues related to the bargaining unit, legitimacy of the authorization cards, or timing of the election, a formal hearing is held by the NLRB to resolve those issues.

▲ **Union Campaigning:** As the economy in the United States moved from a manufacturing to an informational base, the workforce changed from predominantly blue-collar workers, traditional union members, to white-collar workers who have not traditionally been attracted by union membership. The shift in hiring temporary and contract workers to reduce employer costs may also be taking its toll on union numbers. While campaigning strategies vary with each union, the general trend is to find ways of attracting white-collar workers to union membership:

- **Internet:** Many unions have sophisticated websites that provide information for employees who are interested in forming a union.

- **Home visits:** This tactic is most often used when the union is trying to gain initial supporters in the company. It provides an opportunity for organizers to have private conversations with potential inside organizers.

- **Inside organizing:** The most effective organizing process occurs when one or more employees work from within the company to build union support.

- **Salting: Salting** occurs when a union hires a person to apply for a job at an organization they have targeted. Once hired, the employee acts in much the same way as an inside organizer.

- **Meetings:** Union organizing meetings bring together experienced organizers, inside organizers from the company, and employees who are undecided about supporting the organizing process.

- **Leafleting:** The goal of union leaflets is to point out the advantages the union will bring to the workforce and to counter information from management about the benefits of remaining union-free.

- **Media:** When management commits an unfair labor practice or takes any action the union perceives as unfavorable, the union will issue a press release that interprets the action in the most favorable way for the union.

FOR EXAMPLE

In the Media

In 1999, the Union of Needletrades, Industrial, and Textile Employees (UNITE) was conducting an organizing campaign at Loehmann's Department Store in New York City. Just over a month before the scheduled NLRB election, the store fired one of the leaders of the organizing campaign. UNITE issued a press release that concentrated on the fact that the employee had an exemplary work record at the store and was a single mother. The union went on to allege that the store had spied on the employee during her lunch break in order to find a reason to fire her. The union used this as the basis of its media campaign encouraging the public to boycott the store.

- **Picketing:** Picketing occurs when a group of employees patrols the entrance to a business in order to inform customers and the public about disputes, or to prevent deliveries to a business that the union is trying to influence in some way (see Section 13.6 for more).
- **Political involvement:** In some cases, selective support of public officials—either through funding or verbal means—can play a role in union campaigning.

▲ **NLRB Elections:** The purpose of an NLRB election is to determine whether or not a majority of employees in the unit desire to be represented by the union.

UNION ORGANIZING: HOLLYWOOD STYLE

The 1979 movie *Norma Rae* provides a dramatic illustration of the unionization process by depicting the unionization of a garment factory in the South. Based on a true story, the movie follows the efforts of a union organizer from New York to build support for a union in a textile factory in a small southern town. The organizer begins by visiting the homes of some of the workers, distributing leaflets at the front gate of the factory, and enlisting the support of one of the workers who becomes the "inside" organizer. This insider lends credibility to the union representative by introducing him to coworkers, sponsoring organizing meetings, and obtaining signed union authorization cards. In the course of the campaign, management commits several unfair labor practices. One of the final scenes dramatizes the vote count: as the NLRB official observes, representatives for management and the union count each vote.

13.3.3 Making Union Changes

When necessary, employees may request changes to a union arrangement; descriptions of the two methods follow:

▲ **Decertification:** Employees may petition the NLRB for decertification if they are dissatisfied with the union's performance. A decertification petition requires signatures of at least 30 percent of the employees before the NLRB will act upon it. Decertification may also occur because the employee relationship with management has improved, and employees no longer feel the need for representation. It is critical for HR professionals and management to understand that the employer may not encourage or support employees in the decertification process; doing so constitutes an unfair labor practice.

▲ **Deauthorization:** Employees may wish to maintain the union but remove a union security clause, such as dues check-off or maintenance of membership clause. The NLRB will approve deauthorization based on a petition by 30 percent or more of the members of the bargaining unit. As with decertification, employers must not participate in the effort to deauthorize the union as doing so is considered to be an unfair labor practice.

SELF-CHECK

1. List the steps involved in the union-recognition process.
2. Give three examples of union campaigning methods.
3. Union memberships have steadily increased in the past decade. True or false?
4. The purpose of an NLRB election is to decide which employee will be union president. True or false?

13.4 Recognizing Unfair Labor Practices

An **Unfair Labor Practice (ULP)** is an action by an employer or a union that restrains or coerces employees from exercising their rights to organize and bargain collectively or to refrain from doing so. Congress has identified ULPs for both employers and unions.

13.4.1 Employer Unfair Labor Practices

Employers who attempt to restrain or otherwise interfere with the right of employees to organize and bargain collectively can, in a worst-case scenario, be ordered by the NLRB to bargain with a union even if an election did not take place or if the union loses an election. For that reason, it is extremely important for employers to be certain that all supervisory personnel are aware of what constitutes an unfair labor practice. An acronym that is helpful in avoiding prohibited activity is *TIPS*: employers may not **T**hreaten, **I**nterrogate, **P**romise, or **S**py on employees. Employer unfair labor practices defined by the NLRA are as follows:

▲ **Interfere with, restrain, or coerce unionization efforts:** Employers may not interfere in any way with attempts to unionize the workplace, including organizing activity, collective bargaining, or "concerted activity" engaged in by employees for mutual aid or protection. Interfering also includes inhibiting free speech of employees who advocate unionization.

▲ **Dominate or assist a labor organization:** Employers are precluded from forming company unions that are controlled by management and, therefore, do not allow employees an independent representative. Employers are also prohibited from showing favoritism to one union over another.

▲ **Discriminate against employees:** Employers may not discriminate against union members in any of the terms and conditions of employment. This includes taking disciplinary action against employees for participating in union activities.

▲ **Discriminate against NLRB activity:** Employers may not retaliate against employees who have filed charges or participated in an investigation conducted by the NLRB.

▲ **Refuse to bargain in good faith:** Employers must bargain with a union once it has been designated by a majority of the employees and the union has made a demand to bargain.

▲ **Enter into a hot cargo agreement:** It is unlawful for employers and unions to enter into a **hot cargo agreement** in which, at the union's request, employers stop doing business with another employer.

13.4.2 Union Unfair Labor Practices

The LMRA identified the following union actions that were considered ULPs:

▲ **Restrain and coerce employees:** Union conduct that interferes with an employee's right to choose a representative or to refrain from participating in organizing or collective bargaining activity is a ULP. The act identifies some of the coercive behavior that is unlawful, including assaults, threats of violence, and threats to interfere with continued employment. Unions are also held responsible for coercive acts committed by union members in the presence of union representatives if the representatives do not renounce the actions.

▲ **Restrain or coerce employers:** Unions may not refuse to bargain with representatives chosen by the employer to negotiate with the union or fine or expel from the union a supervisor based on the way the supervisor applies the contract during the course of business. Unions may not insist that employers accept contract terms the union has negotiated with other bargaining units.

▲ **Require employers to discriminate:** Unions may not require the employer to terminate an employee for working to decertify the union or require employers to hire only union members or others of whom the union approves.

▲ **Refuse to bargain in good faith:** Unions must meet and confer with employer representatives at reasonable times to negotiate the terms and conditions of the contract.

▲ **Engage in prohibited strikes and boycotts:** Unions may not engage in hot cargo actions or **secondary boycotts**, attempts by labor to convince others to stop doing business with a particular firm because that firm does business with another firm that is the subject of a strike and/or a boycott.

▲ **Charge excessive or discriminatory membership fees:** Membership fees must be reasonable and in line with the members' wages and industry standards.

▲ **Featherbedding:** Unions may not require employers to pay for services that are not rendered. For example, unions may not require employers to continue to pay employees to do jobs that have been rendered obsolete by changes in technology. An example of this is the fireman on a train who fed coal into the fire on a steam engine to keep the water hot enough to run the train. When diesel trains came along, the fireman was no longer needed to run the train. If a union insisted on keeping the firemen on the trains even though they were not necessary, this was known as "featherbedding."

▲ **Organizational and recognitional picketing:** Picketing is discussed later in this chapter in Section 13.6.

13.4.3 Consequences of Unfair Labor Practices

If, as the result of an investigation, an employer or a union has been found to have committed a ULP, the NLRB can order remedial actions to be taken. The NLRB goal is to eliminate the ULP and to undo the effects of the illegal action to the extent possible. One of the requirements is that the offending party post notices in the workplace advising employees that the ULP will be discontinued and describing the actions to be taken to correct the offense.

▲ **Employer remedies** The NLRB may require that the employer disband an employer-dominated union, reinstate employees to positions they held prior to the ULP, or engage in the collective bargaining process and sign a written agreement with the union.

▲ **Union remedies** Unions may be required to agree to reinstatement of employees it caused to be terminated or rejected for employment, refund excessive dues with interest to members, or engage in the collective bargaining process and sign a written agreement with the employer.

13.4.4 Filing an Unfair Labor Practice Charge

ULP charges can be filed by an employee, an employer, or a union representative (the charging party) on a form available from the NLRB. The statute of limitations for ULPs requires that they be filed within six months of the incident. Once the case has been received by the NLRB, the charged party is notified, invited to submit a written statement of the facts and circumstances about the case, and advised that they have the right to counsel. The case is then assigned to a board agent for investigation. The board agent conducts interviews with all parties to the action, as well as with any witnesses, and makes a recommendation to the regional director for disposition of the case. At this stage, the charges may be dismissed if unwarranted or result in a complaint if valid.

Depending on the nature and severity of the offense, the complaint may result in an informal or formal settlement agreement. An informal settlement agreement requires that the charged party will take specified actions to remedy the ULP and does not involve a board order or court decree. A formal settlement involves a complaint issued by the NLRB against the charged party and results in a board order or court hearing.

FOR EXAMPLE

Unfair Picketing

A tactic sometimes used by unions to pressure employers into taking some kind of action is to conduct a mock funeral procession—including casket and "grim reaper"—in front of an employer's facility. The employer is typically a hospital. By implying that patients admitted to the hospital are likely to leave in a casket, the union puts pressure on the hospital to stop doing business with a nonunion contractor. In a 2006 ruling, the National Labor Relations Board held that conducting a mock funeral procession in front of a Florida hospital was a form of picketing in violation of the secondary boycott law.

SELF-CHECK

1. Define *unfair labor practice*.
2. *Featherbedding* is an unfair labor practice committed by employers. True or false?
3. Explain the meaning of TIPS.

13.5 Collective Bargaining

The National Labor Relations Act imposes a duty to bargain on employers and unions. Mandatory subjects for the bargaining process include wages, hours, terms and conditions of employment, the agreement itself, and any questions that arise from the agreement.

▲ **Collective bargaining:** Method of determining wages, hours and other conditions of employment through direct negotiations between the union and employer; typically results in a written contract.

Bad faith in the bargaining process can be evidenced by a lack of concessions on issues, refusing to advance proposals or to bargain, stalling tactics, or withholding information that is important to the process. Evidence of bad faith by management in the bargaining process can also be evidenced by attempts to circumvent the union representative by going directly to employees with proposals before they have been presented to the union.

13.5.1 Collective Bargaining Strategies

HR professionals should be aware of the four basic negotiating strategies used in union environments:

▲ **Single-unit bargaining:** The most common strategy, single-unit bargaining occurs when one union meets with one employer to bargain.
▲ **Parallel bargaining:** In parallel bargaining, the union negotiates with one employer at a time. Once a contract has been reached with this employer, the union uses the gains made during the negotiation as a base for negotiating with the next employer.
▲ **Multi-employer bargaining:** In multi-employer bargaining, the union negotiates with more than one employer in an industry or region at a time. This situation can occur when temporary workers are part of a

client employer's bargaining unit and the union negotiates with both the temp agency and the client employer on employment issues.

▲ **Multi-unit bargaining:** Multi-unit bargaining, or coordinated bargaining, occurs when several unions represent different bargaining units in the company. An example of this occurs in the airline industry, when the employer negotiates with the unions representing pilots, flight attendants, and mechanics or other employee classes. This allows the employer to coordinate negotiations on mandatory and permissive bargaining subjects while allowing the unions to cooperate on issues that have similar meaning to their various members.

13.5.2 Collective Bargaining Agreement (CBA)

The **Collective Bargaining Agreement (CBA)** is a contract governing the employment relationship for a specified period of time. The clauses contained in the CBA will, of course, be reflective of the bargaining topics in individual companies; some of the clauses found in many contracts include the following:

▲ **Wages, hours, terms, and conditions of employment:** The clauses that describe the wages, medical and other benefits, overtime, hours, and other conditions of employment are the backbone of the CBA.

▲ **Union security clauses:** The union security clause requires union members to provide financial support to the union. A security clause helps to ensure that the union will be financially able to carry out its bargaining obligations.

  • A **union shop clause** requires that all employees join the union within a grace period specified by the contract, but no fewer than thirty days, or, in the construction industry, seven days.

  • An **agency shop clause** specifies that all employees must either join the union or pay union dues if they choose not to join the union.

  • A **closed shop clause** requires that all new hires be members of the union before they are hired; illegal except in the construction industry.

  • A **maintenance of membership clause** allows employees to choose whether or not to join the union, but once they join, they must remain members until the expiration of the contract. The employee must notify the union to discontinue membership within 30 days of the contract expiration.

▲ **No strike/no lockout clause:** These clauses are considered very important to both unions and management because they provide economic protection from work stoppages on both sides. Strikes and lockouts are discussed in Section 13.6 of this chapter.

▲ **Contract administration:** This clause covers how the contract will be administered over its duration. Procedures for disciplinary actions, grievance resolution, and arbitration, as well as agreements on how clauses may be modified during the contract term, can be included in this clause.

▲ **Dues check-off:** Most unions prefer to have employees agree to automatic deduction of their union dues. To be enforceable, employees must give written authorization for the deductions.

▲ **Zipper clause:** A **zipper clause** is an agreement between the parties that the CBA is the entire agreement between them and that anything not in the agreement is not part of the agreement. The purpose of this clause is to prevent reopening of negotiations during the term of the contract.

13.5.3 Resolving Grievances

When disagreements occur in a union environment, the grievance process described in the CBA provides the framework for resolving them. The framework describes the steps to be taken and the time frames within which actions must be implemented to either resolve or reply to the grievance.

Many grievances can be resolved at the first step of the process with the immediate supervisor, grievant, and union steward working together. If resolution is not possible at that level, a union official takes the dispute to the next level of company management, where the grievant is represented by the union. If the dispute is not resolved at the second level, a member of the union grievance committee meets with the next level of management in the company. Grievances that are serious enough to be unsolved at the highest management level in the process then go to a third party for resolution. Depending on the terms of the CBA, this may involve binding arbitration, as is the case in the majority of contracts, or it may utilize mediation or another form of alternative dispute resolution.

▲ **Binding arbitration:** In the union environment, binding arbitration is used to resolve conflicts without resorting to work stoppages.

▲ **Compulsory arbitration:** The process mandated by legal statute to resolve disputes in the public sector where labor strikes are prohibited.

▲ **Mediation:** The process used to mediate disputes in a union environment is the same as it is in a nonunion environment. With the aid of the mediator, the parties to the disagreement are able to develop a mutually acceptable solution.

> **FOR EXAMPLE**
>
> **Playing Fair**
>
> In the United States, some of the recent, more notable, Collective Bargaining Agreements (CBAs) have involved major professional sports leagues. A history of poor relations between the players' unions and owners of all the various major leagues, as well as because of the tremendous amounts of money involved, had made it increasingly difficult to work out agreements. In fact, the NHL was the first major North American sports league to lose an entire season (2004–2005) to labor issues; other breakdowns in contract talks have resulted in lockouts of players and many shortened seasons. Major League Baseball has experienced similar periods of disagreements between players and owners. There were eight work stoppages from 1972 to the strike that caused the cancellation of the 1994 World Series.

SELF-CHECK

1. Define *collective bargaining*.
2. Explain the difference between *binding arbitration* and *compulsory arbitration*.
3. List the four basic union negotiating strategies.
4. Which is a type of union security clause?
   a. closed shop
   b. zipper
   c. no strike
   d. dues checkoff

13.6 Identifying Union Actions

For a variety of reasons, such as when communication between union and management breaks down and tempers flare, or when workplace conditions become so hazardous that employees are afraid they will be maimed or seriously injured on the job, one party or the other may determine that the only course of action left to them is a work stoppage. HR professionals should familiarize themselves with the following actions, some more common than others:

▲ **Lockouts:** A **lockout** occurs when management shuts down operations to keep the union from working. This can happen for several reasons. For example, union members may be engaging in a work slowdown, and it may be costing management more to have the employees working slowly than it would cost to shut down the operation.

▲ **Boycotts: Boycotts** occur when the union and the employees in the bargaining unit work together against an employer to make their dissatisfaction with the employer's actions known or to try to force the employer into recognizing the union or conceding to the demands of the union.

▲ **Strikes:** A **strike** occurs when a union decides to stop working. Whether a strike is lawful or unlawful depends on the purpose of the strike.

- A strike in support of a ULP committed by the union is an unfair labor practice and therefore an unlawful strike.
- A strike that occurs in violation of a no-strike clause in a CBA is not a protected activity, and employees engaging in this type of activity may be terminated or disciplined.
- Strikers who engage in serious misconduct during a strike, including violence, threats of violence, physically blocking someone from entering or leaving the place of business, or attacking management personnel will cause a strike to be deemed unlawful.
- Work slowdowns are considered unlawful strikes and may result in disciplinary action, including termination.
- A **wildcat strike** is one that occurs in violation of a contract clause prohibiting strikes during the term of the contract.
- A **sit-down strike,** in which employees stop working and stay in the building, is considered an unlawful strike.

▲ **Picketing:** Picketing—when union members patrol near a place of business—can be a lawful activity and a way for unions to advertise

---

FOR EXAMPLE

Case of California Lockout

In February 2004, a huge five-month strike and lockout of supermarket workers in southern California ended in defeat. A many as 70,000 workers, members of several locals affiliated with the United Food & Commercial Workers Union (UFCW), were involved in the 138-day action. In the end, workers overwhelmingly voted to accept a new contract that included major losses in health care and wages. Although the supermarkets lost billions in profits, they succeeded in beating the strike and imposing the cuts.

their message. Although picketing often occurs in connection with a strike or work stoppage, it is not the same thing as a strike. The difference is that picketing occurs to simply inform other parties about issues under dispute, while a strike occurs when the employees stop working.

PICKETING PRIMER

The National Labor Review Board recognizes three types of picketing:

▲ **Organizational picketing** occurs when the union wants to attract employees to become members and authorize the union to represent them with the employer.

▲ **Recognitional picketing** occurs when the union wants the employer to recognize the union as the employee's representative for collective bargaining purposes.

▲ **Informational picketing** is done to truthfully advise the public that an employer is a union-free workplace.

SELF-CHECK

1. Explain the difference between a *lockout* and a *strike*.
2. Define *boycott*.
3. *Picketing* is another word for *striking*. True or false?

SUMMARY

Human resource professionals should be prepared for the changes that occur when a union is involved in an employment relationship. With a union, the focus moves from employee relations to labor relations, and it now involves a third party, the union, in the relationship. In such situations, HR professionals must have a clear and comprehensive knowledge of the numerous labor laws designed to protect the rights of union employees. The National Labor Relations Act gives employees certain rights, including the right to unionize, join unions, bargain collectively, and conduct lawful strikes. An employer facing union activity may not threaten, interrogate, promise, or spy on employees during any phase of the organizing process. These or other actions taken by an employer to coerce employees from exercising their rights is considered an unfair labor practice. By having a comprehensive knowledge of how unions function, an employer can more capably enter into contract negotiations as well as prevent any possible charges of unfair labor practices along the way. HR professionals should be aware of the negotiating strategies used in collective bargaining; in addition, a familiarity with a union's grievance process is also very important. Because union membership has seen a decline in recent years, employers should be aware of any union efforts to organize and attract new members. As is the case in any employer-employee relationship, the most effective way to avoid problems or grievances is to treat employees fairly and with respect.

KEY TERMS

Agency shop clause	All employees must either join the union or pay union dues if they choose not to join the union.
Authorization card	The means by which to determine that there is sufficient support for a union to hold an election.
Binding Arbitration	The process used to resolve conflicts without resorting to work stoppages.
Boycott	When the union and the employees work against an employer to make their dissatisfaction with the employer's actions known.
Closed shop clause	Requires that all new hires must be members of the union before they are hired.
Collective bargaining	Method of determining wages, hours and other conditions of employment through direct negotiations between the union and employer.
Collective Bargaining Agreement (CBA)	A contract developed as a result of collective bargaining.
Compulsory arbitration	The process mandated by legal statute to resolve disputes in the public sector where labor strikes are prohibited.
Featherbedding	When unions require employers to pay for services that are not rendered.
Hot cargo agreement	When employers stop doing business with another employer at a union's request.
Informational picketing	Picketing to advise the public that an employer is a union-free workplace.

Injunctions	Court orders that either require or forbid an action by one party against another.
Labor relations	The relationship between employers and employees who are represented by unions.
Lockout	When management shuts down operations to keep a union from working.
Maintenance of membership clause	Employees may choose whether or not to join the union, but once they join, they must remain members until the expiration of the contract.
Mediation	With the aid of the mediator, the parties to the disagreement are able to develop a mutually acceptable solution.
National Labor Relations Board (NLRB)	Conducts elections and prevents and remedies unfair labor practices.
Organizational picketing	Done to attract employees to become members.
Picketing	Patrolling near a place of business by union members, often to increase the pressure on the employer to come to an agreement with the union.
Recognitional picketing	When a union wants an employer to recognize the union as the employee's representative for collective bargaining purposes.
Salting	When a union hires a person to apply for a job at an organization they have targeted.
Secondary boycotts	Attempts by labor to convince others to stop doing business with a particular firm because that firm does business with another firm that is the subject of a strike and/or a boycott.
Sit-down strike	Employees stop working and stay in the building; considered an unlawful strike.
Strike	When a union decides to stop working.
Unfair Labor Practice (ULP)	An action by an employer or a union that restrains or coerces employees from exercising their rights to organize and bargain collectively or to refrain from doing so.
Union	An organized association of workers who have united to represent their collective views for wages, hours, and working conditions.

Union shop clause	Requires that all employees join the union within a grace period specified by a contract.
Union steward	The person union members elect to represent them to management with grievances and other requests (also known as shop steward).
Wildcat strike	A work stoppage that occurs in violation of a contract clause prohibiting strikes during the term of the contract.
Yellow dog contracts	Agreements used by employers to prevent employees from joining unions.
Zipper clause	An agreement between parties that anything not in the CBA is not part of the agreement.

ASSESS YOUR UNDERSTANDING

Go to www.wiley.com/college/messmer to assess your knowledge of labor relations.

Measure your learning by comparing pre-test and post-test results.

Summary Questions

1. A union defends the rights of employers in labor disputes. True or false?
2. In which decade did union activity peak?
   - **(a)** 1930s
   - **(b)** 1950s
   - **(c)** 1960s
   - **(d)** 1990s
3. Which of the following is an example of a lawful strike?
   - **(a)** when a no-strike clause is written into a contract
   - **(b)** when union members engage in misconduct
   - **(c)** when an employer has committed an unfair labor practice
   - **(d)** when a union has committed an unfair labor practice
4. A yellow dog contract is
   - **(a)** an injunction.
   - **(b)** an anti-corruption law.
   - **(c)** an agreement against picketing.
   - **(d)** an agreement preventing employees from joining a union.
5. The National Labor Review Board investigates actions against both employers and unions. True or false?
6. Name the law that was originally written for the railroad industry but now covers the airline industry as well.
7. A petition to the NLRB is the first stop in a union organization process. True or false?
8. Salting is a practice in which
   - **(a)** the union hires an individual to publicize its reasons for targeting an employer for unionization.
   - **(b)** the union hires an individual to distribute leaflets to employees as they are leaving work at the end of the day.
   - **(c)** the union hires an individual to picket the employer's business.
   - **(d)** the union hires an individual to apply for a job with an employer and begin to organize the company.

9. If employees no longer want a union to represent them, they may petition the NLRB for

   (a) decertification.

   (b) deauthorization.

   (c) contract bar.

   (d) statutory bar.

10. A hot cargo agreement

   (a) is unlawful for unions.

   (b) is unlawful for employers.

   (c) is unlawful for both employers and unions.

   (d) is not an unfair labor practice.

11. Union membership fees should be the same for all industries. True or false?

12. The statute of limitations for filing an unfair labor complaint is

   (a) 60 days.

   (b) three months.

   (c) six months.

   (d) one year.

13. A union security clause that requires all employees to join the union or pay dues if they don't join is

   (a) an agency shop clause.

   (b) a union shop clause.

   (c) a closed shop clause.

   (d) a maintenance of membership clause.

14. Name two ways in which union grievances can be resolved.

15. Which type of negotiating strategy is most common?

   (a) single unit

   (b) parallel

   (c) multi-employer

   (d) multi-unit

16. A wildcat strike is an unlawful strike. True or false?

17. The goal of organizational picketing is to

   (a) advise the public of a union-free workplace.

   (b) gain union recognition for collective bargaining.

   (c) attract new members of a union.

   (d) prevent management from working.

Applying This Chapter

1. One of your business competitors has recently become unionized. What steps should your union-free organization take to keep up relations with its employees?

2. You've just received a letter from a union claiming to have the support of more than sixty percent of your employees. The union now wants to be recognized as the employees' exclusive bargaining agent. As an employer, evaluate what choices you have at this stage of the organizing process.

3. Assume that labor relations at your hotel have improved so much that many service union members have started to discuss the potential for change—perhaps even dropping the union altogether. Name the two possible options for change. Also, what must management do to avoid the chance of committing an unfair labor practice?

4. Potential employees of the Smith County Hospital are being pressured to join the union before they are hired. Assess what, if any, contractual clause is being violated, and what recourse is available to hospital management.

5. Employees of a refrigerator manufacturer have filed complaints with their union about poor working conditions at the factory. Explain the likely grievance process and indicate the role of a union supervisor in handling the grievance.

YOU TRY IT

Out of jurisdiction

In order for the National Labor Review Board to provide assistance to workers, they must be within NLRB jurisdiction. Using information on the NLRB website, www.nlrb.gov, determine which workers are excluded from coverage by the National Labor Review Act, which governs the NLRB. List at least six examples of such workers.

Equal Opportunity ULPs

In its work to promote ethics in public life, the National Legal and Policy Center (NLPC) publishes a Union Corruption Update. Using the center's website, www.nlpc.org, including the corruption update, find both an example of a union's unfair labor practice as well as an employer's ULP.

Collective Bargaining at Work

A collective bargaining agreement is the result of negotiations between a union and an employer, typically to resolve issues of wages, hours, and working conditions. Consider your own organization, its workers, and its working environment and create an outline for a hypothetical CBA. Draw from examples of real-life agreements.

- What are the most important issues for employees and employers?
- Which issues are likely to be most contentious?

APPENDIX A
Professional HR Certifications

Professional certification indicates that an individual has met requirements established by a national certifying body for that profession. A number of professional certifications are available to HR practitioners. Some are awarded to specialists in areas such as staffing, compensation and benefits, and training; others are awarded to generalist professionals whose work encompasses multiple areas of human resource responsibilities. Those listed here are ones that will be most often encountered during the course of a career.

Generalist Certifications

The first HR certifications were earned in 1976; by May 2003, more than 68,000 HR generalists had earned professional certification. Today's certification process, which has evolved over time, consists of three levels of certification, Professional in Human Resources (PHR), Senior Professional in Human Resources (SPHR), and Global Professional in Human Resources (GPHR).

The certification process allows practitioners to demonstrate their mastery of the profession by meeting standards set by fellow practitioners who work in the field each day.

EXAM REQUIREMENTS

HRCI has set some requirements that must be met by candidates for the PHR, SPHR, and GPHR exams. Check their site, www.hrci.org, for the most up-to-date information regarding exam requirements.

Compensation and Benefit Certifications

Compensation and benefit professionals are certified by two different organizations: WorldatWork, which was previously known as the American Compensation Association, and the International Foundation of Employment Benefit Plans. WorldatWork certifies professionals at three levels, described as follows.

Certified Compensation Professional (CCP)

Candidates for CCP certification must demonstrate competence in nine areas, and the certification process requires candidates to pass exams in each of the areas. Six of the exams are designed to cover a wide variety of basic compensation knowledge, including the management of total rewards programs, knowledge of compensation and benefit regulations, fundamentals of benefit programs, job analysis, documentation and evaluation, and quantitative analysis methods. In addition to exams that measure basic compensation knowledge, candidates must select three areas of specialty, such as international benefits, mergers and acquisitions, or communicating with employees about total rewards (among others).

Certified Benefits Professional (CBP)

Like the CCP, the CBP certification requires candidates to pass nine exams to demonstrate their knowledge of various benefit programs.

Global Remuneration Professional (GRP)

Earning the GRP requires candidates to demonstrate their knowledge of remuneration techniques that apply to organizations with operations around the world. It consists of a series of exams focused on global application of compensation and benefit practices.

Information about compensation and benefit examinations is available on the WorldatWork website: www.worldatwork.org.

Employee benefits specialists can also earn certifications from the International Foundation of Employment Benefit Plans (IFEBP), in partnership with the Wharton School of Business at the University of Pennsylvania (for U.S. candidates) and with Dalhousie University in Nova Scotia (for Canadian candidates). This organization recently revised its certifications to include four levels, described as follows.

Certified Employee Benefits Specialist (CEBS)

The CEBS designation is earned by individuals who complete coursework in eight areas and earn a passing score on a comprehensive examination that covers all aspects of employee benefits programs.

Other Designations

The IFEBP has revised its certification program by adding three new designations. The Compensation Management Specialist (CMS), Group Benefits Associate (GBA), and Retirement Plans Associate (RPA). These three designations are designed to acknowledge individuals who have mastered knowledge in each area of specialty.

Staffing Certifications

Staffing professionals formed an association known as the National Association of Personnel Services (NAPS), which sponsors two professional certifications:

Certified Personnel Consultant (CPC)

Candidates for the CPC certification must pass a certification exam designed to measure knowledge of employment laws, government regulations, ethical standards, and best business practices.

Certified Temporary-Staffing Specialist (CTS)

The CTS exam covers topics similar to those on the CPC exam, but focuses on how they affect temporary service agencies.

In addition to these certifications, NAPS also sponsors a certification for recruiters who specialize in placing physicians, the Physician Recruiting Consultant (PRC) certification. Additional information about NAPS and these certifications is available on its website at www.recruitinglife.com.

Training Certifications

The ASTD is the professional association for training and development professionals. This association sponsors two certificate programs, as follows.

Certified Performance Technologist (CPT)

The International Society for Performance Improvement (ISPI) developed the CPT certification to measure candidates on 10 Standards of Performance Technology. These standards include the ability to focus on results, to analyze situations within the context of the larger organization, to add value to programs, and to collaborate with clients in developing programs, among others.

Human Performance Improvement (HPI)

The HPI certification is awarded to candidates who successfully complete six courses, covering topics that include analyzing and improving human performance at work; selecting, managing, and evaluating interventions used to improve performance; and moving from a focus on traditional training techniques to performance improvement consulting.

Information about the ASTD certification programs is available on the ASTD website at www.astd.org.

APPENDIX B
Interviewing Candidates

What makes an interview question "good"? The answer, simply, is that a "good question" does two things:

▲ It gives you the specific information you need to make a sound hiring decision.

▲ It helps you gain insight into how the candidate's mind and emotions work.

Avoid timeworn, cliché questions, such as "What are your strengths and weaknesses?" or "Where do you see yourself in the next five years?" or "If you were an animal, which one would it be?" Instead develop a list of questions designed to elicit responses that will be most helpful in evaluating a candidate's suitability for your position and organization. Following are fifteen to get you started, along with ideas on what to look for in the answers.

▲ **Can you tell me a little about yourself?** A well-prepared candidate has a well-rehearsed answer. A confident applicant can give a brief summary of his or her strengths, significant achievements, and career goals. The interviewer's main job? To make sure that the answers are consistent with the applicant's resume. A rambling answer with few specifics may indicate a poorly focused or incompetent candidate.

▲ **What interests you about this job and what skills and strengths can you bring to it?** Note that the question is not "What are your skills and strengths?" but "What skills and strengths can you bring to the job?" The answer is yet another way to gauge how much interest the applicant has in the job and how well prepared he or she is for the interview. Stronger candidates should be able to correlate their skills with specific job requirements: "I think my experience as a foreign correspondent will be of great help in marketing products to overseas customers." They will answer the question in the context of contributions they can make to the company.

▲ **Can you tell me a little about your current job?** Strong candidates should be able to give a short and precise summary of duties and responsibilities. How they answer this question can help an interviewer determine their passion and enthusiasm for their work and their sense of personal accountability. Be wary of applicants who bad-mouth or blame their employers. If they're not loyal to their current employer, how can you expect them to be loyal to you?

▲ **In a way that anyone could understand, can you describe a professional success you are proud of?** This question is especially good when interviewing someone for a technical position, such as a systems analyst or tax accountant. The answer shows the applicant's ability to explain what they do so that anyone can understand it. Do they avoid jargon in their description? Do they get their points across clearly? Failure to do so may be a sign that the individuals can't step out of their "world" sufficiently to work with people in other departments, which is a growing necessity in many organizations today.

▲ **How have you changed the nature of your current job?** A convincing answer here shows adaptability and a willingness to "take the bull by the horns," if necessary. An individual who chose to do a job differently from other people also shows creativity and resourcefulness. The question gives candidates a chance to talk about such contributions as efficiencies they brought about or cost savings they achieved. If a candidate says he didn't change the nature of the job, that response can indicate something as well.

▲ **What was the most difficult decision you ever had to make on the job?** Notice the intentionally vague aspect of this question. It's not hypothetical. It's real. What you're looking for is the person's decision-making style and how it fits into your company culture. Someone who admits that firing a subordinate was difficult demonstrates compassion, and those who successfully decided to approach a coworker over a conflict may turn out to be great team players. Individuals who admit a mistake they've made exhibit honesty and open-mindedness.

   Also listen how people went about making the decision. Seeking the advice of others, for example, may mean that they are team-centered. This question is an especially important one when interviewing a candidate for a middle- or senior-level management position.

▲ **Why did you decide to pursue a new job?** This question is just a different way of asking, "What are you looking for in a job?" Some candidates come so well rehearsed they are never at a loss for an answer. Sometimes, phrasing the question in a different way can cause them to go "off script."

▲ **I see that you've been unemployed for the past eight months. Why did you leave your last job, and what have you been doing since then?** This question is important, but it shouldn't seem accusatory. Generally speaking, people don't leave jobs voluntarily without another one waiting in the wings, but it happens. It isn't really unusual for highly competent people to find themselves unemployed through no fault of their own. Keep an open mind. But try to get specific, factual answers that can be verified later. Candidates with a spotty employment history, at the very least, ought to be able to account for all extended periods of unemployment and to demonstrate whether they used that time productively—getting an advanced degree, for example.

▲ **Who was your best boss ever and why? Who was the worst, and looking back, what could you have done to make that relationship better?** These two are more penetrating questions than one may think. Among other things, the answers give insight into how the candidate views and responds to supervision. A reflective, responsive answer to the second part of the question may indicate a loyal employee capable of rising above an unpleasant supervisory situation and/or learning from past mistakes, both highly desirable qualities. A bitter, critical answer may indicate someone who holds grudges or simply can't get along with certain personality types.

▲ **Which do you enjoy the most: working alone with information or working with other people?** The ideal answer here is "both." People who say they like working with information are obviously a good choice for technical positions, but it may be a red flag if they don't also mention their like for communicating and collaborating with other individuals, which is increasingly a function of even technical jobs. An excellent candidate might say the different perspectives within a group produce more innovative ideas than one person working alone can, but without information, a team can't get very far.

▲ **What sort of things do you think your current (past) company could do to be more successful?** This one is a great "big picture" question. With it, an interviewer is probing to find out whether the candidate has a clear understanding of his current or past employer's missions and goals and whether he thinks in terms of those goals. Candidates who can't answer this question well are demonstrating a lack of depth and interest, which can quite likely carry over into a new organization. Sometimes the answer to this question also reveals hidden bitterness or anger at an employer.

▲ **Can you describe a typical day at work in your last job?** Strong candidates can give specific details that can be verified later, but the main point of this question is to see how the applicant's current (or most recent) routine compares with the requirements of the job in question. How interviewees describe their duties can prove highly revealing. Do you sense any real enthusiasm or interest? Do the details match the information you already have? Look for enthusiasm and some indication that the applicant connects his current duties with company goals.

▲ **What sort of work environment do you prefer? What brings out your best performance?** Probe for specifics. Find out whether this person is going to fit into the company. If a corporate culture is collegial and team-centered, don't go for someone who answers, "I like to be left alone to do my work." Be aware of unrealistic expectations or potential future clashes. ("My plan is to spend a couple months in the mail room and then apply for the presidency of the company.") People rarely, if ever, work at their best in all situations. Candidates who say otherwise aren't being honest.

▲ **How do you handle conflict? Can you give me an example of how you handled a workplace conflict in the past?** Look for candidates who try to be reasonable but nonetheless stand up for what's right. Unfortunately, most candidates say the right things, which is why specifics are good. Be suspicious if the answer is too predictable. While some people may be naturally easygoing, candidates who say that they never get into conflict situations are either dishonest or delusional.

▲ **How would you respond if you were put in a situation you felt presented a conflict of interest or was unethical? Have you ever had this experience in previous positions?** Given the publicity surrounding the collapse of Enron and other corporate scandals, no rational candidate today is going to say that sometimes it's okay to be unethical. But how individuals approach this question and anecdotes they relay can offer valuable insights as to how they may respond if faced with such a situation.

In addition to an opportunity to showcase their qualifications, savvy candidates also use the interview to find out as much as they can about the position and company, so many come prepared with questions of their own. Don't interpret questions as disruptive: They're a show of interest and professionalism.

APPENDIX C
Substance Abuse and Drug Testing

Drug testing can be a divisive workplace issue, so employers must give careful consideration to a number of issues prior to implementing a program in their organization. As with all other employment-related testing, drug tests should be related to the job functions being performed; for example, jobs that require the use of machinery, equipment, or vehicles as part of regular job duties. (Chapter 4 covers drug and other testing for job candidates.)

Substance Abuse in the Workplace

Employees who are substance abusers, whether they are abusing on the premises or simply come to work under the influence of drugs or alcohol, are often responsible for increased absenteeism and are more likely to be the cause of workplace accidents, injuries, or deaths in the workplace. At the extreme, abusers may become violent and disruptive to operations. Employees who are under the influence while at work can expose their employers to costly lawsuits when they endanger the lives of coworkers, vendors, and customers. Situations created by substance abusers can result in lower morale among employees who need to pick up the slack for a coworker who is frequently absent or unable to perform at an acceptable level. These issues add to employer health care and workers' compensation costs.

It is important to note that employees who are recovering substance abusers are protected by the Americans with Disabilities Act (ADA) as long as they are in recovery; if they "fall off the wagon" and begin using again; they are no longer protected by ADA requirements.

Unless employers receive funds from federal contracts, subcontracts, or grants, they are not required by law to provide a drug-free working environment. Many employers choose to do so, however, because it makes good business sense and reduces the costs associated with substance abuse. There are six components for an effective substance abuse program in the workplace:

▲ Support for the substance abuse policy from top management. (As with any policy, this is the most important component.)

▲ A written policy clearly stating that substance abuse will not be tolerated in the workplace.

▲ Training for managers and supervisors to ensure that they understand and can explain the policy, are able to recognize the signs of substance abuse, understand the importance of documenting poor performance, and know what steps to take when they become aware of a substance abuser.

▲ Education programs for new hires and employees to inform them of the policy and explain the consequences for violations. If the organization has a drug testing program, it should be explained prior to employment and during orientation. Employees should be made aware of resources in the community or through the employee assistance program (EAP), as well as the effects of substance abuse on themselves, their families, and the costs to the employer.

▲ An EAP that provides confidential counseling for substance abusers as needed.

▲ An ongoing, fair, and consistent drug testing program that complies with federal, state, and local laws and union contracts. The program should identify who will be tested, when tests will occur, which drugs will be tested for, and what happens if the test is positive.

Establish a Testing Program

Employers should begin a drug-testing program by developing a policy for the organization. The policy should consider issues such as state or local laws, the substances to test for, which employees are to be tested, the procedures to be used, what consequences will occur, and how the policy is communicated to employees.

Maintain Fairness and Consistency

First and foremost, the program must be applied fairly and consistently in the organization. Employers may choose to test employees in all jobs at all levels, or they may select employees in job groups that require, for example, the use of machinery or vehicles as part of their regular duties. If a single job group is subjected to testing, all employees in that group must be equally eligible for testing. If an employer decides to test all workers involved in the operation of production machinery, for example, all the employees in that group must be equally likely to be tested.

Determine Consequences

Prior to implementing a drug testing program, it's important to consider the consequences that employees will face if they test positive for drug abuse. Will the company have a zero-tolerance policy, so that a single instance results in termination? Or will there be some other consequence such as a suspension or required counseling? Whatever consequences are chosen, the employer must be willing to implement them fairly and consistently to avoid charges of discrimination.

Set Testing Parameters

Employers must also determine which drugs will be included in the test process. Most often, employers test for marijuana, cocaine, amphetamines, opiates, and PCP. The decision about which drugs are tested helps to determine the testing method to be used, whether it is based on a sample of blood or urine, or uses a hair follicle or fingernail sample.

Consider Timing

Another issue to be considered is when testing will be conducted. The following table describes five options for conducting tests.

Drug Test Timing Options

Option	When Used
Applicant	Applicants may be required to take and pass a drug test *only after a job offer* has been made. The offer may be contingent upon a successful result, but the test may not be required until the offer has been accepted.
Random	Tests may be conducted randomly, with employees selected arbitrarily, as long as all employees in the group are equally likely to be selected. Some states place restrictions on random testing based on privacy concerns.
Post-accident	Tests may be conducted after an accident occurs. It is a good idea to establish what types of accidents will require testing; for example, whether minor accidents (such as tripping and falling) will require a test, or only more serious accidents, such as those involving medical attention or hospitalization.

(continued)

(continued)	
Reasonable suspicion	When supervisors notice employees behaving unusually or if they have physical symptoms associated with drug or alcohol use (such as dilated pupils or slurred speech), they may require employees to submit to a drug test. This type of testing requires that supervisors be trained to recognize symptoms and behaviors that are commonly associated with drug abuse.
Regular schedule	Tests may be conducted on a regular basis, although this allows employees who normally abuse substances to abstain for a period of time prior to the test or to purchase products designed to mask drug use for the test.

Employers should be aware that the increased use of drug testing programs has spawned a number of businesses that sell products and information designed to mask drug use and allow abusers to pass drug tests. These businesses offer products that can thwart blood, urine, and hair follicle testing, so employers must take steps to ensure that the drug testing facilities they use can detect and prevent the use of these products in their testing programs.

APPENDIX D
Useful HR Resources

Take advantage of the many nonprofit organizations whose missions, services, and activities relate to the human resources function. Some of these organizations offer a great deal of information through their websites.

Benefits

Employee Benefit Research Institute (EBRI)
2121 K Street, NW, Suite 600
Washington, DC 20037-1896
Phone: 202-659-0670
Fax: 202-775-6312
web: www.ebri.org
The Employee Benefit Research Institute is the source of a wide array of benefits facts and figures, web links to its own and other online resources, and a range of programs that make benefits information easily available.

Compensation

Employers Council on Flexible Compensation (ECFC)
927 15th Street NW, Suite 1000
Washington, DC 20005
Phone: 202-659-4300
Fax: 202-371-1467
Web: www.ecfc.org
The Employers Council on Flexible Compensation provides information on flexible compensation programs to members, national opinion leaders, and the general public to help create a positive climate for the growth of flexible compensation.

Contingent Workers

American Staffing Association
277 S. Washington Street, Suite 200
Alexandria, VA 22314
Phone: 703-253-2020
Fax: 703-253-2053
Web: www.americanstaffing.net
The American Staffing Association has been promoting flexible employment opportunities since its founding in 1966. Its members provide a wide range of employment-related services and solutions, including temporary and contract staffing, recruiting and permanent placement, outsourcing, training, and human resource consulting.

Employee Assistance Programs

Employee Assistance Professionals Association
4350 North Fairfax Drive, Suite 410
Arlington, VA 22203
Phone: 703-387-1000
Fax: 703-522-4585
Web: www.eapassn.org
Established in 1971, the Employee Assistance Professionals Association publishes the Journal of Employee Assistance and offers training and other resources to enhance the skills and success of its members and the stature of the employee assistance profession.

Equal Employment Opportunity

Equal Employment Advisory Council (EEAC)
1015 15th St. NW, Suite 1200
Washington, DC 20005
Phone: 202-789-8650
Fax: 202-789-2291
Web: www.eeac.org
The Equal Employment Advisory Council, founded in 1976, is the nation's largest nonprofit association of employers dedicated exclusively to the advancement of practical and effective programs to eliminate workplace discrimination. Members rely on the EEAC's staff of attorneys and compliance professionals to help them meet their EEO and affirmative action compliance obligations. Membership is corporate, meaning that anyone employed by a member company is eligible to benefit from EEAC's array of member services.

General HR Management

American Management Association
1601 Broadway
New York, NY 10019-7420
Phone: 212-586-8100
Fax: 212-903-8168
Web: www.amanet.org
The American Management Association provides a full range of management development and educational services to individuals, companies, and government agencies worldwide. The organization features seminars, conferences, current issues forums and briefings, as well as books and publications, research, and print and online self-study courses.

Society for Human Resource Management (SHRM)
1800 Duke St.
Alexandria, VA 22314
Phone: 800-283-SHRM (7476); 703-548-3440
Fax: 703-535-6490
Web: www.shrm.org
The Society for Human Resource Management (SHRM) is the world's largest association devoted to human resource management. Representing more than 200,000 individual members, the Society's mission is to serve the needs of HR professionals by providing the most essential and comprehensive resources available. SHRM has more than 560 affiliate chapters, both in the United States and abroad, and provides additional programming and networking opportunities in local areas.

WorldatWork
14040 N. Northsight Blvd.
Scottsdale, AZ 85260
Phone: 877-951-9191 (toll free); 480-922-2020
Fax: 866-816-2962 (toll free); 480-483-8352
web: www.worldatwork.org
Founded in 1955, WorldatWork focuses on human resources disciplines associated with attracting, motivating, and retaining employees. The WorldatWork family of organizations provides education, certifications, publications, knowledge resources, surveys, conferences, research, and networking opportunities.

Information Technology

International Association for Human Resource
Information Management (IHRIM)
P.O. Box 1086
Burlington, MA 01803-1086
Phone: 800-804-3983; 781-791-9488
Fax: 781-998-8011
Web: www.ihrim.org

The International Association for Human Resource Information Management provides HR technology professionals with news, knowledge, and networking opportunities. IHRIM is a community of practitioners, vendors, consultants, students, and faculty.

Training and Workforce Development

American Society for Training and Development (ASTD)
1640 King St., Box 1443
Alexandria, VA 22313-2043
Phone: 703-683-8100
Fax: 703-683-8103
Web: www.astd.org

The American Society for Training & Development is the world's largest association dedicated to workplace learning and performance professionals. Its members and associates come from more than 100 countries and thousands of organizations of all types and sizes.

GLOSSARY

ADDIE process Acronym for Analysis, Design, Development, Implementation, and Evaluation; an instructional design model that provides an outline to follow when developing training programs.

Age-based discrimination Unfair treatment against a person because of his/her age.

Agency shop clause All employees must either join the union or pay union dues if they choose not to join the union.

Alternate work arrangements Any scheduling pattern that deviates from the traditional workweek.

Alternative Dispute Resolution (ADR) An alternative to battles in court; involves mediation or arbitration.

Anniversary reviews Performance appraisals scheduled on the anniversary of the employee's date of hire.

Applicant tracking system Software application that can post job openings on various websites, automate resume scanning, generate letters, and perform other functions.

Appraisals Part of a management process in which managers monitor employee performance, note which areas need to be improved, and then communicate assessments in a constructive way.

Arbitration A neutral third party listens to both sides of the dispute; unlike a mediator, an arbitrator has the power to impose a financial settlement.

Authorization card The means by which to determine that there is sufficient support for a union to hold an election.

Background checks Employee evaluation tools such as criminal checks, academic degree verifications, and workers' compensation reports.

Base Plan   Health insurance that covers certain services, usually in connection with hospitalization.

Behavioral interviewing   Questioning technique using open-ended questions related to candidates' past experiences on the job.

Behaviorally Anchored Rating Scale (BARS)   Evaluation system designed to emphasize the behavior, traits, and skills needed to successfully perform a job.

Benefit   Any form of indirect compensation that isn't part of an employee's basic pay or directly connected to job performance.

Benefits   Items offered to employees in addition to their base wage or salary; examples include health insurance, stock options, and retirement plans.

Binding Arbitration   The process used to resolve conflicts without resorting to work stoppages.

Biological hazards   Bacteria, molds, contaminated water, and dust that are known to cause illness in workers; most often the result of mining and industrial operations.

Blind ads   An online posting or classified ad that doesn't identify the company and typically directs replies to a post office box number.

Blood-borne pathogen standard   Requires employers to develop an exposure control plan of how to prevent or reduce the effects of exposure to pathogens.

Bona Fide Occupational Qualification (BFOQ)   Job requirements that are reasonably necessary to meet the normal operations of a business.

Bonus   A reward for a job well done; usually financial, but may include rewarding time off, free membership in a local health club, or discounts on merchandise.

Bottom-up communication   Information that flows from employees up through an organization.

Boycott   When the union and the employees work against an employer to make their dissatisfaction with the employer's actions known.

Brown-bag lunch   An informal way for senior executives to meet with and talk to small groups of employees.

Buddy program   By pairing a veteran employee with a new employee, an employer makes sure that new employees have a smooth transition into an organization.

Burnout   When workers wear down from stress and become unable to cope with workday demands.

Cafeteria benefits   Flexible benefits that give employees a menu of choices.

Candidate management system   Software application that can post job openings on various websites, automate resume scanning, generate letters, and perform other functions.

Central tendency   Evaluation bias that occurs when a supervisor does not identify those employees who are performing at a very high or very low level, leaving all employees with an "average" assessed.

Chemical hazards   Hazards such as asbestos, corrosives, pesticides, gas fumes, or solvents that pose a physical or health risk to workers.

Cloning effect   Hiring someone in your image even though someone with your particular mix of skills and attributes isn't qualified for that particular job.

Closed shop clause   Requires that all new hires must be members of the union before they are hired.

Closed-ended question   Question that calls for a simple, informational answer.

Code of ethics   Company policies that place a strong emphasis on the behavior of their employees.

Collective bargaining   Method of determining wages, hours and other conditions of employment through direct negotiations between the union and employer.

Collective Bargaining Agreement (CBA)   A contract developed as a result of collective bargaining.

Commissions   A percentage of the sales price of a service or product that salespeople receive in addition to (or in lieu of) salary.

Compensation   All the rewards that employees receive in exchange for their work, including base pay, bonuses, and incentives.

Competency modeling   Determining the mix of skills, attributes, and attitudes that produce superior performance in the operational functions of a company.

Compliance Safety and Health Officer (CSHO)   An individual trained on OSHA standards who conducts workplace inspections.

Compressed work week   Employees work the normal number of hours but complete those hours in fewer than five days.

Compulsory arbitration   The process mandated by legal statute to resolve disputes in the public sector where labor strikes are prohibited.

Contingency search firms   Recruiting focus is on mid- to upper-level positions usually in a particular field or profession.

Contingent workers   Temporary or contract workers.

Cost of labor   The cost to attract and retain individuals with the skills needed by an organization.

Credentials   Degrees and licenses acknowledging that a candidate has passed a particular test or completed a specific field of study.

Critical behaviors   Specific behaviors deemed necessary to perform a particular job competently.

Critical incidents method   Performance appraisal technique built around a list of specific behaviors deemed necessary to perform a particular job competently.

Defined benefit plan   An employer-sponsored retirement plan that promises to pay a specified amount to each person who retires after a set number of years of service.

Defined contribution plan   A retirement plan wherein a certain amount or percentage of money is set aside each year for the benefit of the employee.

Deliverables   Specific job goals or targets.

Dependent care account   Employees can set aside a maximum of $5,000 to be used to care for dependent children or elders.

Direct compensation   Salaries or wages, incentive awards, bonus payments, sales commissions, and other monetary compensation paid directly to employees.

Disabled person   Any person who has a physical or mental impairment which substantially limits one or more major life activities.

Discrimination   Unfair treatment of a person or group on the basis of prejudice.

Disparate impact   Employer actions that aren't intended to discriminate but have the effect of doing so.

Disparate treatment   Intentional acts by an employer to discriminate.

Diversity training   Employee guidance that teaches them to increase sensitivity toward others.

Domestic partners   Opposite-sex or same-sex nonmarried partners.

Early retirement   When retirement is elected before the normal retirement age; a method of reducing payroll costs.

E-learning   The use of computer and online technology to house and deliver training content.

Employee Assistance Programs (EAPs)   A mechanism for helping employees deal with certain personal problems (such as alcohol abuse).

Employee empowerment   Philosophy that employees ought to have as much control and autonomy as is reasonably possible in the performance of their day-to-day tasks.

Employee focus groups   Group of employees who meet to discuss what a company needs to do to achieve its strategic goals and what skills are required to meet this challenge.

Employee relations   The policies and practices that are concerned with the management and regulation of relationships in an organization.

Employee training   Everything an organization does to upgrade the skills and improve the overall job performance of employees, both in the short term and long term.

Employment agencies   Typically recruiting generalists that focus on entry- and mid-level jobs in a range of industries.

Employment-at-will   Employee or employer can terminate a relationship with no liability if there was no express contract for a definite term governing the employment.

Entitlement philosophy   Salary and promotion decisions are based on length of service; this philosophy is exemplified in a union environment.

Environmental health hazards   Chemical, physical, and biological dangers in the workplace.

Equal Opportunity Employment Commission (EEOC)   The federal agency responsible for enforcing federal antidiscrimination laws in employment.

Equity   Plan that provides benefits to employees in the form of stock option plans, or by awarding stock to employees directly or at perferred rates.

Ergonomic injury   An injury that is related to the way the physical environment is designed.

Ethics   A set of rules or principles that define right and wrong conduct.

Evaluations   Another word for performance appraisal.

Executive search firms   Recruiting focus is on high level executives, up to and including CEOs.

Exempt workers   Employees that receive a flat weekly, monthly, or annual salary, regardless of the number of hours they work over a given period.

External equity   Compares jobs in the organization to other similar jobs in other organizations to make sure that the organization's wages and salaries are sufficient to attract the qualified employees it needs.

Fair Labor Standards Act (FLSA)   Regulation enacted in 1938 that remains a major influence on basis compensation issues for U.S. businesses.

Family Medical Leave Act   Created to help employees balance the needs of their families with the demands of their jobs.

Featherbedding   When unions require employers to pay for services that are not rendered.

Flexible Spending Accounts (FSAs)   Accounts that allow employees to set aside pretax funds for medical expenses they plan to incur during the calendar year.

Flextime   Any arrangement that gives employees options on structuring their work day or work week.

Flow sheet   A document that lists the steps in the evaluation process with spaces for the date and initials of the person completing the step.

Focal reviews   Performance appraisals given at one time during a review cycle, regardless of individual dates of hire.

Forced comparison   Ranking appraisal method in which employees are compared to other employees and ranked by the number of times they're identified as the best.

Forced distribution   Employees are ranked along a standard statistical distribution, or bell curve.

Forced-choice methods   Evaluation method with which evaluators choose one of two statements that best describes the employee; alternatively, evaluators select a description that may fall somewhere in between.

Furlough   Generally used in unionized environments to temporarily lay off employees; employees often return to work on a certain date or in stages.

Gatekeeper   A primary physician who decides whether a member needs to seek specialty services within the network or services outside the network.

General duty standard   Applies to all businesses and requires business owners to provide a safe work environment for their employees.

Generalists   People who possess skills in several areas rather than in one particular specialty.

Grievance procedure   A disciplinary process that provides a means for dealing with problem behavior among employees.

Group incentives   Programs used to increase productivity, encourage teamwork, and share financial rewards with employees; common group incentives include profit sharing and stock ownership.

Halo effect   A phrase used to describe a common phenomenon in hiring in which the interviewer becomes so enraptured by one particular aspect of the candidate—that it colors all of the interviewer's other judgments.

Hazard communication standard   Requires employers to inform employees of the dangers of chemicals used in the workplace.

Headhunters   Recruiting focus is on high level executives, up to and including CEOs.

Health Maintenance Organizations (HMOs)   Healthcare option that offers a wide range of medical services but limits choices to those specialists or organizations that are part of the network (also known as HMOs).

Health Savings Accounts (HSAs)   Designed to help individuals save for future qualified medical and retiree health expenses on a tax-free basis.

Hot cargo agreement   When employers stop doing business with another employer at a union's request.

Human Resource Information Systems (HRIS)   Software designed for human resources management purposes.

Human resources management   The decisions, activities, and processes that meet the basic needs and support the work performance of employees.

Hypothetical question   Question that invites the candidate to resolve an imaginary situation or react to a given situation.

Incentive pay   Programs that reward employees for individual and/or organizational results.

Incentives   A tool used to boost productivity; an incentive comes before work is done.

Indemnity plans   Insurance programs (also known as fee-for-service plans) that reimburse members for defined benefits.

Indirect compensation   A type of monetary compensation that consists of benefits paid by the organization on behalf of employees, such as medical insurance, workers' compensation, or mandated benefits.

Informational picketing   Picketing to advise the public that an employer is a union-free workplace.

In-house classroom training   A group of employees gathers in a classroom and is led through the program by an instructor; the traditional and most familiar form of training.

Injunctions   Court orders that either require or forbid an action by one party against another.

Intellectual capital   The knowledge, applied experience, and professional skills that translate into customer relationships and provide an organization with a competitive edge in the marketplace.

Internal equity   The worth of a job to a company; value is based on the content of the job, its level of responsibility, and how much impact the decisions in the job have on an organization.

Job analysis   Process of gathering information about various aspects of a job, including reporting relationships, interactions with others, qualifications, work environment, and the knowledge, skills, and attributes (KSAs) needed to perform the job successfully.

Job description   A written document that is produced as the result of a job analysis. It contains information that identifies the job, its essential functions, and the job specifications or competencies that enable an individual to be successful in the position.

Job rating checklist   A prepared list of statements or questions that relate to specific aspects of job performance.

Job satisfaction   How content an individual is with his or her job.

Job-sharing   Two part-time employees share the same full-time job.

Knowledge workers   An employee who possesses the skills and knowledge needed to perform the jobs and functions most affected by technological advances, tasks that in turn require significant levels of education.

Knowledge, Skills, Abilities (KSAs)   The qualifications that are needed by an individual in order to perform successfully in a position.

Labor market   Sources from which an organization recruits new employees.

Labor relations   The relationship between employers and employees who are represented by unions.

Lateral communication   Communication that takes place between employees in different departments within the organization.

Layoffs   Termination of employees, but in cases when the people being let go haven't done anything to warrant losing their jobs.

Leading question   Question asked in such a way that the answer you're looking for is obvious.

Leased workers   Temporary employees that work on a full-time basis; provided by an outside employment agency.

Leave of absence   An arrangement giving employees extended time off (usually without pay); employee still maintains employment status.

Lifestyle benefits   Relatively inexpensive rewards or services that make life a little easier for employees.

Lockout   When management shuts down operations to keep a union from working.

Lockout/tagout standard   Designed to reduce injuries and deaths by preventing machinery or equipment from starting unexpectedly during repairs and maintenance.

Maintenance of membership clause   Employees may choose whether or not to join the union, but once they join, they must remain members until the expiration of the contract.

Major Medical   Healthcare option that covers such services as routine doctors' visits and certain tests.

Management By Objectives (MBO)   Appraisal system that focuses on results and the activities and skills that define an employee's job.

Management By Walking Around (MBWA)   A way for managers to talk to employees about working conditions and processes.

Mass layoff   A layoff that affects 500 or more workers or 50 or more workers if they comprise at least 33 percent of the active, full-time workforce.

Mediation   Process in which a neutral third party is brought in to help two parties come up with a solution that is acceptable to both parties.

Medicare   A federal health insurance program for people sixty-five and over.

Mentors   Experienced employees chosen to coach less experienced employees; generally a long-term relationship.

Multi-rater assessments   An employee and her supervisors and coworkers are asked to complete detailed questionnaires on the employee.

National Institute of Occupational Safety and Health (NIOSH)   Agency charged with researching and evaluating workplace hazards; suggests ways of eliminating risks.

National Labor Relations Board (NLRB)   Conducts elections and prevents and remedies unfair labor practices.

Nonexempt workers   Employees paid on an hourly basis (though some receive salaries) and are eligible for overtime pay if they work more than forty hours in a given week.

Occupational noise exposure standard   Sets allowable levels of workplace noise and identifies procedures for measuring noise.

Occupational Safety and Health Act of 1970   Federal legislation requiring employers to protect workers from injury or illness.

Occupational Safety and Health Administration (OSHA)   Agency that sets and enforces safety standards for virtually every business in the United States.

Offshoring   When a function may be moved to a remote location out of the country.

Ombudsman   An impartial person not involved in a dispute who speaks with both parties and suggests alternative solutions.

Onboarding   Coordination of a new hire process; includes orientation, review of job expectations, and other resources to help new employees.

Open-door policy   Strategy to encourage employees to come forward with questions and concerns about work issues.

Open-ended question   Question that requires thought and obliges the candidate to reveal attitudes or opinions.

Organizational culture   Establishes standards of behavior, many of which are unwritten, for all employees.

Organizational inbreeding   The effects of recruiting from within a company for too long.

Organizational picketing   Done to attract employees to become members.

Outplacement specialists   Companies that help dismissed employees, usually middle managers and above, regroup and find new jobs.

Outsourcing   When a company turns over an entire function (payroll, for example) to an outside specialist.

Peer review panel   Dispute-resolution method in which management and non-management personnel listen to disputing parties and make decisions.

Pension   A sum of money paid regularly as a retirement benefit.

People needs   The requirements of a workforce, ranging from a safe working environment to fair compensation and competitive benefits.

Performance-based philosophy   Salary increases and promotions are awarded to those employees who contribute to the achievement of organization goals.

Perquisites   Special benefits not made available to the general employee population.

Personal protective equipment standards   Requirement that employers provide appropriate garments and equipment for dealing with different types of hazards; also requires employers to train workers in the proper use and maintenance of the equipment.

Phased retirement options   Program that allows tenured employees to gradually ease their way out of the organization by reducing the number of hours they work.

Physical hazards   Elements such as electrical currents, excessive noise, too much or too little light, radiation, and vibrations that can have negative effects on worker health.

Picketing   Patrolling near a place of business by union members, often to increase the pressure on the employer to come to an agreement with the union.

Preferred Provider Organizations (PPOs)   Healthcare that gives employees a range of choices about doctors (also known as PPOs).

Proactive   Approach of acting in anticipation of future problems, needs, or changes.

Professional Employment Organizations (PEOs)   Outside agency that provides temporary workers or other employees to a company.

Qualifications   The skills, attributes, or credentials a person needs to perform a task.

Racial bias   A preformed negative opinion or attitude toward a group of persons who possess common physical characteristics (color of skin, facial features; etc.) that distinguish them as a distinct division of humankind, eg, Asians, Blacks, Whites.

Raises   Increases in base salary or rate of pay, as opposed to one-time or periodic awards.

Ranking methods   Evaluation technique that compares employees in a group to one another; three variations used.

Reasonable cause   To have knowledge of facts that would cause a reasonable person, knowing the same facts, to reasonably conclude the same thing.

Recency   Bias that occurs when supervisors use only the most recent performance results as the basis for an evaluation.

Recognitional picketing   When a union wants an employer to recognize the union as the employee's representative for collective bargaining purposes.

Restricted stock   Ownership in a company with rights to vote and receive dividends without the right to transfer or sell the shares until the shares are vested.

Reviews   Another word for performance appraisal.

Right-to-sue notice   Issued by the EEOC when it finds reasonable cause for an individual to file a lawsuit against his or her company.

Safety and health plan   Strategy that identifies and assesses workplace hazards, and describes the steps taken to correct those hazards (also known as an injury and illness prevention program).

Salary   Pay arrangements of employees who receive their compensation as a flat amount, regardless of how many hours they work.

Salting   When a union hires a person to apply for a job at an organization they have targeted.

Secondary boycotts   Attempts by labor to convince others to stop doing business with a particular firm because that firm does business with another firm that is the subject of a strike and/or a boycott.

Severance agreement   A statement that addresses confidential agreements and releases a company from legal liabilities.

Severance pay   Money in addition to wages and any other money that employers owe employees at termination.

Sexual harassment   Any form of harassment that has sexual overtones.

Sit-down strike   Employees stop working and stay in the building; considered an unlawful strike.

Social Security   A system to provide basic retirement income for workers who have contributed to the plan.

Soft skills   Such skills as an aptitude for communicating with people of all levels, skill sets, and backgrounds; the ability to work well in teams; and other factors, such as a talent for efficient and creative problem-solving.

Specialist   A person who specializes in one area of human resources or other field.

Staffing companies   Companies that can help workers get back into the workforce; sometimes specializing in particular industries.

Staffing firm   Fee-based recruiting company that focuses on mid- to upper-level positions, usually in a particular field of profession.

Staffing plan   The way an organization recruits, hires, retains, promotes, and terminates employees.

Stock option   Program that gives employees at publicly held companies the right to purchase shares in the company at a time of their own choosing, but at a price that is set at the time the option is awarded.

Straight ranking   Appraisal method in which employees are simply listed in order of ranking.

Strategic needs   Those actions or measures that ensure the successful attainment of an organization's goals or mission.

Strategic staffing   The process of putting together a combination of human resources—internal and external—that are strategically keyed to the needs of the business and the realities of the labor market.

Strategic thinkers   People who set objectives and get work done, while anticipating future issues; examine trends and long-term needs.

Strike   When a union decides to stop working.

Task   What an employee does in a job position—from computing taxes to baking the donuts.

Telecommuting   Any work arrangement in which employees regularly work out of their homes or other locations all or part of the work week.

Tenure   Time spent in a job grade or position.

Termination-at-will   Also known as employment-at-will.

360-degree assessments   Also known as multi-rater assessments.

Top-down communication   Information that flows from the organization to employees.

Total compensation   All types of direct cash compensation.

Total rewards   Monetary compensation (direct and indirect) and nonmonetary compensation, unique and beneficial aspects of working for a particular employer.

Unemployment insurance   Provides basic income for workers who become unemployed through no fault of their own.

Unfair Labor Practice (ULP)   An action by an employer or a union that restrains or coerces employees from exercising their rights to organize and bargain collectively or to refrain from doing so.

Union   An organized association of workers who have united to represent their collective views for wages, hours, and working conditions.

Union shop clause   Requires that all employees join the union within a grace period specified by a contract.

Union steward   The person union members elect to represent them to management with grievances and other requests (also known as shop steward).

Variable compensation   Programs that reward employees for individual and/or organizational results.

Variable pay   Pay tied to specific performance goals and includes commissions, bonuses, and incentives.

Vesting   An employee must stay with the company for a specified time before exercising stock options.

Weighted   The process of giving elements in an application form certain value, putting more emphasis on qualifications that may influence job performance.

Weighted rating system   A number is used to reflect the relative importance of each criterion being evaluated.

Wildcat strike   A work stoppage that occurs in violation of a contract clause prohibiting strikes during the term of the contract.

Workers' compensation   Insurance that provides protection for workers who suffer injuries or become ill on the job.

Workforce diversity   The effort to allow and encourage diversity in the workplace.

Wrongful termination   When an employer terminates someone for a reason prohibited by statute or breaches a contract.

Yellow dog contracts   Agreements used by employers to prevent employees from joining unions.

Zipper clause   An agreement between parties that anything not in the CBA is not part of the agreement.

INDEX